MW01599230

SAFE SPACE

A True Story of Faith, Betrayal,
and the Power of the Force

Nicholas Harrison

One Printers Way
Altona, MB R0G 0B0
Canada

www.friesenpress.com

Copyright © 2021 by Nicholas Harrison
First Edition — 2021

All rights reserved.

Additional Contributors
Collette Berg, Editor
Pia Guerra, Illustrator

No part of this book may be reproduced or used in any manner without written permission of the copyright owner except for the use of quotations in a book review. For more information, address: info@nicholasjharrison.com

The events and conversations in this book have been set down to the best of the author's ability. Some names and details have been changed to protect the privacy of individuals.

Cover design © 2020 by Pia Guerra
Author photo by Kevin Clark Studios
Star Wars Saved My Life photo by Tim Matheson
Droid illustrations by Olivia Piper Harrison
Aurebesh font by Neale Davidson

Throughout this book, the author has made countless references to Star Wars films and the universe George Lucas created. Although this book is not affiliated with George Lucas, Lucasfilm Ltd., or The Walt Disney Company, the author is forever grateful for the existence of their films and acknowledges that the intellectual property of the Star Wars films and the entire Star Wars universe belongs to them.

No part of this publication may be reproduced in any form, or by any means, electronic or mechanical, including photocopying, recording, or any information browsing, storage, or retrieval system, without permission in writing from FriesenPress.

ISBN
978-1-7775930-1-8 (Hardcover)
978-1-7775930-0-1 (Paperback)
978-1-7775930-2-5 (eBook)

1. FAMILY & RELATIONSHIPS, ABUSE, CHILD ABUSE

Distributed to the trade by The Ingram Book Company

FOREWORD

This is a tale told from a place that is unfortunately very near and sadly not so long ago. A tale told with honesty and integrity. Its raw story provokes horror, humour, and heartfelt empathy in equal measure.

True stories of inspirational resilience are rare. The requisite vulnerability and authenticity to tell personal tales of trauma and redemption take enormous character and courage. This is such a tale, and one accessibly framed within the context of the enabling role and healing potential of popular culture.

Safe Space is a story of gut-churning and heart-rending personal tragedy combined with the saving grace of Star Wars, R2D2, and the path of the Jedi.

When I first met Nic, I had no inkling of his backstory. I came across his name at an author's festival while in casual conversation with a close friend of his. I was encouraged to contact Nic, but this was for a very different context.

I was working on a book about what the effects of a lifetime of Batman might've had on the brain of Bruce Wayne. (You know, the fictional character who suffers horrific childhood trauma but then avows a lifetime mission requiring arduous training to overcome and rise above as the Dark Knight Guardian of Gotham?) Truth, as it turns out, and as demonstrated in *Safe Space*, can be strangely more powerful than fiction.

I did reach out to ask Nic about mundane things like his injury history during a career performing and coordinating stunts in film and television: What kind of injuries have you had? How have they affected you? Blah blah blah. It now seems simple and kind of superficial.

But, in the course of corresponding with him, I discovered that I had actually stumbled across a real-life version of Bruce Wayne *and* Batman: that popular culture alter ego and superhero who rose above, rolled into a real human.

Nic's story reveals how the inspirational power of imagination and commitment embodied by the Jedi Knights in Star Wars enabled him to overcome horrific childhood abuse.

It's a story that forces us to face the worst and most inhumane—but also the redemptive and best—parts about being human. Star Wars brought Nic to martial arts, and his training reinforced the role of Jedi determination to provide meaning that infiltrated all aspects of his life.

He changed suffering to surviving and thriving.

He combined the path of the sword with that of the lightsaber.

In *Man's Search for Meaning*, Viktor Frankl wrote about the horror of life in a Nazi concentration camp, saying, "In some ways suffering ceases to be suffering at the moment it finds a meaning ..." Nic Harrison discovered a meaningful way to address his own trauma and suffering. His resilience is supported by the power of popular culture and has enabled him to emerge from it and rise above like a true Jedi.

This is a story that honours the true capacity for inspiration to fire the resilience of the human spirit. It's proof that the actions and reactions of each and every one of us possess the power to change worlds. It's up to us to choose the dark side or the light side.

Just like *Star Wars*, this is a powerful story that will linger, that will trouble and inspire, long after the telling of the tale.

— E. Paul Zehr, PhD
Author, *Becoming Batman:*
The Possibility of a Superhero

INTRODUCTION

Safe Space chronicles my history of enduring abuse and confronting my monsters despite the odds against me. When I was working on my PhD at the University of British Columbia, I met Dr. Ernest Mathijs. He has written multiple books on fandom and cult cinema, and we had several discussions about films and fandom, including my passion for all things Star Wars. When I finished writing this book, I asked him if he would write a piece to contextualize it and help readers understand that film fandom can have a healing effect on the soul. I was excited and humbled when he agreed. I am honoured to include his article alongside my work.

MEMORIES, MOMENTS, AND THE REAL-LIFE DISTINCTION OF TRUE FANDOM

by Ernest Mathijs, PhD

Safe Space is a witness to the power of fandom.

For far too long, fandom of popular culture was seen as silly or dangerous. From the fanatic followings of sects and the idolatry that characterized the Middle Ages (recounted so colourfully by my PhD supervisor, a professor in medieval philosophies and a specialist on heresies), via the Werther Fever fandom that surrounded Johann Wolfgang Goethe's *The Sorrows of Young Werther*, to denunciations of comic book fandom as "deviant" in the 1950s, fandom has been vilified. Through the censorship of subversive films (like those of David Cronenberg), fandom has often found itself in the corner of the outsider and the outcast.

Much has changed since. Ever since Henry Jenkins and others in the early 1990s argued fervently that fandom is not a pathology but a power, fandom has been seen differently. Maybe this is still not yet the case in the eyes of the general public, that sees any deviation from regulatory norms (however rigid), moderation (however frugal), and prescribed duty (however slavish) as excessive. But then that type of general public is, as *Safe Space* shows, increasingly less a part of today's world.

Fandom liberates. It has the ability to allow us as consumers and agents of popular culture to take charge of our own processes of making meaning (not just to dislike and like as one sees fit, but to have agency)—of taking control of our own lives by choosing the metaphors by which we live.

Put differently, Star Wars is what I make it to be. *Safe Space* is a book that is both a testament to fandom and a testimony of its emancipatory abilities. In telling his personal life story, in a direct voice with no holds barred, yet with a sense of hope, Nic Harrison uses Star Wars to make sense of, and give a place in his world to his life, past and present. The metaphor of Star Wars in that story is essential. When I say Star Wars, I mean the Star Wars universe. And that difference matters, because a universe has a scope beyond one's immediate experience: it is a cultural frame of reference that includes instrumental, expressive, cognitive, affective, and normative orientations. It inhabits a worldview. *Safe Space* uses Star Wars as a compass to make distinctions.

DISTINCTION AND DISINTERESTEDNESS

Full disclosure: I am a member of the department that Nic, pardon me, Dr. Harrison, graduated from, at the University of British Columbia. I was a member of the program he attended, and I recall, with great fondness, talking with Nic about movie audiences and cult fandom—one of my specialties.

I remember vividly how one day Nic came into my office and shared with me his excitement about obtaining a real Indiana Jones fedora. A real one, he explained, because there were so many knockoffs. Nic, I hope I remember this correctly! Because I have since developed a knack for distinguishing between real Indiana Jones fedoras and not-so-real ones. It has lifted me up in the ranks of Indiana Jones connoisseurs. I am still a lowly amateur but no longer a bottom feeder.

At that moment, Nic struck me as the kind of person I knew was a real fan—because to real fans these things matter. Let me put that differently: to real fans a distinction between true and false matters, between right and wrong. All too often, this sharp sense of distinction is relegated to one of aesthetic taste. But, as Pierre Bourdieu's research on the hierarchies of taste has taught us, taste is a difference maker. And these distinctions, and we all know this, have a moral dimension.

Safe Space showcases Nic's sense of that distinction. It runs through the descriptions, observations, and impressions he is sharing. It informs his ability to report with what Jerome Stolnitz would call critical and compassionate "disinterestedness." Disinterestedness needs to be seen here not as a refusal to engage with particular impressions but as a sense of focus. In *Safe Space*, Nic does that, literally, all the times his self tells himself to "stay on target." The preciseness of a fan has made it possible for Nic to write this book.

Fans also enact, perform, that distinction and that disinterestedness in the face of adversity. To see a fan stand up and speak out on behalf of their object of desire is not adorable—it is admirable; it is not defensive, but it is affirmative; and it is brave. *Safe Space* is a brave book. With the earnestness and sense of distinction of a fan behind it, it dares to name what is often left unsaid.

THE ABJECT: THINGS UNSAID

Let me be precise here about "things unmentioned," and use one example from *Safe Space*. Nic writes about 'spit,' phlegm, as a tool of oppression, and the descriptions he uses are of visceral realness. Spit is only one of the descriptions in *Safe Space*, but it is exemplary. In academic and theoretical terms, via 'spit,' Nic touches on the abject— the aspects of cultural taboo which cannot (or can hardly) be named, and which escape language and description. I study horror films and their audiences, and scary movies are filled with abject moments, with moments of taboo: sexual, morbid, hygienic, dietary, name it. Taboos are primarily concerned with cleanliness and purity, and the abject threatens that. It signals a danger. Bodily fluids play a primary role as articulations of that danger. That is because bodily fluids remind us of the fragility of the border between the public body of myself (my outside, that which I control) and my private body (the intimate, my innards, that which is, for most of us, untouched unless for medical reasons, or by choice in the case of an intimate relation). In horror films, a violated body—that is, one that witnesses the non-consensual disruption of the security of the border between the outside of the body and its inside—is the site of disgust. That is why horror films hit a nerve. And that is also why horror movies teach lessons. Melodrama and erotic movies do that too: they too showcase bodily fluids, such as tears, sweat, or, well, you can guess. Because of the abject, bodily fluids mark the edge of what we tolerate. That is why we discipline their appearance; it is what we have private bathrooms for, and hospitals; it is why we 'train' from an early age to control ourselves and not 'show' what goes on inside us. It is also what makes telling a story such as Nic's so difficult—difficult to tell and difficult to read.

'Spit' is such a bodily fluid, and in *Safe Space* it is a signal of danger. It alerted me, the horror veteran, to danger around the corner. But, as I tell my students, we must acknowledge this danger, name it, and face it. It is an act of bravery to do so. And *Safe Space* does this. In a way only a fan with a sense of distinction could.

MEMORY

Safe Space, then, is a compass, a focus, for saying things that were previously unsaid, via Star Wars. And in being that, *Safe Space* is a unique memoir.

Safe Space is a book of memories, of things and events that happened and that are recounted, reported, by a witness. All too often events past are left alone, forgotten, or ignored. But, as Nursing Professor Allison Phinney says, quoting Timothy Findley: "If we cannot remember anything, how can we possibly know who we are?"

The memory of the past makes the present relevant—makes it alive.

Safe Space does that too, when Nic writes that he aims to live in the present. I am pretty sure he means an informed present, a present that does not let itself be robbed of its meaning because of its shallow ignorance or refusal to acknowledge what has been. There are too many writers who cancel the past and celebrate 'forgetting.'

Virginia Woolf wrote that "memory is the seamstress." In *Safe Space*, Nic writes about memories as waypoints. In a chapter on 'memory' in her book *Media Reception Studies*, the American film historian and leading figure in gender studies Janet Staiger reports on research, by Lynn Spigel and Henry Jenkins, on adults watching (and re-watching) old films and shows and relaying how much they meant to them—and how much they continue to mean. The example she relays is that of *Batman*, the television show. The re-watching, she observes, evokes memories of originally watching, and those, in turn, lead the viewers to recall how much the shows meant to them—not only at the time, but since then, as transitional moments (a moment of "taking his first step into a much larger world" to use Nic's—and George Lucas's—words), rites of passage, or of stages of coming to terms with one's past towards larger social meanings about one's own identity and place in the world.

Fast forward to today, when much more recent research demonstrates how audiences self-describing as vulnerable have made their viewing experiences (and those experiences' everyday life importance) into crucial memories of media and popular culture, *especially* memories embroidered around instances and trajectories of fandom.

I'll admit I am not the biggest fan of *Star Wars*. But I vividly remember watching *The Empire Strikes Back* and *The Return of the Jedi* in theatres, with a sense of anticipation and exhilaration. There was no denying this was a *mimetic* moment: a moment when one's private life synched with public life, when the cues from a film about small-scale rebellion versus vast bureaucracies lined up with the clues I had as a young teenager about life in the real world, filled with report cards, judging adults, and annoying administrative hurdles.

The fact that I was primed for this mimetic moment by numerous stories about *Star Wars* and its universe (in the Dutch comic book magazine *Eppo*) perhaps smoothened the moment. But it was a 'live' and captivating moment nonetheless. So, call me a fan at that moment.

MOMENTS

Memories have the tendency to crystallize around material and tactile moments: moments of touch, of bodies, of proximity. It is no coincidence smells stay with us because they demand closeness. I was in my early thirties when I saw *The Straight Story*, David Lynch's pedestrian-paced film about two alienated brothers. A few days before the film, my grandmother had passed away. She had been living in my parents' house for the last decade or so, and we had been close (she was close to everyone who knew her, a warm person). But the fact she was 'gone' did not hit me until I saw Dean Stockwell's face appear at the end of *The Straight Story*. And in that moment, I changed. There was nothing to see, really: I looked the same, and moved the same; but something had shifted profoundly. Maybe it was the moment I 'finally grew up,' 'I woke up,' 'I saw clearly,' 'I was triggered,' ... whatever terms come to mind ... because within the month, I finished my PhD, got a job (as a secretary), and then pursued an academic life.

These moments matter. The aggregate of such moments can make up a path, if the right metaphor binds them. In *Safe Space*, Nic carves out such a trajectory of moments, via the fan-distinctive focus on both sad and joyful memories.

A moment is supposed to last only three to seven seconds in film. Or even one to three seconds. But not longer. That is the time it takes for an actor to get 'in the moment,' for the crew to 'take a moment' to problem solve on the spot, or to improvise. It is the time that measures the average shot length across film history. Outside that span, a film is regarded as either compressing or stretching time for aesthetic reasons—to make a point. I would like to put forward that these 'normal' moments are at least equally exceptional. It all depends on how 'normal' the perceiver makes the moment. For me, Dean Stockwell's moment is everlasting. As *Safe Space* shows, some moments last longer, some are only instances.

In *Safe Space*, moments are cherished. They are not just the stones with which the story is built—they *are* the story. Much like the author's credo to "live in the moment," *Safe Space* lives in its moments. This gives this book a unique style, a flow that glides from instance to instance and that hops from incident to incident.

Moments happen rather quickly. Nic, I am borrowing this thought from you, because it runs through your book. Because they happen rather quickly, we tend to minimize them. But in those moments lie lifelong feelings. *Safe Space* is filled with such moments.

EXUBERANCE

Finally, this. Every record needs to have a fun side, and every fan appreciates a rabbit hole or Easter egg. There are a few in *Safe Space*, waiting to be discovered by readers. For me, the rabbit hole was the mention of 'Uptown Funk' and *Mary Poppins*, within the wider community of cosplay (and especially the 501st). I teach a course at UBC on cult cinema, and a parade of the 501st adorns one of the slides of the session on cult blockbusters. It always fascinates students. Further down in the same course we discuss "Scary Mary Poppins" (I'll let you discover for yourself what that is), and I show a montage of classical Hollywood musical moves and dances to the tune of 'Uptown Funk.' Each time, the class is riveted. I am not listing this to show some sort of synchronicity. Instead, I think these examples, these little mentions, allow us to enjoy just how connected films and film-viewing can make us. To some, these 'little things' may seem silly, but they are essential. As Nic writes, they are moments of infectious exuberance. And exuberance is key to life.

Disgusted by the horrors of World War I, German philosopher Ernst Bloch tasked himself with writing *The Spirit of Utopia*, a work that has strongly influenced thinking about the role of cultural expressions in society. In the book, Bloch dissects the world and argues for expressive exuberance. I can only translate that as 'joy of life.' *Safe Space* does the same. Nic has written a book that springs with vitality and that enjoys being alive.

Ernest Mathijs is Professor of Cinema and Media Studies at the University of British Columbia.

PREFACE

Thank you for reading *Safe Space: A True Story of Faith, Betrayal, and the Power of the Force.* This book is the result of a decade of writing about how Star Wars saved my life. It began as a research paper at the University of British Columbia for my PhD advisor, Jerry Wasserman. I used my own survivor's story as a research subject on how popular culture can be viewed through a therapeutic lens for people who have experienced severe childhood trauma. After Jerry read my paper, he asked if I wanted to switch my dissertation focus to that subject.

I did not.

I thought that would be the end of it, but my destiny was about to take a different path. A couple years later, I posted my paper on Facebook and a friend, Ken Hollands, asked me if I ever thought of turning my story into a one-person play. In 2017, *How Star Wars Saved My Life* premiered at Performance Works in Vancouver, BC. Now, I find myself having expanded my story into this humble work you hold in your hands.

I have written about actual events and people in my life. I have taken the liberty of changing many names and places within this book to protect their privacy; I have also chosen to leave the names of others unchanged as a way of honouring them. In doing just that, I have demonstrated I am not an unbiased writer. I have my flaws, and this book is an example of them. To the best of my abilities, I have attempted a chronological approach; however, there is no doubt some sequencing of events might not be true to the timeline in which they happened. I have taken liberties to help the narrative that follows flow. Much like the Star Wars universe I often discuss, my story is full of heroes and villains, allies and foes, who hinder and help. This book has been written without the consent or authorization of any person affiliated with Lucasfilm Ltd. or The Walt Disney Company, and I acknowledge that the intellectual property of the entire Star Wars universe belongs to them.

This book is about my personal journey of extreme trauma and survival from childhood through my adulthood, and how the Star Wars franchise has saved and shaped my life. As a survivor of sexual abuse from Catholic priests, I feel it is important to speak out against organized pedophilia and the systems that remain in place to protect serial pedophiles. I discuss how I was groomed and exploited for sex, how I was a victim of beatings and other traumatic abuse, and how society has allowed such systematic abuse to carry on without any real justice against such sickening crimes. I also illustrate the long-lasting effects of abuse—how it lives on through emotional scarring long after the abuse itself has ended.

I am reminded of my past every day, and it has been a long journey from victim to survivor. Years of feeling subhuman—unworthy of living as a result of the crimes perpetrated against me—has resulted in the writing of this book. Only now, well into my life, do I feel worthy of the love and protection that should be felt by every child born in the galaxy.

May this book find you balance in the Force.

May the Force be with you as it is with me.

This is the way.

For my mother, Pearl.
She has always been strong and caring.
Her love and encouragement over the years have been
a constant source of strength for me.
She is my General Leia.

maxima debetur puero reverentia
We owe the greatest respect to the child.

— Juvenal

PROLOGUE

*A long time ago in a galaxy
far, far away ...*

— Title Card, *A New Hope*

I was in and out of consciousness for several weeks. I had continual nightmares and fragmented dreams. My parents told me that I almost died, yet I have no memory of that. I do remember dreaming I was in a boat circling a black hole and feeling the temptation to drift into it. A voice echoed in the blackness.

Run, Luke!

Listening to these words, I suddenly found a paddle in my hands and paddled against the increasing strength of the current trying to pull me into blackness. Then I felt hands around my waist and a thrusting sensation of pain. I could feel myself being thrown into a wall and falling down the stairs, smashing my head onto the floor. When I picked myself up, I was wearing a cassock and was standing in front of a crowded congregation in a church. I was covered in blood, and they pointed at me, laughing.

Trust your feelings!

I could feel the doctor's cold stethoscope pressing against my chest. Injections in my arms. More blackness. Yet, through it all, I heard my mentors calling out to me.

Let go, Luke. Trust in the Force.

I opened my eyes. I was in my room. My parents were there looking at me, but they didn't speak. It took all of my energy, but I managed to say, "The Force is with me." My mom started to cry. I had no idea how long I had been in bed, but I had lost almost a hundred pounds.

I had awoken memories within as I faced death in my sleep. The memories of sexual abuse and the physical pain I had endured were growing. Yet, in that blackness, it was my love of *Star Wars* that kept me fighting to live.

I was in grade twelve and was desperately looking forward to graduation and to finally being able to leave my hometown. As I slowly regained my strength, I was told that I would likely not be graduating, as I had missed too much school. But I knew I had to get away. I studied and prepared for my final exams while my teachers told me I would not pass.

I did not pray to God for help. Instead, I turned to the Force. I could feel my regeneration as I closed my eyes and breathed. I had to leave the darkness for the unknown. I knew that if I didn't leave after graduation, I would never get out of that town.

I passed my courses with honours, and by August of that year I was in my car driving to university. The Force was with me. And yet, the darkness of my dreams and my memories haunted me still. As my hometown faded away behind me, I hoped that the dark side within me would fade away too.

Soon I would learn that the dark side was not something I could simply run away from. The paths between the light and the dark sides of the Force are not so easily maintained—especially for me who had been given a push into the darkness by my early mentors.

To be a Jedi, I would learn, is a lifelong journey.

1
BEGINNINGS

If there's a bright centre to the universe, you're on the planet that it's farthest from.

— Luke Skywalker, *A New Hope*

I love Star Wars. It has had a huge impact on my life, and it has brought me immense joy and happiness.

I will warn you now that I am a nerd. Perhaps the term *geek* may apply and is better suited, but truly I am, above all things, a nerd. I still have a few of my original Star Wars toys from my childhood that have managed to remain with me through the years. Only the most durable ones have made it this far. The paint may be chipped, the faces on the action figures may have faded over time, and there may be a few missing parts here and there; but they remain among some of my most precious curios.

As an adult I have continued to accumulate memorabilia. My assortment of lightsabers continues to grow as I seek out unique hilts and blades that I can duel with. I dare say my costume collection has increased dramatically.

I remember the costumes of my youth—going to the local K-Mart and Woolco, and finding the vinyl masked Star Wars characters. My parents never bought me any of those commercially made costumes. They took pride in homemade costuming. As much as I wanted to be

Luke or a Rebel pilot, I instead dressed up as the Red Baron or a gypsy each Halloween.

Now, as a grown man, I finally have the costumes I dreamt of as a child. My obsessive-compulsive disorder has contributed to my painstaking quest to ensure that the costumes I now have meet or exceed their screen-used cousins. At the time of writing this, my costumes include Darth Vader, an Imperial officer, a death trooper, Rebel pilots (from both *Rogue One* and *A New Hope*), Chewbacca, and a Jedi. In addition, I have built a fully functional and authentic R2-D2.

As I wrote above, I am truly a nerd.

I can honestly say I've watched the original Star Wars films hundreds of times. I used to know every single line of dialogue in every film—and have demonstrated this knowledge much to the chagrin of anyone who foolishly thought watching with me was a good idea.

Because of my obsession with detail, I find myself being more melancholic with every Halloween that passes. When my children were younger, I loved dressing up with them and taking them around the neighbourhood. I have dressed up with my children as various Star Wars characters over the years including (but not limited to) Boba Fett, Rebel pilots, stormtroopers, Darth Vader, biker scouts, and my favourite—the Jedi Knight. Not Luke or Obi-Wan, but rather a generic Jedi. I have been asked by confused adults if I would also like some candy.

"A Jedi craves not these things."

Why did I do this? Why did I go to great lengths to ensure my children and I had cool Halloween costumes? I love my children. I love sharing events with my children. And—even if it's only for a minute—I love feeling as though I am somehow part of the Star Wars universe.

Star Wars is not just a series of films to me. It's a way of life. I am a professional actor, stunt coordinator, and fight director, and my decision to pursue these careers has been solidly rooted within the realm of Star Wars. My skill as a swordsman I attribute to my childhood determination to be like Luke Skywalker, and I am always most comfortable when I have a lightsaber or sword in my hand. As a drama teacher I often find ways to weave Star Wars references into my lessons. I am sure this frustrates some students, but my students are all well aware that, as a teacher, I am a Jedi.

When I was nine years old my mother surprised me at the local pharmacy when she bought me my very first *Star Wars* action figure, R2-D2.

It was October of 1977 in Hopeless—the town I grew up in in Northern British Columbia, far north of a town named Hope. The ongoing joke among the town's residents was to tell visitors that we lived "beyond Hope"—which is somewhat accurate. I will not reveal the town's actual name, so from here on I will refer to the town of my childhood simply as *Hopeless*. *Star Wars* had been out for a number of months, was still in the local theatre, and I was hooked.

Now, for those who do not know who (or what) R2-D2 is, let me attempt to explain. R2 is a cute blue and white droid with a round silver dome that stands roughly three feet tall. Even though he only beeps and chirps electronically, his counterpart C3PO and Luke Skywalker are able to understand him. R2 is what is known in the Star Wars universe as an astromech, or service droid, capable of many tasks such as co-piloting starfighters, recording important messages, concealing lightsabers, and getting people out of very sticky situations.

Most of my original Star Wars toys are now gone, but R2 continues to stay with me and has been with me for many adventures—as a child and as an adult. R2 was there when I endured physical fights in school. I would clutch him as I walked home, and it was somehow comforting. R2 was there when I graduated high school, through university, and through my time living in England. R2 was with me when I was married and has been to the Soviet Union with me when I was performing. He shared a spot in my Black Knight costume in *Scooby-Doo 2*. R2 accompanied me when I was in the hospital with my dying father, for the birth of my children, and when I have spent endless hours marking students' papers. He was there when I had to take my beloved cat, Socrates, to the vet to be put down, and when I was granted my PhD.

R2 has been witness to my greatest achievements and my lowest moments. And though I had boxed up my other toys as a teenager, my childhood attachment to him kept my robot always diligently by my side. He has been my touchstone through most of my life. He is well worn—a little deformed from the years of being carried in my pockets. He is my constant companion. I have ranted to him when I have been upset and when I have tried to think things out. He has also become a very important part of this testament of mine about abuse. If you ever want to challenge me to his whereabouts all you have to do is ask to see him. He is always either on me, in my house with me, or in my car. He is never far away.

I know it is materialistic of me, but that first Star Wars gift from my mother was so much more than just a gift. That day she bought me a lifelong friend—my companion droid. He is my security—my witness to events. R2 was the first toy I owned from the Star Wars series, and he is now the last one left, having escaped the plight of my other toys.

My R2 is special to me. He represents the hope I had as a child for something new and for happier times. More importantly, he was a gift from my mother—physical proof of her love for me. If only we knew as adults the power of such moments as those we experience as children.

R2 was at one time my world—my safe space. Now he is a reminder of my past. He is lovable, loyal, and he is my droid. R2 is my touch-stone. I love that droid so much. You see, the gift of that special action figure when I was nine came at a time when I was in need of comfort and friendship.

I am getting ahead of myself. You see, this is the story of how one science fiction franchise—Star Wars—saved my life, and how it provided the safe space for me to become the Jedi I am today.

2

FAMILY

Luke's just not a farmer, Owen. He has too much of his father in him ...

— Aunt Beru, *A New Hope*

The Force is with us. It binds us, surrounds us, and holds the galaxy together. Each of us has a beginning, a middle, and an end in this world. As far as we know, we do not choose who we are born to or what our lives will be. From the moment we are born, we are in a constant state of learning that continues until our last breath. Our parents or guardians are, in most cases, the first role models we pattern our behaviour after.

My father was born Anglican. He was the son of an American pioneer and an English nurse. My dad grew up "in the bush," as he would say. He lived a pioneer's life. When he was born, he made the journey from the hospital to his home in a saddlebag on his mother's horse.

His mother, Esther, had come from a family in England that was former aristocracy—or so the rumour went. As it became easier to search ancestry, I did some research on my grandmother and discovered that, in fact, Esther's genealogy is ridiculously blue-blooded. I wish my dad had lived long enough to know he was a descendant of kings and queens. He would have found it funny. My dad was a very gentle and humble man.

He made his living as a welder—at least I knew him to be a welder throughout my life. He had also been a barge captain, a truck driver, a pilot, and a plumber. He served Canada as a paratrooper during the Second World War. He did not become a paratrooper because he wanted to jump out of planes and be sent on dangerous missions. He wanted to be a paratrooper in 1941 because it paid more than a regular soldier's pay. At that time, he was the head of his family. His father and mother had both died—his father from cancer and his mother from suicide.

I've learned that his father, my grandfather, was not a pleasant man: an alcoholic who beat his wife and children. When my dad was old enough to protect his mother, he would offer himself up to his father to take beatings instead of her. He told me of how he was tied to a bed and whipped with his father's belt. I am thankful that I never received such cruel and terrible punishment from my dad.

Eventually Esther reached her breaking point and drowned herself in the waters of Ootsa Lake. After that, my dad sent most of his army pay to his siblings. Being a paratrooper would give him extra spending money, so he signed up for the First Canadian Parachute Battalion.

Over the years of my childhood, I would hear funny stories from my dad about his time in the service; however, he never shared battle stories with me. Those stories were off limits.

I knew my dad's profession to be that of a welder. He could fix anything that was broken. If he couldn't fix it, he would simply replicate it. As a welder, he was an artist. I once showed him a sword I had that needed repair. He looked at it and informed me that the hilt was brass and that it could not be welded as it was a soft metal. Instead, he asked me if he could keep it for a week. He ended up returning to me an exact reproduction of my damaged sword in stainless steel. It was much stronger and resilient than the original stage sword I had asked him to repair.

He became my personal sword maker. At the time of his death, he had made me over one hundred swords for my use as a professional fight director.

My mom came from a different background. She was a combination of Mennonite German, Austrian, and Jew.

My mom's father was a station agent for the Canadian National Railway. He was an immigrant from Austria. As a daughter of immigrants, my mom was no stranger to hard work. During the Second World War, she was only eight when she had her first job; she had an affinity for numbers and would do bookkeeping for the owner of a local restaurant. She was paid in extra rations that she would bring home to her family—extra butter, cheese, and sugar were exchanged for her expertise at keeping books at eight years old.

In her twenties she became a bank teller and eventually became a bank executive. She was popular amongst her clients, and it was her hard work ethic that accelerated her climb up the corporate ladder, taking on positions that were commonly only held by men. My mom continues to be an incredible person.

My parents met in the small town of Hopeless. Where is Hopeless, you may ask? Well, if there is a bright centre to the universe, then Hopeless is the town that is farthest from it. My mom was married to my dad's best friend. My dad, who was recently divorced, made a point of going to her wicket at the bank whenever he needed help cashing his cheques. The chemistry between my parents was so strong that my mom left her husband and eventually married my dad.

It was there in Hopeless that my parents found a new hope together. They both had had children through their previous marriages; however, I was *their* only child. You have no idea how much I love my parents.

Although I was my parents' only full biological child, their marriage provided me with four half sisters and one half brother. My dad had three children who lived with their mother whom I never even met until I was much older. My mom had two daughters who were in and out of my life growing up. Margorie was significantly older than me and thus was not a large part of my childhood. Melissa, however, was only a handful of years older and lived with us.

Melissa would never let me forget that I was only her *half* brother. She forced me to serve her when we were alone. She would hit me, call me names, and berate me in front of her friends. She empowered herself at my expense.

Her story is not mine to tell, and she cannot defend herself in this book, so you are naturally exposed to opinions and bias from my perspective. As for my other siblings, I have not seen them or spoken with them in years. I don't believe I would even recognize any of them if I was to see them on the street. They have never been a significant part of my life, and I don't expect this to change.

My parents were the first to show me the power of the Force. I would, of course, learn more about the Force when I was nine years old—through the Star Wars films. To me, the Force is love. As Obi-Wan Kenobi tells young Luke, "It is an energy field created by all living things. It surrounds us and penetrates us. It binds the galaxy together." A Jedi's strength flows from this Force.

It is my philosophy that in order to be a Jedi you must live in the past, present, and future in harmony. Our memories are our guides, and they can be powerful allies, or they can be our most dire foes. It's what and how we learn from them that guides us towards the darkness or towards the light, or to the careful balance in between.

∃ MEMORIES

The belonging you seek is not behind you. It is ahead.

— Maz Kanata,
The Force Awakens

I occasionally find myself lost in my thoughts for no apparent reason. My memories can be triggered by sound or smell. For instance, there is a particular smell near the entrance gates at Disneyland that always triggers my memory of being there for the first time, when I was ten years old. It never fails to bring me back to the day I first arrived there with my family in my youth.

Everyone has an earliest memory. Sometimes we hide them away and forget about them over time. Sometimes they come back—and sometimes they simply slip away into the ether of time. The memories from my early childhood come to me in flashes. My earliest memory is firmly embedded in my heart. It is the building of my playhouse, The Trapper John.

It is late summer. The warm breeze from the day continues into the evening. The smell of the tall grass fills the air. I must be three, maybe four, years old. My dad and some of his friends are building me a log cabin—a real log cabin. It is not one of those plastic ordered-through-the-mail-catalogue kind of cabins, but a *real* miniature log cabin. My dad has skinned the trees himself. He's making it for me. He's even made a wooden door for it with a proper wood handle. The logs seem to fit together without nails. It's just carved wood.

He works through the dusk, and as the darkness falls my dad and his friends make a large bonfire as they continue to work on the cabin. The heat from the flames warms my face, and I am happy—so happy—that nothing else matters in this moment. The snapping, popping, hiss of the flames is magical. I look up into the night sky and watch the glowing embers float towards the stars. I start to wonder if the floating embers become stars as they slip into the night sky. This night is full of wonder and love and magic.

A darker memory I have is from when I must have been only three.

It is winter. My parents are rushing to get me dressed in a snowsuit in the kitchen. There is lots of yelling and I feel overwhelmed. My mom is being rough with my arms as she forces them through the arms of the snowsuit. The radio is on—it's always on in the kitchen. There is more activity surrounding me and then the door closes, and I am standing alone. I look out the window and see their car driving away. I cry. I have been abandoned. I don't think it's for long. The door opens and my mother rushes in. I have been found. I feel the combination of anger and joy as she takes me in her arms and holds me tightly.

There is another memory that I can recall from my early childhood. It's a fond memory, but it's a different kind of joy from the one I just mentioned.

It is fall. I wake up early so I can watch television and say goodbye to my dad before he leaves for work. We only get two channels in our small town, and they don't even go on the air until about six o'clock in the morning.

I am lying on the living room floor. The green and blue shag carpet warms my chest and stomach. Before me, I have a mug of hot chocolate and a plate of buttered toast. Have you ever experienced the amazing taste that is achieved through dipping buttered toast into hot chocolate? It is a delicious combination of sweet and savoury—though I admit I have not done this in many years.

The black and white test pattern on the television flickers off and is replaced by the theme song of my first favourite cartoon. In later years

I would enjoy *Scooby-Doo, Yogi Bear,* and Disney shorts, but at this age my favourite cartoon—or show, for that matter—is *Mighty Mouse.* The theme song remains in my memory:

> *Mister Trouble never hangs around*
> *When he hears this mighty sound.*
> *"Here I come to save the day"*
> *That means that Mighty Mouse is on the way.*
> *Yes sir, when there is wrong to right*
> *Mighty Mouse will join the fight.*
> *On the sea or on the land*
> *He gets the situation well in hand.*

I was so obsessed with this Terrytoons classic that I even dressed as Mighty Mouse for Halloween one year. I remember wearing grey long underwear with a tail sewn on the back and a yellow "M" stitched on the front of the chest. Mouse ears were stitched onto an old wool hat we had. I wish there were pictures of this creation, but, alas, I am resigned to the flashes of these memories within me.

Mighty Mouse had amazing superpowers. He could fly, had super strength, and had invulnerability. He had X-ray vision and was fond of another mouse named Pearl Pureheart. His arch-nemesis was a cat named Oil Can Harry. From what I can remember, Oil Can Harry was always trapping Pearl Pureheart, and Mighty Mouse would always come to the rescue at precisely the right time.

I loved how Mighty Mouse could fly. I had recurring dreams where I was running down the street by my house and I would trip—but instead of hitting the ground I would suddenly fly up and around the neighbourhood. The dreams were so intense and realistic that at times I believed I really had this power. Mighty Mouse was my hero.

As I grew older, my parents were faced with the challenge of where to send me for my education. There was a public school in our neighbourhood, but my mom did not want me to go to that school as it was considered a rough place. We did not live in the best area of town.

Today, that area has been labelled a bad neighbourhood, the economic depression in the town having worsened over time.

My parents believed that I should attend the prestigious private school in our small town—the esteemed Blessed Virgin of the Bleeding Heart Elementary. We were not a Catholic family, but religious education and indoctrination was part of the package when attending this traditional Catholic school. It was there that I learned the customs and rituals of the Catholic faith and eventually was assimilated into the religion.

The priests and brothers who ran the school always kept a watchful eye over their flock. Every day began the same way. Students from all the grades—or at least the primary grades—would assemble in the church basement and organize themselves in their various divisions. Students would then sing the national anthem, followed by 'God Save the Queen.' Announcements and school business would follow, and then the assembly would end with the students reciting the Lord's Prayer in monotone before being sent to class.

My memory of my education at the school is a blur of events, with vivid recollections of various moments. I can remember the faces of some of the students from the old photographs, but their names come and go. Names such as Thomas, Kim, Teresa, Vincent, and Randall burn in my memory still.

The school's population was made of several different factions. First, there were the sons and daughters of the prominent Catholic families who paid for their children to attend the school. Next, there were the children from the poor Catholic families who were "permitted" to attend. Then, there were the Indigenous children who were casualties and holdovers from the residential school system who remained in the Church's care. Finally, there were a few—not many—like me and my half sister, whose non-religious parents really did want a better start in life for their children and paid the most for us non-Catholics to attend.

I can recall the school in vivid detail—the walls were dull and grey, the floors dark green, and the humming of the fluorescent lighting provided a monotone background soundscape throughout the school day. Our uniforms consisted of light-blue shirts, dark-blue pants, black socks, and black shoes. The halls of the school were patrolled by the priests in their flowing black robes and white collars.

Our headmaster was Brother Ignatious. He had receding grey hair, dead grey eyes, and was a tall and ominous man. He was a brother belonging to the Oblates of Mary Immaculate—a missionary order. Ignatious took his role as headmaster seriously and ruled the school using tactics of fear and intimidation.

My first of many encounters with Ignatious began shortly after I started attending the school at age five.

4
AND SO, TO SCHOOL

Truly wonderful, the mind of a child is.

— Yoda, *Attack of the Clones*

Everything at the school was new to me. My blue dress shirt was not nearly as comfortable as T-shirts or sweaters. It was going to take time to get comfortable in my new school uniform.

My kindergarten teacher was Miss O'Donnell. She was young and had blue eyes with jet black hair, and she was from Galway in Ireland. She had an accent that was soothing and relaxing; I loved listening to her speak. She began class each morning by playing Cat Stevens's 'Morning Has Broken.' Sometimes she would take out her guitar and play along as the record scratched out the song on her portable turn-table. One morning she played it over and over and had us sing along with her. I remember her as a kindly woman. She was soft-spoken, but there was a sadness and melancholy about her.

One day I was unable to finish an in-class assignment on time, and Miss O'Donnell sent me into the hall to wait for Brother Ignatious. I stood outside the class with my back against the wall and remained at attention as we had been taught to do. This was my first time being sent outside the class, so I stood in the dark hall and waited for what seemed like an eternity. The fluorescent lights hummed in the background.

Eventually Ignatious appeared at the end of the hall and made his way towards me, his black oxford shoes echoed in the hall as heel met linoleum. He asked me why I was waiting in the hall for him. What had I done to be there? I could not think of anything I had done wrong and really was not sure why I was sent to wait. He leaned in so close that I could smell his breath. It smelled of stale coffee and rancid milk.

Ignatious asked me to hold out my writing hand. I was so scared that I had to think for a moment which one it was. I used both (to the chagrin of Miss O'Donnell) but decided it was best to go with my favoured drawing hand.

I presented my right hand to him. He clutched my wrist with his left hand, and he produced a thick leather strap from behind his back. I now know the strap was professionally made by the Tawes company. The company made professional punishment tools for private schools all over the world. Ignatious's Tawes made a swooshing sound as he moved it through the air. Three times he "attempted" to strike the palm of my hand.

Each time he "missed."

He made the most of the moment, turning the event into a theatrical act. Each time that he missed my hand he pretended to have a conversation with God. He alleviated the tension by making it seem funny to me that he was missing my hand. He looked up and asked God why he kept missing and told God he was going to do better and try again. Each time he missed he commented that the Virgin Mary must really not want him to punish me, and he couldn't understand why I was having such luck in being spared.

After his third attempt, he told me that God told him I was a sweet child and that it must have been a mistake for me to be waiting in the hall for him. He tightened his grip on my wrist as he relayed God's message to me. He looked up and asked God if he had the right child, and acted as if God was answering him, all the while holding my wrist firmly.

His hold seemed to last for a long time. Finally, Ignatious released his grip and sent me back into class, patting my backside gently as I returned.

I have thought about that incident a lot since it happened. Was it just a sick game Ignatious enjoyed playing with the new children at the school? As a child I thought that maybe the Blessed Mother or the baby Jesus were really looking out for me. Maybe they *had* somehow prevented the strap from striking the palm of my hand.

When I was older, I thought that maybe in that moment I was somehow able to *force* the strap away from striking its intended target. The Force, perhaps? Or maybe it was a Sith mind trick. The Sith, as I would eventually learn at eleven years of age from my Burger King collector glass, are the followers and devotees of the dark side of the Force that Darth Vader belonged to ... and possibly that Ignatious belonged to as well.

5

FATHER VITUS

*I need someone to show me
my place in all this.*

— Rey, *The Last Jedi*

In sharp contrast to Brother Ignatious was Father Vitus. Father Vitus did not have as intense features as Ignatious. He was a taller, more slender man. He had white hair, wore glasses, and had a happier disposition than Ignatious.

Vitus effortlessly made friends with my parents, making several casual visits to our home. He came to know my parents very well and then visited us on a regular basis. He became so familiar with them that he would borrow my parents' car on occasion.

He often had two or three Indigenous children in his company. I always felt afraid when the children were with him. They seemed angry and did not speak much, and when they did speak, it was so quietly that I could not easily hear or understand them. The children, I would learn later, were wards of the Church, and Vitus became a surrogate father to them. Vitus shared that their parents were either dead, drug-addicted, or too irresponsible and drunk to care for their children, so the Church was taking on the responsibility of raising them.

I remember the day he brought two new children into our house. He told us he had just taken them from a remote community four hours away. They were only about three or four—a brother and a sister—and they were very quiet. I tried to show them some of my toys in our living room while Vitus visited with my parents in the kitchen. They grabbed the toys from me and played roughly with them, trying to remove the heads off some toys and the wheels from others. They spoke to each other in a language I had never heard of before; it was not English or French. Vitus had ears like a hawk. He came into the room and shouted at them.

"No!"

The children became silent once more. I had no idea what I had just witnessed. He grabbed them each by their upper arms and looked into their eyes as he continued to yell at them.

"Don't start anymore of that nonsense!"

He then returned to the kitchen as though nothing had happened and made light of the situation.

"No rest for the wicked. It's my duty to tame the savage little beasts."

The children sat quietly on the floor in the living room as Father Vitus sat in the kitchen telling more stories about "Indians."

"The funniest thing is when I am asked to perform marriages, and the squaws show up at the church, and they are dressed in white. In white. Heaven knows that's the last colour they should be wearing. I mean some of them have their own children as ring bearers. Oh, the hypocrisy."

He enjoyed telling jokes and making fun of the Indigenous children in the North. Once he even told my mom that he knew how the whole "Indian issue" could be resolved.

"You see, Pearl, we have a church cat. She's a good mouser. Whenever she is knocked up by a tom, we wait for her to have her litter. As soon as that's done, I take the kittens and toss them into a sack, tie it nice and tight, and take a drive to the bridge. I just throw the sack over the railing and the problem is solved. My cat is back to mousing and there are no kittens to deal with. That's how you control the feral cat situation. It's a simple solution, really."

As an adult I really don't know how my parents were able to tolerate his demeaning, sickening, and racist attitude. As a child I did not fully understand the extent of the racism inherent within Vitus. All I really thought about him was that he was kind of funny, awkward, and oddly charismatic.

Father Vitus would often drop in unannounced for visits with my family. If he arrived near dinnertime, he would always be welcome to join us, and we would set a place for him at the table. My mom was flattered that a priest had made friends with us and thought that his willingness to spend time with us must be a good omen. She would do everything she could to make him comfortable when he visited.

Vitus would lead us in saying grace when he dined with us. We were not inherently a religious family and never said grace at dinnertime. (We did, however, say thanks at the table on Thanksgiving and Christmas dinners, as more of a tradition than out of religious piety.) When Vitus said grace at our house, it lacked the ceremony and the severity of the prayers I had become accustomed to at the school. His grace was funny.

He would stand before us and say, "Rub-a-dub-dub. Three men in a tub. Thanks for the grub." He would then sit down and begin to eat.

He was quick with jokes as well. One story I can recall him telling my parents was that of a devout Catholic woman who was married and had fifteen children. Her husband died and she quickly remarried and had another fifteen children. Her second husband passed away after the birth of her last child, and she died a few years later. When she died, the priest at her funeral stated, "At least they're together now."

One of her children put up her hand and said, "Excuse me, Father, do you mean her first or second husband?"

The priest replied, "I mean her legs."

I was too young to understand the joke, but my parents thought it was hilarious—perhaps only because it was a priest who was telling it.

Vitus was really not a typical priest. He seemed more like a fun-loving spiritual adventurer—a man who loved spending time with the non-Catholic families ... all the while sizing up their children and earning familial trust.

ō
FLYING

I'm going to be a pilot.
Best in the galaxy.

— Han Solo, *Solo*

It was early October.

I'm in the schoolyard. The weather is cool. Sunny, but cool. Father Vitus is on duty during recess. I love the swings. Like Mighty Mouse I can, if only for a moment, fly. I pump my legs harder and harder until I feel the cool breeze on my face and imagine I am soaring over the mountains, up to the sky, and into the universe. I am free! Higher and higher I soar. I feel I am like Mighty Mouse. No! I *am* Mighty Mouse. I am so powerful. My legs are jets. I am actually flying. I can fly! I can—

In the middle of my fantastic flying fantasy, I sense that someone is watching me. I open my eyes and look down. I am being watched. It's Randall. My heart beats a little faster. I don't like Randall much. He's bigger than I am, and he is always bossy. For some reason he seems to always be in a bad mood. Randall stands directly in front of the swings, and as I glide back and forth, he continues to stare at me. I know what he wants. He wants the swing.

"Hey! Get off my swing!" he shouts.

I feel the universe I have been flying in start to slip away. Suddenly my legs are no longer jets. They begin to lose their power as I try pathetically to keep my spot on the swing.

"Get. Off. Now!"

I attempt to make my case as I continue to glide in front of him. "You want me off the swing? But I just got on."

Randall contorts his face. A deep guttural sound emanates from his throat. He takes a breath in as he arches his body back, then suddenly spits his phlegm at me. His first attempt barely misses me.

"Ewwwww. Don't spit at me." My command goes unheeded.

A second volley is launched towards me, hitting the chain above my hand. His targeting is getting better.

"Don't spit at me!" I plead. I can't see where his third attempt has landed. I don't think it's hit me. No, I am pretty sure I am still okay.

"Don't! Randall! Pleeeeease!" I am panicked and am begging now. My luck is sure to run out shortly.

Randall launches a final phlegm attack. A hit! A hit! A palpable hit! He has struck me right in the chest. I look down in horror to see the slimy green discharge start to make its way down my brown and beige ISPO jacket.

I immediately bring my feet down and leap off the swing. I begin to gag. My only hope is to find a leaf. I can use a leaf to wipe it off. I look over my shoulder and see Randall take over the swing. He attempts to spit on me again. I move myself out of range.

I manage to get most of the residue off my jacket with some of the orange maple leaves scattered over the playground. I look back at Randall on the swing. He is pumping his legs so hard that it looks as if he will spin over the bar of the swings. There is no chance I will be able to get another turn today. He pumps his legs harder and harder as he laughs with the enjoyment of simulated flight.

I sit on the ground out of spitting distance—alone—and start to cry. I long to be home. I remember how my dad would make me hot chocolate and buttered toast while I waited for Mighty Mouse to start. I wish Mighty Mouse was here with me now. I really could use a hero.

"There, there. Why so sad?"

I look up to see Father Vitus looking down at me. He looks especially tall from my angle. The sun behind him turns him into a dark silhouette before me. I look down.

"Randall spit on me." I pause. Vitus doesn't say a word, so I awkwardly continue. "I was on the swing, but Randall wanted me to get off. So, he spit on me ..." I point to where I had been hit, "... all over my jacket."

Vitus looks towards the swings. He adjusts his black hat as he leers at Randall. He looks back to me. "I will deal with that little savage later."

Father Vitus then changes his tone. His concern turns to reassurance. "I know what may make you feel better ... candy. Here, take my arm and I will help you up."

He extends his gloved hand towards me, and I take it. He pulls me to my feet.

"Now, just reach inside my pocket here." He indicates to the front pocket of his trousers. "Go ahead. Don't be afraid. I have lots of candy in there."

I remain still. He reasons his seemingly odd request to settle my apprehension.

"I don't want to take my gloves off, so you will just have to reach inside yourself."

I have never put my hand inside someone else's pocket before. Father Vitus takes my hand and guides it towards the opening of the front pocket of his black trousers. His pockets are deep. I find what I am sure is a wrapped candy at the bottom of his pocket. He turns his hips towards me as I begin removing my hand. Something in his pants brushes against my clenched fist. It all happens rather quickly.

I open my hand and look at my prize. It's one of those terrible Halloween-wrapped molasses candies. The wrapper is orange, yellow, white, and black, and it has what I think is a bad drawing of a witch and a ghost on it. It's the kind of candy that pulls the fillings out of your teeth when you try to chew it.

Vitus smiles and pats me on the head as he walks away, resuming his recess patrol. I sit in my solitude and unwrap my wax-paper treat. I cannot seem to get all of the paper off before popping the candy into my mouth. My stomach feels funny, but the sweetness of the candy tastes good. I look back over my shoulder and see Randall spitting on any kid that gets too close to him on the swings. Randall may have taken the swing, but at least I have candy.

THE WRATH OF IGNATIOUS

*Let me give you some advice.
Assume everyone will betray you,
and you'll never be disappointed.*

— Tobias Beckett, *Solo*

Memories, like waypoints, continue to map the paths we take during our lives. The following memory is another such marker in my life.

A few days later, I was out in the school's courtyard during lunchtime. The school's priests took turns patrolling the school grounds, and during this particular lunch, it was Brother Ignatious who was on patrol.

I find myself wandering through the open field at the back of the school, pacing by myself. I am sure we have all once seen—or have been—that child: looking down, mesmerized by their boots, or distracted by the many wondrous rocks that can be found on the ground—wandering away, unknowingly, from the flock of other children.

Yes, today that child is me. The textures of the rocks are interesting. Some smooth, some rough. The colours muted but varied. I like looking down and seeing how the earth feels beneath my feet. I am often alone during lunch, though it doesn't really bother me. I have many things to occupy my mind, and I am content, more or less.

I happen to look up to see Brother Ignatious walking deliberately towards me. His long black coat flows behind him as he moves steadily with determination. His thick Irish accent cuts through the air.

"Nicholas. Come here. Now." His grey eyes narrow. Something seems to have upset him.

I look behind me to make sure there is no clear and present danger that I may be oblivious to. It starts to sink in that maybe it's me he's upset with. Maybe I am not allowed to be out in the field alone.

Ignatious gets closer. He stops before me and wipes the perspiration from his brow with a white handkerchief he pulls from his pocket. He folds it and returns it to its place.

"Randall told me you lied to Father Vitus about him spitting on you."

I am slightly confused. "He *did* spit on me."

I appear to have said the wrong thing. But it was the truth.

Ignatious curls his lip. "More lies, Nicholas?" His County Cork lilt makes his accusations sound more like an Irish folk song than scolding.

I try to explain. "He—"

"Quiet! Liars deserve to be punished. I thought you would be better than this. Jesus, Mary, and Joseph! I am so upset that you would resort to lying."

Brother Ignatious pulls out his trusty strap, seemingly from nowhere. Before I have any time to react, his free hand snatches my right wrist, squeezing it so tightly that I cannot even close my own hand. Ignatious looks right through me with his grey eyes.

"So, are you calling Randall a liar?"

I am confused by this line of questioning. I don't know what to say except the truth.

"He is, yes."

Ignatious brings the strap down hard upon my hand.

Whap! I shriek, feeling the first bite of his strap cutting into my small hand. The sting of the strap's leather immediately produces tears. I am in pain and shock.

Whap! My hand burns. My cheeks glow red from the combination of the pain from the strap and the humiliation of the situation. I see a small gathering of children behind Ignatious as he continues with his discipline. Some are laughing, some are trying not to look, but just like passing a car wreck at the side of the road, they cannot help but to watch the scene unfold. I see Randall over Ignatious's shoulder. His schadenfreude is epic as he doubles over laughing at my sudden and swift courtyard punishment.

Whap! The third bite of the heavy leather on my palm is dull and hard.

Ignatious releases my wrist, sheaths his strap, and resumes his patrol. The crowd of gawking children immediately disperses as he turns around. Even Randall is quick to leave the scene and run back towards the abandoned swings in the distance.

I look down at my hand. I can see the finger marks where Ignatious had been clutching my wrist so tightly. My young brain tries to make sense of the strapping. Three times. I remember that the Catholics are drawn to the number three. Three strikes to my palm. Palm Sunday. The signs of the cross. Three. The three strikes for the Father, and the Son, and the Holy Ghost. Three. The number of completion that expresses a beginning, a middle, and an end. I find another rationale for the three. Three strikes to my soul for fear, anger, and aggression.

I could feel my innocence ebbing away. I had never been spanked or hit at home. This was a new experience for me. It felt as though my soul was cracking.

Memories. Waypoints on our life's journey. I wish there were some destinations that I could erase, or simply let slip off my map. Unfortunately, these memories remain burned in my brain—lingering phantoms from years past that, to this day, haunt me during times of insecurity and loneliness.

I began receiving the strap on a more consistent basis. Each time I was strapped, I was told how upset God was with me and that I would have to work much harder to earn God's love. Sometimes strappings happened in the privacy of the headmaster's office. Sometimes I was forced to lay across Ignatious's lap while he removed my pants to strap my exposed skin.

By November of my kindergarten year, many children in my class had been strapped. Sometimes strappings were held by appointment. During such occasions, formal strappings were often accompanied by a number of Hail Marys on the rosary, followed by writing lines on the chalkboard with the hand that had just been strapped.

The priests kept strapping us, and we, young problem solvers that we were, kept trying to find new ways to deal with the pain.

8
SURVIVING THE STRAP

In a dark place we find ourselves
... a little more knowledge
might light our way.

— Yoda, *Revenge of the Sith*

The children in my class shared solutions by which we could either neutralize the pain of the strap, or—at the very least—significantly reduce it. The solutions ranged from the bizarre to the disgusting. There are three that still come to mind:

1. Apple juice. I have no idea where this idea materialized among the school's population, but it was a fix that was handed down from the older kids to the new initiates. Children who were about to get the strap were advised to pour apple juice over the palms of their hands. The rationale for this was that somehow the apple juice would absorb the pain from the strap. It was suggested that if it did not immediately prevent the pain, it would work after several applications. As one can imagine, this treatment had no effectiveness. If anything, the extra wetness on the palm only intensified the sting from the heavy leather.

2. Apples. The second method of preventing pain while being strapped was a variation of the technique above. Rather than

apple juice, children scheduled for a strapping were advised to use an actual apple. By taking a bite out of the apple and rubbing the exposed apple flesh over the palm, the pain would again be dissipated by the magic properties of the apple.

3. Spit. The third common approach to eliminating the sting from the strap involved the compliance from a fellow student. The concept was that the spit from another person on the palm of the hand would act as a buffer between the leather of the strap and the palm of the hand. The thicker the phlegm, the better the result. Children who were just becoming sick or just recovering from a cold were the best designates to offer potential pain-free strap success.

Apples featured heavily in the techniques. I am sure this has something to do with the prevalence of the apple in the Old Testament. The apple represents the forbidden fruit and temptation for Adam and Eve, as well as knowledge, the fall of man, and original sin. Needless to say, none of these techniques were effective, and number three was especially disgusting.

Brother Ignatious was the chief administrator of the strap. Depending on the severity of the situation, a student could get anywhere from one to twenty strikes on the hand or buttocks.

One child, Vincent, was strapped so hard that a few bones in his right hand broke. He was then forced to write lines with that same hand. He could not stop crying out in pain, and his shrieks could be heard through the halls of the school. I remember seeing his hand bandaged up the next day and thought to myself that his fingers looked like thick sausages. His parents were devout Catholics and, instead of comforting the boy, had struck him again at home for being strapped at school. After all, if the headmaster had done that then there must have been good cause.

Ignatious possessed more than one type of strap. I particularly recall two different straps amongst his collection. He carried a small, thick strap with him when he was on duty patrolling the schoolyard. In his office he had a longer strap with a split tail. That strap was used primarily for striking both hands at once as well as for striking the buttocks. It had a wrist strap, so the user didn't have to worry about losing the strap in the middle of a session of administering discipline. That one hurt the most. It stung and could easily shatter smaller bones. Other priests had different methods of corporal punishment varying from yardsticks, to canes, to electrical cords. But Ignatious was the strap-man.

I had witnessed neighbourhood kids being strapped with a belt: a single piece of flimsy leather. I can still picture Kenny, my next-door neighbour, playing with me in his yard and watching his dad run out of the house taking off his belt. This is horrific, but after what I had experienced at school, it seemed to me a rather meek attempt at discipline.

Ignatious was a pro. His straps were *made* for discipline.

⊑
GROOMING

It's a trap!

— Admiral Ackbar,
Return of the Jedi

Despite Brother Ignatious being the chief administrator of the strap, he seemed pleasant enough when not doling out punishments in the schoolyard or in his office. I remember him often singing or whistling Irish ditties when wandering the yard. His favourite was 'Molly Malone.'

In Dublin's fair city,
Where the girls are so pretty
I first set my eyes on sweet Molly Malone ...

Father Vitus was a favourite amongst the children of the school as he was known to give us candy if we followed the rules. *His* rules.

I remember seeing a boy come out of the rectory one day with a giant blue and white lollipop. It was, as we referred to that particular type of candy, an "all-day sucker." He had tried to hide it from us, but trying to hide candy from other kids at school is futile.

Being able to get candy like that sucker required students to know the specific rules. Word spread that there was free candy to be had and that Vitus was the hookup. The rules were simple enough:

1. Father Vitus was the only "candy-man." We were not to approach any other priest to ask for candy, as that may jeopardize our mission to acquire candy from Vitus in the future.

2. Children were only permitted to approach Vitus during recess or lunch—and only when he was on duty during those times. No other times were permitted as that may arouse undesired suspicion.

3. If Vitus was on patrol, children would have to approach him and whisper into his ear that they had a secret. The secret was that they wanted candy.

A time would then be arranged to meet with Vitus to get the candy. Initial meeting places were established outdoors, but those lucky enough to be his regular clientele were eventually advised of more secluded meeting locations that would allow the transfer of candy to be done in private. This was done, it was said, to reduce the risk of jealousy from children who were not in the know.

It was imperative for children to follow the rules, and to keep them a secret, to keep the candy supply train running. The size of the treats varied. Some children received smaller treats than others. It all depended on how loyal you proved yourself to be. The more loyal to Vitus, the grander the prize.

My kindergarten year was full of mixed messages. I was told some days that I was a sweet child. Other days I was told that God hated me. Sometimes I received the strap without knowing exactly why I had been singled out. I was rewarded for keeping secrets with the priests. I was strapped if my uniform was not properly worn, if I sang out of order, or if I forgot the words to songs or lines to prayers. I had experienced pain and absolute fear for the first time from an agent of God—and it happened frequently. By the end of my first year at Blessed Virgin of the Bleeding Heart Elementary, I learned how terror destroys hope.

Grade one was made even more intense with the arrival of Brother Tische. His weapon of choice was the bamboo cane. His targets were the backs of hands, the arms, and the buttocks. Children were sent to the broom closet to sit in the dark during class if they had committed the crimes of having dirty fingernails or having spoken out of turn.

I am getting better at being in small, dark places, but it has taken a long time for me not to get too anxious when I find myself in such a space. The smell of stale air mixed with the moist, mouldy smell from mops instantly brings me back to the feeling of helplessness and fear that I experienced each time I was sent to the closet for having dirty fingernails.

Being hit on the palm by the strap was one kind of pain. Being struck on the back of your knuckles with a bamboo cane had a different feeling but was equally painful. Tische reinforced Ignatious's ridicule by telling me over and over what a dirty boy I was and how I would have to work very hard to earn God's love. I didn't know how I could be so inherently bad. I had not felt like a bad person before I went to school, but the priests were making me believe I was a terrible human being, deserving of all the punishments that befell me.

Another Brother—Pierelli—preferred a more pugilistic approach to his punishments, using his bare fists when disciplining students. He never struck my face—as that would have likely raised suspicion—but instead enjoyed punching me in the stomach. He had a way of making me feel that I needed to be hit in order for God to love me.

I still possess a letter I wrote to him telling him how I "missed his punches." Somehow, being hit was a sign that I was worthy of God's love. While painful, his punches did not hurt as much as the cane or the strap.

I began to lash out in my drawings. The mixed messages of discipline and love were overwhelming. My favourite colours to use were black and red.

As I look back on some of the drawings that survived my experience at the school, it is obvious what was happening. Of course, I am now looking back with the knowledge of my abuse, but it is all there in the primitive drawings—sad expressions, red scribbling over the genitalia, and oversized phallic shapes dominated my early artwork. They represent the visual screams for help chronicling my personal hell. My artistic archives are a testament to the turmoil and the pain of my early childhood.

10
WINTER IS COMING

R2 says that the chances of survival are seven hundred seventy-five ... to one. Actually, R2 has been known to make mistakes ... from time to time.

— C3P0,
The Empire Strikes Back

Winters were cold in Northern Canada. It was not uncommon for temperatures to dip below minus thirty degrees. Uncovered skin was susceptible to frostbite within minutes of exposure, and then there was the real yearly danger of children sticking their tongues on the cold metal bars of the schoolyard equipment.

Each winter, three or four children fell for the dare to stick their tongues on the monkey bars. It provided great amusement to the children observing, but pain for those who were coerced to attempt the feat. If you are familiar with the 1983 movie *A Christmas Story*, there is a scene that chronicles this commonplace act of schoolyard stupidity in most winter towns.

Venturing outside during the extreme cold provided too much opportunity for accidents. During such cold spells, students at the school were forced to spend recess and lunch in the school basement.

The school also held evening fundraisers in the wintertime. One such fundraiser happened on a cold December night. The wind chill factor had brought the outside temperature down to below minus forty degrees. Children could pay two dollars to get a hotdog and hot chocolate, and to watch *Ma and Pa Kettle Back on the Farm*.

I enter the coatroom and remove my cap, parka, snow pants, and mittens, and hang them in an orderly fashion on the hook. I place my boots on the mud rack, so they don't get the entire floor wet as they thaw. Two nuns sit at the table at the entrance to the basement. I take my two-dollar bill and pay my admission fee. One of the sisters tears two tickets for me to take to the concession to select my hotdog and drink.

"One hotdog and one hot chocolate please."

Brother Pierelli is running the concession. He pulls a wiener from the giant pot on the stove and puts it into a bun. He then takes a small Styrofoam cup and pours a translucent liquid into it. It smells like hot chocolate but is very watered down. I pour some ketchup on my hotdog and turn away.

Pierelli yells at me. "Nicholas!"

I remember that I have forgotten to hand over the tickets for my items. I set them down and feel my cheeks getting hot. "I am sorry Brother Pierelli." I hand him the tickets.

"Just remember," he warns me, "forgetfulness can create a separation from God. And that, my lad, is a significant characteristic of a sin."

Embarrassed and slightly confused, I sit down in the back row of bleachers with my provisions, ready to watch Ma and Pa Kettle and their fifteen children. I don't want to be near the other children after my interaction with Brother Pierelli at the concession. I just want to enjoy my food and watch the movie alone. The hot-chocolate-flavoured water is extremely hot and burns the roof of my mouth. The lights are turned off and everyone settles as the movie starts.

Safe Space

Father Vitus appears out of nowhere and sits next to me at the back of the basement. Most of the children have moved closer to the projector screen much like moths around a lightbulb. It's very dark at the back. Vitus appears to be enjoying the film as he sits and watches for several minutes beside me. He rubs his hands on the top of his pants, reaches into his front trouser pocket, and pulls out a humbug. I can hear the candy clacking against his teeth as he sucks on it while I try to enjoy the movie.

He slides closer and closer to me. He eventually gets so close his thigh presses against mine. I feel increasingly uneasy. He reaches over and grabs my free hand and holds it over his groin and pushes himself against my palm. I am now terrified. I try to pull my hand away as he does this. He's not even looking at me—he just sits, watching the movie play on as I struggle silently against him. I don't know what he is trying to do, but it does not feel good.

I finally free myself from his grip and Vitus suddenly stands up and walks away, leaving me alone on the bench. Who can I tell about this? He is a priest, an agent of God. My parents trust him. Who would believe me? I am just a kid. How can I explain what he did?

It dawns on me that I am alone. I can share this with no one. I feel scared. I am in the dark, and I feel as though I am nothing. I want to forget, yet I remember Pierelli's warning about forgetfulness being a sin.

For the first time in my life, I feel lost.

11
TAKING SHOTS AND GETTING SKUNKED

He was the best star pilot in the galaxy, and a cunning warrior ... And he was a good friend.

— Obi-Wan Kenobi,
A New Hope

During the severe temperature dips in the North during winter months, exposed skin can freeze within minutes. If you have ever taken a breath quickly through your nose in such temperatures, you know how painful it can be. In such circumstances, people take quick, shallow breaths in the short time they venture outdoors.

During the weekends in the winter, we would frequent a property that my parents owned in a remote northern community. It was situated on a large freshwater lake that was over one hundred kilometres long. The severe winters froze the ice solid, making it a great (and safe) time to ice fish, target shoot, or cross-country ski—all of which I did with my family.

My father flew a Stinson aircraft, and in the winter, he put skis on the airplane to land and take off on the lake. I loved flying with him. He was a good pilot, and he always took extra care when I accompanied him. As I was then in the second grade, my father wanted to teach me how to properly use a firearm. On clear days we would fly over the lake and find quiet places to land where we would set up cans to shoot for target practice.

I took my shooting exercises very seriously. Deep down I felt that I could use the skill to protect myself—perhaps I would need to bring my father's rifle to school in order to keep people away from me if they continued trying to hurt me. I was sure that if I pulled a rifle on Brother Ignatious, he would stop strapping me—and that sounded like a good idea.

I had once snuck into my parents' room and took the rifle from their closet. I wanted to see if I could put the .22 in my pants in order to sneak it to school. As it was a rifle, it was too long for me to success-fully conceal. Looking back, that was a very good thing.

I did once take one of my grandfather's 30.06 bullets to school and tried to make it go off by striking it against some rocks, but I had no success. I even asked my dad for some grenades as a Christmas present once. My parents thought it was funny that I would want them, not knowing why I was asking. I am thankful that I did not have access to smaller firearms in my home, as I am sure I would have tried to bring them to school to stop the pain that was being inflicted upon me and my soul.

On a cold weekend in December, my dad took me out for a routine session of target practice. My dad was a highly skilled marksman. He had earned his marksmanship merits during his days as a paratrooper during the Second World War. We left early in the morning—"at first light," as my dad would say—and flew for a bit. My dad liked to drop the plane when we flew—the plane suddenly falling in the air—giving me the feeling one gets during a big drop on a roller coaster. He knew I was all for the excitement of the drops and sudden turns, so he would amuse me with these minor aerobatic stunts.

After we had been flying for approximately forty minutes, we found an isolated area on the lake behind an uninhabited island. It was remote enough to do target practice without disturbing anyone in the early morning. We landed and found a good direction to shoot in—snowbanks in front of cutbanks: this ensured that our bullets would not accidentally strike anything other than what we were aiming to hit. My dad always told me that a marksman is responsible for anything they hit. It was imperative that we took every precaution to not hit anything we were not intending to.

I set up a row of cans that we had brought along for the practice. My dad was a big supporter of the "pack it in, pack it out" policy long before it became a commonplace practice with hikers and campers. He took out the .22-calibre rifle he kept in the airplane for emergencies. The rifle, he claimed, was mine. When he was growing up in the woods, it was a necessity for every young boy to have a rifle and learn how to live off the land. He wanted to pass on the tradition of teaching good survival skills to me, should I ever need them.

My dad grew up in the 1920s in a now-forgotten community known as Ootsa Lake. The community was a settlement for hunters, pioneers, and settlers. It had been flooded in the 1950s for a dam that was built in the North. The remnants of my dad's childhood cabin were left under water and remain so today.

My dad had bought me a BB gun the previous year and had taught me the safety and procedure for handling any kind of rifle. I was now ready to move up to an actual firearm, and my dad taught me how to load the .22-pump action rifle.

It started to snow just as we started to practise. If you have lived in northern communities during the winter, you will know that the snow, as it falls, acts like a sort of muffler—deadening sounds around. It creates an eerie deafness to the environment around you. It was just my dad and me and the sharp crackling of the .22 that could be heard on this particular snowy day.

After about five minutes of practice (I had been doing pretty well—especially since we did not rely on scopes when we were shooting), a strange pungent smell filled the air. A skunk must have been in the area and was scared by the sounds of the rifle. We continued to shoot, but the smell became stronger.

My dad put his hand on my shoulder and asked me to be quiet. He thought he had heard something. We walked quietly towards the targets. As we got closer, we saw it. A skunk, not much bigger than a kitten, was lying just behind the targets I had set up. It was caught in someone's trap, no more than ten or fifteen feet away from our targets.

The small skunk was emaciated. It was common for trappers to set traps with bait to lure small game. It was apparent that the skunk, foraging for food, was the unlucky victim of one of these traps, having both hind legs caught in it. The trap must have shattered the small animal's legs instantly. It appeared to have been there for some time and looked like it had made an attempt to eat its legs away to free itself from the trap's unforgiving steel jaws. What was left of the lower body was bloody and skeletal. It must have drifted into unconsciousness and was near death before we had arrived. There was no saving the creature.

My dad was upset to see this animal squealing in fear and pain as it laid there, trying even then to escape as it had been awoken by our practice. I was holding the rifle. My father's command was serious and direct.

"For God's sake, shoot it."

I had never killed a living thing before. My skill at target practice was now being put to the test, but this time to take a suffering life. I began to shake as I brought the stock up to my shoulder.

"Shoot it."

I took aim and squeezed the trigger. The skunk banked sharply to the left and dropped still. A split second later, it was up again and squealing in even more pain.

"God damn it. Put it out of its misery!"

I had to take a second shot. I was trembling now and started to cry as I squeezed the trigger again. Once again, the skunk drooped but popped back up and continued crying out. I was making the last moments of this creature's life excruciatingly painful.

"Jesus Christ," my dad said as he grabbed the rifle from me, shoving me aside. With an action that can only be explained as that of a trained woodsman, hunter, and soldier, my dad reloaded the rifle and fired it so quickly I was shocked. The animal was killed instantly. My dad did the only thing that could be done and put it out of its misery and suffering. I, on the other hand, had been responsible only for escalating its pain during the last moments of its life.

I had never killed anything before. My hands were shaking so badly that I thought they would never stop. My heart was racing so fast. I had failed in my pathetic attempt to show mercy to that suffering creature. I felt sick to my stomach. My dad did what he had to do. As we walked over to the lifeless body of the small skunk, hot tears streamed down my cheeks. I had only grazed the skunk with my shots, but my dad was able to kill it with a single shot. I asked him if we should bury it. He told me that the ground was too frozen to bury it and it would be found by other predators and eaten. He pried the trap open and let the lifeless body drop into the snow. Black and red, it lay on the cold white blanket of the ground.

My dad could see that I was in no condition to continue target practice. He put his free arm around me and walked me back to the airplane. He put the rifle away and we collected everything we had set out, leaving only the corpse of the skunk behind.

A few years later I would use my marksman skills at Circus Circus, in Nevada, to win a plethora of stuffed animals, but that day was the last time I ever harmed a living animal. My desire to shoot to kill had vanished.

As we flew away, I looked out the widow of the cockpit. The skunk's dead body was a tiny black dot surround by specks of red. Food for wolves. I regretted the pain I had caused that little creature. I was even more upset that I had failed my dad. I had tried to do what he asked of me but failed in my attempts. Killing the skunk was the humane thing to do—the only thing that could be done—and I had only caused it more suffering.

We never spoke of that day again. It was the last time my dad and I went out to practise shooting. My childhood was being ripped away from me at school, and I had just witnessed the death of another living thing. I grew up a little more as I witnessed, firsthand, the preciousness and fragility of life.

12
WINTER HAS COME

If once you start down the dark path,
forever will it dominate your destiny ...

— Yoda,
The Empire Strikes Back

Later that same winter, I was given the news that I was lucky enough to be fitted for a cassock and surplice. As part of my religious indoctrination, I was finally going to be an altar boy. I thought that perhaps that meant that I would not have to endure any more "incidents" with the priests. I thought that maybe I had finally graduated from that.

Father Vitus leads me down a corridor that connects the main school annex to the Blessed Virgin Cathedral. We pass a few private chambers, and it suddenly becomes clear where we are heading. I stop. The teachers have made it clear that no students are allowed to enter the rectory. This area is explicitly reserved for nuns and priests.

"Children aren't allowed in the rectory," I say in an attempt to remind the Father.

Vitus looks down at me and smiles reassuringly.

"They are on special occasions. After all it is not every day that someone like you gets to be an altar boy."

What he says is true. I had not expected to be selected for such service. I had been told by the "real" Catholic kids that the altar boy position was something only permitted for kids who were born Catholic. I had been baptized as a Catholic and had my first official communion when I was in grade one. I felt proud that I had been given an opportunity that not many "converted" Catholics were given.

The Pope spoke once about the important role that altar servers play during religious services. He stated that mass was a way for altar servers to be closer to Jesus. Vitus had decided it was my turn to be opened up to the glory of God.

Father Vitus opens the creaky door to the rectory.

"Wait here," he whispers, slipping inside and quietly closing the door.

I am not sure what to expect of the cassock and surplice fitting. I would be lying if I said I did not feel a sense of pride. It feels as though I am on the precipice of achieving something great. I can feel the butterflies in my stomach and think to myself that this is going to be a day long remembered. I am sure even Mighty Mouse would be proud.

The door opens once more.

"This way," says Vitus, smiling.

Yes, indeed, *a day long remembered,* I think to myself, as his smile is warm and comforting.

He leads me past the modest communal kitchen and down another hall into a small room with a single bed.

"Where are we?"

"My private quarters."

The room is orange, blue, and white. There is a small desk against the wall to my left. A small collection of books, a lamp, and a rosary are scattered across the desk. The bed rests directly across from the door. It has an orange blanket on top and it is neatly made. A crucifix hangs on the wall beside the door. It is a small and modest room.

I have a bad feeling about this all of a sudden. Something does not feel right. Vitus closes the door and locks it.

Click. He stands in front of me and begins to undress me. Small beads of sweat line his brow. I feel paralyzed. I can't move. I am in a state of shock and disbelief. This is not what I am expecting.

"What ... what ... are you doing, Father?"

"Fitting you for a cassock. It's important that we get the right fit the first time."

"Where is the cassock? What does it look like?" I am getting increasingly nervous.

He does not respond.

I look around the room. There is no cassock in sight. Perhaps it's in the closet. He unbuttons my shirt and undoes my pants. He then pulls my pants down to my ankles. I am starting to get very scared. Something is terribly wrong about this. I don't know what to do or what to say. I have temporarily forgotten how to move.

"Yes, this will do nicely."

He turns away from me and starts to fumble with his clothes. I can hear the unbuckling of his belt. I look at the wall and see Jesus on the crucifix staring back at me. Vitus turns around and exposes himself to me as he folds his white underwear beneath his testicles. I am so scared and embarrassed. I have never seen anyone naked before. His penis, half erect, looks mean and terrifying. He wraps his hand over his penis and appears to begin punching himself over and over in the groin.

"This is what men do," he says.

His breathing gets heavier, and his face becomes red. A pungent smell fills the room. I become frozen, unable to move.

"Watch me!"

He grunts as he makes me watch him stroke his penis over and over. He then grabs my small hand, placing it around his erect penis and jerks my hand rapidly back and forth. Within seconds he pushes me away and doubles over, grabbing his handkerchief. He quickly covers his penis with it as he drops to his knees. It looks like he is dying.

Indeed, this is a day that will be long remembered.

I stand before him, frightened and feeling sick. He stops moving and just lies on the floor, doubled over. I start to think that maybe he actually *is* dead or dying. I pull my pants back up and get dressed as quickly as

I can. I feel so many emotions flooding me at once. Everything seems eerily silent. I don't dare speak out loud, but secretly I thank God for killing him. I ask the Blessed Virgin to send him to Hell for me.

I feel the hatred and the fear swelling inside me. I raise my hand that had been wrapped around him and smell his sickly, musty odour.

Suddenly there is a noise—a groan. I look down.

Shit.

A sign of life. Vitus isn't dead after all. He looks up at me with rage in his eyes. I look to the crucifix, and Jesus looks mockingly back at me. Vitus composes himself as he starts wiping something off the floor and his pants with his handkerchief.

"You tell no one of this," he barks at me, his tone becoming more ominous. "Don't you dare say anything about what happened here. *Nothing* happened here. Do you understand? You stupid child. Look what you made me do. If you tell anyone of this, God will kill you. Get out. Now."

I run out the door. I am scared shitless. I feel a sharp pain in my stomach as I run down the hall and feel as though I am going to throw up. Questions swirl around in my mind like a raging tempest.

Why was I alone in there with him? Where are the nuns?

I run out of the rectory and into the washroom, and I barely make it to the toilet in time as I throw up. I smell my hands and take in that sickly, musty smell, and I immediately throw up again. I flush the toilet and rush to the sink to wash my hands. They don't feel clean. I wash them again and again with more and more soap. It doesn't help. I do this again and again for several minutes, feeling as though I will never get them clean. I only stop once the soap dispenser is empty. The basin is full of suds and my hands are sore from scrubbing them so hard. My mind races.

Was this the work of a man of God?

Why me?

What was I doing to cause all of this?

Was I being punished because I was a bad boy?

I feel my shame cut through me like a knife.

Another waypoint had been placed on my life's map. My life was forever altered as a result of that event. I was heading into much darker times. A much more dangerous course was set before me, and I had no idea how to navigate it.

The abuse only accelerated from that time onwards. The strappings became more frequent. Brother Ignatious began strapping me in the privacy of his office. Each time I received a strapping, I was reminded of how upset God was with me.

Ignatious would force me to lie across his lap, and he would strap my (sometimes exposed) buttocks. There were times when I could feel his erection within his pants digging into my stomach as he was strapping me. He told me that I was a dirty boy and that I would have to work harder to gain God's love.

What saddens me is that I believed him. I could tell no one. So, to suppress the guilt and shame of what was happening to me at school, I began to feed my shame with food. I overate at home. I gained weight. I cried a lot—silently, afraid to make noises. I even tried to kill myself.

13
MISERABLE MEMORIES

Fear leads to anger ... anger leads to hate ... hate leads to suffering.

— Yoda, *The Phantom Menace*

Miserable Memories.
Things I remember. Like flashes in a horror film.
Don't make a noise. Don't make a noise. Shhhhhhhh ...

Lullabies.

Hush little baby ... don't you cry ...
Mother's going to bake you a fattening pie ...
Got to speak—
Eat another Wigwam.
Try to tell.
Snickers ... Smarties ... Cuban Lunch ... Eat-More.
Wagon Wheels covered in peanut butter.
Mr. Big ... Wunderbar ... O Henry!
Ice cream. Chocolate shakes.
DQ sundaes.

Every bad taste in my mouth meant another chocolate bar at home.
With every bad mouthful at school, I found that chocolate could

take away the bitter taste. This was obviously my fault, wasn't it? If it happens again, eat a peanut butter cup ... or onion rings ... or both. Or Captain Crunch on top of mint ice cream ... soothes the burn in the throat.

Embarrassed.
Ashamed.
Worthless.
     Piece.
        Of.
        Shit.
Don't tell.
Secrets. Silence.

Silent Night, Holy Night,
All the shame, all the fright.
Trust us mother and give us your child,
Holy innocent, tender and mild.
Weep in heavenly peace.
Weep your fat ass to sleep.

I was often told that God hated me, and that I was a dirty boy. It was the duty of the priests to punish me for my sins. I *made* the priests do this to me.

I was continually told that if I ever were to tell anyone, God would never be able to love me or my family—and he would destroy us for what I had forced the priests to do. He would hate me for what I was doing to them.

Please don't.
No.
Try to pull away.
No.
Hands on the back of my head ... closer ...
NO!

Close my mouth. Shut my teeth. Keep them shut.
Strong adult hands—thumbs poke through.
No. NO! Can't breathe ... I can't. I CAN'T!
Help me, get me out of here. OUT! OUT! Somebody? Anybody?
Nobody? ...
Help me? Why am I so alone?

Snickers.
Smarties.
Cuban Lunch.
Eat-More.
Chocolate masks the taste.
No mess ... no trace ...
Inside me is the mess—huge mess.

Stop crying, he said. YOU DID THIS TO ME, he said. Here, have
some candy, he said. Have some candy. Don't tell. God is watching,
he said.

Mr. Big.
Wunderbar.
O Henry!
Eat-More.

Have some candy. Bury my shame. Embarrassed.
Worthless.
      Piece.
         Of.
         Shit.

Time to end it.
Take some pills.
Time to put yourself to sleep, you …
Worthless.
           Piece.
                  Of.
                  Shit.

But Bayer Chewables just don't cut it.
Hold my head under water.
Too weak to end it. Breathe.

Try again. Head under water.
Too weak to hold it.
Just can't end it.

Worthless.

Wigwam, Aero, Kit Kat!
That's it!
Feed the pain. Feed the shame.
Worthless.
           Piece.
                  Of.
                  Shit!

14
MORE CHOCOLATE,
FAT BOY?

It's not a problem if you don't look up.

— Jyn Erso, *Rogue One*

Darkness overwhelmed me. Darkness and fear. With each encounter the darkness continued to fester. My pain worsened. My wounds became septic, and no cessation of suppuration was likely. I would go home and cry. I would turn my pain into reading, trying to escape into my mind. I was trying to fly in my mind like Mighty Mouse, but I was not able to get off the ground. Rage and shame engulfed me.

I tried several times to get up the courage to tell my dad and my mom about what was happening at school. Inside I was silently hoping to be rescued. I wanted to be saved from my physical and psychological torment. On the outside I was feeding my guilt and shame with whatever I could put in my mouth. Food was my comfort. All I wanted was to be numb, and it was working.

My mom became increasingly frustrated with my sudden weight gain. It was getting harder for her to find pants that fit me. I had only one pair of pants that were not part of my school uniform. They were elasticized and had windmills embroidered on the back pockets. It wasn't long before I couldn't do them up.

One Saturday morning my mom needed to go to a nearby town, and I was taking too long to get dressed. I couldn't make the pants fit. She started to yell at me, at one point trying to do up my pants for me. Then it came out. Her frustration and anger could no longer be controlled. She shouted at me:

"Have another chocolate bar, fat boy!"

Silence.

My mom and I looked at each other. She looked down and I tried to suck in my stomach in one last attempt to do up my pants. It proved impossible. I stood in my room and looked at my protruding stomach. I *was* fat. I was disgusting. I was everything the priests told me I was. If God didn't love me, it was clear my parents would find me repulsive as well. Her words proved her disgust for me. I heard them over and over in my head.

Have another chocolate bar, fat boy!

There are moments that imprint deeply upon one's memories. This is one of the big ones for me, because it was my mother who said this to me. This was the woman who bought me the junk food to exacerbate my addiction. She made sure the freezer was full of ice cream and the cupboards were full of Count Chocula, Captain Crunch, Wagon Wheels, and peanut butter.

These had become my coping foods, my friends, and without them I would be alone with the guilt and shame of the abuse that I brought upon myself. Without them, I would have no place to hide my horrible secrets.

Have another chocolate bar, fat boy!

After my mom blurted out the comment, I could tell immediately that she wished she could have taken it back. The look on her face said it all. She was also struggling. She was dealing with stress as a female bank executive in a male-dominated profession, a daughter that was a runaway, a husband often away for weeks at a time, and now an obese son unable to fit into child-size clothing. She left my bedroom but then returned, reassuring me we would find some new pants on our excursion.

I remember being in the change room at a clothing store later that day, attempting to try on several pairs of pants. Nothing fit. I can still hear the clerk speaking to my mom on the other side of the door, his voice so loud that everyone in the store could hear his opinion of me.

"I'm sorry, there's nothing that fits him. He's going to need men's-size pants, but we can hem the legs. It happens with fat kids."

I stood in the change room; tears rolled down my cheeks as I quietly sobbed—a skill I learned at school so as not to draw attention to the pain I was feeling inside. My windmill pants were on the chair beside me—pants I had worn without being able to do up the top button because I was "too fat" to fit.

My mom tried to reason with me on the hour-long drive home, offering healthy alternatives to the chocolate bars and ice cream. Celery and carrots would just not provide the comfort I so desperately needed from the saturated fats and cocoa butter my junk food bounty offered. A life of obesity was the price I was willing to pay to prevent my family from being destroyed by God.

I had the responsibility of protecting my family, and my sacrifice of childhood freedom was a small price to pay for their lives.

15
MUSIC, THE FOOD OF LOVE

I felt a great disturbance in the Force ... as if millions of voices suddenly cried out in terror and were suddenly silenced. I fear something terrible has happened.

— Obi-Wan Kenobi,
A New Hope

In addition to being headmaster of Blessed Virgin of the Bleeding Heart Elementary, Brother Ignatious was also the choirmaster. My parents would often laugh about him dressed as a bumble bee during one concert, wiggling with us children as we sang the bee song. They thought he had a great sense of humour and loved that he was able to laugh at himself in public.

It's lunchtime. Ignatious plucks me from the schoolyard with a little more anger than usual and takes me into the gymnasium to get me ready for the upcoming concert. I hate choir. Brother Ignatious often singles me out because I sing off-key, but I really can't hear that.

He locks the door to the entrance as he leads me into the wings of the gymnasium.

"I don't want you embarrassing me with your singing. Today I am going to fix that."

As we step up on the stage, I see the pommel horse and other gymnastics equipment. I stop walking, but Ignatious keeps hold of me and moves me forcibly towards the pommel horse. As we get closer, he shoves me down hard, so I am splayed over the device. With both hands he pulls off my pants and underwear. I try to scramble up, but he pins my chest to the top of the pommel horse with one hand as he quickly unbuckles his pants with the other. He presses up hard against me.

"No!"

I try to struggle with him, but he is too determined and strong for me. He punches me in the back of my head, which stuns me. He then grabs my mouth with his punching hand as he moves himself into position with his other hand, lining himself up. I am overpowered and feel him rip into me. Tears roll down my face. I become limp, giving up. Resisting only made it hurt more. He spits on himself to make it easier for him to enter me. He does so with urgency and anger.

He is raping me.

Worthless.
    Piece.
        Of.
        Shit!

He finishes after a few thrusts and throws me to the stage floor.

"Get out of here! God will kill you if you tell anyone."

I pull up my pants and struggle to get up.

"Out!"

I run off the stage and out of the gymnasium. I hear him whistling as though nothing had happened.

She died of a fever
And sure, no one could save her
And that was the end of sweet Molly Malone ...

I am in terrible pain. It's hard for me to walk, stand, or sit. Brother Tische becomes upset with me because I cannot stop fidgeting. He canes me in front of the class because of my inability to sit still.

When I am finally in the safety of my home, I try to get up the courage to tell my parents everything that has been happening at school. I desperately want to tell them everything. But I know it would mean the death of my family if I said a word to them.

I sit in the bathroom at home and panic as I bleed on the toilet paper. The bleeding won't stop. I want to tell my parents so badly what has been happening to me. I try to get up the courage to tell them. More blood. If I tell them what is happening, then my family will be destroyed by God. The blood on the toilet paper was a sign of what will come if I dare speak out.

The pain is overwhelming. I start to think I am dying. I have to do something. Maybe if my parents see it, they will do something. I don't have to tell them what happened. Maybe they will know.

My parents are watching the evening news. My heart is pounding.

"Hey Mom, Dad? I think there's something wrong."

My mom looks at me. "What is it?"

Not sure how to respond, I say, "My bum is bleeding."

"John, will you have a look," my mom says, not expressing any concern. My dad takes me in the bathroom and rather awkwardly asks me to sit down on the toilet and bend forward so he can examine me. I oblige, hoping he will know what has happened.

"You're probably wiping too hard."

That's it?

I can't tell him what happened. I have to accept his diagnosis. I was hoping for him to discover what had happened.

"Just have a bath. That will make you feel better."

He closes the door to the bathroom. I turn on the water. I wish I could tell them what is happening. I cannot. God will kill me. God will kill my family if I do. It is now apparent to me that this is my problem—alone.

It is my horrible secret.

10
THE HOLY TRINITY
OF TERROR

*We seem to be made to
suffer. It's our lot in life.*

— C3P0, *A New Hope*

It was not long after the rape that the physical and sexual abuse escalated. I had three main abusers—Brother Tische, Brother Ignatious, and Father Vitus. Each employed different methodologies in the way they practised their abuse upon me.

Brother Tische was a physical abuser. Of course, at the time that I attended school, it was not unheard of for teachers to administer classroom discipline. Brother Tische took order very seriously.

Every morning we began class by placing our hands on our desks—palms down. Tische would inspect our fingernails to make sure they were trimmed and clean. He favoured his bamboo cane in class and used it as a pointer as well as an instrument of discipline. When he found a student who had not met his high standards, he would ask the student to hold their hands steady above their desk. He would then strike each hand separately. At times, Tische would forego the bamboo cane and use a wooden yardstick. By choosing the yardstick, he had the option to strike the back of the hand with the flat, broad part of the stick. He preferred using the edge, however. It was much more painful and did not flex as much as the broad side.

Discipline in Tische's class was not limited to the use of the cane or yardstick. He sometimes slapped students who were not taking his lessons seriously. For me, the most frightening punishment was the closet.

His class was in a corner room on the second floor of the school. In the corner opposite the windows, there was a broom closet. Students who disrupted the class were locked in the small closet after they had been struck. There was no light in the closet. I remember there only being a few mops, a broom, some cleaning equipment, and a bucket. Students would use the bucket as a makeshift stool to wait out their punishment. On a few occasions, students had to relieve themselves in the bucket as they would only be let out when Brother Tische had determined that justice was served. In the event of an unscheduled bathroom break in the closet, the offending student was forced to empty the piss bucket in the washroom and then return to the closet with the emptied bucket for an extended period. Sometimes students wet themselves while waiting to spare themselves the humiliation.

Brother Ignatious preferred the strap when publicly punishing students. Behind closed doors he was much more aggressive. While the hands were the main target of the strap, he would at times have students lay across his lap. He would remove the pants of the child and strike the bare buttocks with his hand, cane, or strap.

Sometimes he would hold the student in place on his lap and push down on the kidneys of the child while his erection burrowed into their stomach. Sometimes he would make the students kneel before him while he sat in his oak chair. He would remove his belt and wrap it around the neck of his victim. He could control the student this way and ensure that there would be no biting of his manhood. I cannot say if this was the way he punished all students—I can only account for my punishments with him.

He forced his penis into my mouth several times over the years. He would sometimes grab my jaw, forcing his thumb into my mouth while holding my jaw hinge—another way he could prevent me from biting off his penis. I learned to hate him and fear him for what he did to me. I still bear the scar from his wrath.

One day he took me down the hall from his office after unsuccessfully penetrating me. He was angry. There were stairs that led to the basement of the school. When we reached the stairwell, Ignatious grabbed me by the neck and threw me down the stairs. I hit the wall after flying down the first flight. My body redirected itself down the second flight to my right. I landed on the linoleum of the basement, breaking my fall with my chin. Blood ran down my neck and onto my shirt. Brother Ignatious forced me to clean up the trail of blood that was left on the floor from my fall before anyone else could see it. I am convinced to this day that he was trying to kill me.

Father Vitus kept reminding me that I was a dirty boy, and that he was obligated to do what he did to purify me for God. I was told that if I was to ever tell anyone what had happened to me, my family would be destroyed by God.

I feared Vitus. His physical and sexual attacks on me were not overtly violent, but they were coercive. He tried to be gentle with me and to coax me to perform the acts he made me do to him. When I cried, he would get mad, and *that* was when he became rough with me. He often ended these sessions by giving me candy and sometimes rosaries and other religious icons. It was as though he felt obliged to pay me off. I was nothing more than a child prostitute to him—one that he was seemingly wanting to have a relationship with. He was the only one who persistently tried to kiss and hug me—something that I never reciprocated. I was a child. I hated the feeling of wet lips on my skin. I can still smell his breath of stale candy and cigarettes. He would sometimes cry after he finished pleasing himself, before yelling at me to leave him. I hated and feared all three of these men, but it was Vitus that confused me the most.

I feared that I would never be free. It was my lot in life to serve these men in the name of God if I was going to save my family from his wrath. I toyed with the idea of death as a path to protect my family. My sacrifice would save them. Such serious contemplation for a child not even ten years old.

I shudder each time I watch the scene in *A New Hope* when Princess Leia is in her cell and Darth Vader enters with the torture probe, saying, "And now, Your Highness, we will discuss the location of your hidden Rebel base." The door closes behind him and we are left to our imaginations as to what happened to her during the interrogation. Having lived through several forms of torture, my imagination is very vivid when it comes to such scenes.

I started to have a recurring nightmare. It was always the same. I can still remember it all these years later. It was so intense that I would wake up in bed trying to scream but was unable to make any noise. The nightmare was in black and white. In the dream I was a small white ball, rolling through a labyrinth. After some time, a giant black ball would appear and start chasing me through the maze. As I twisted and turned through the maze, the giant black ball continued to get closer and closer, casting its shadow over me. I would try harder and harder to roll faster and faster, until I turned and ran into a dead end. I would turn to see the black ball speeding towards me, getting faster and faster until I could feel it on top of me, ready to crush me ... And then I would wake, unable to sleep.

A simple dream, though it terrified me as a child. It continues to make me feel anxious as I write about it. Looking back, I can see what it was that I was scared of. I was feeling trapped with no escape. There was never going to be a way out of that hell.

17
ART OF PRECIOUS SCARS

The Force is strong with this one.

— Darth Vader, *A New Hope*

In 2018, when the news of the revelation that over one thousand children were abused in Pennsylvania at the hands of three hundred Catholic priests, it was shocking, horrific, but sadly not surprising. This is happening more and more often. People are now starting to give credence to the stories that are coming out. It almost seems that a week doesn't go by without a new story appearing about yet further abuse at the hands of those who pretend to do God's work. There is one word that I can come up with for that, and that is *sickening*.

People who are fortunate enough not to have endured abuse are puzzled as to why it takes so long for people to expose the truth about what happened to them decades earlier. It's simple. It boils down to fear and shame. I can only speak directly to the abuse I endured as a child, but sadly it is similar for other survivors.

I was groomed for the abuse. Many of the priests who abuse children are serial abusers. Their tactics are extended over a period of time. If a pedophile priest was to simply grab a child and rape them, they would most likely be caught out. They know that. It begins by finding the most vulnerable in the pack. They are skilled hunters and know what to look for. They seek out the children not so popular, who crave attention. They look for the mild and the awkward. It's all part of their sick game.

Several months went by before I was sexually assaulted at my school. It began with corporal punishment and the repetition of telling me that I needed to earn God's love. At five years old, this was all rather overwhelming.

The next thing they do to ensure their survival as pedophile predators is to make sure the children they target will keep their dirty secret. For me it was the constant "God will kill you if you tell anyone," and "You're a dirty boy and need to earn God's love." Perhaps the worst thing I was told was that if I was to ever tell, God would kill my family.

God will kill your family.

Imagine being a small child and being told that by a man who claims to have a direct line to God. No wonder people are struck into silence through fear and intimidation.

It wasn't until fourth grade that I was finally freed from the Catholic school, and it wasn't until many years afterward that my mom would find out about the extent of the abuse. To this day I still hold back details of some of the worst rapes that happened to me.

What is the result of being abused and raped as a child? For the longest time, I had little self-esteem. I felt (and sometimes still do feel) as though I was not worthy of success. I felt a need to constantly prove to people that I was a good person. I wanted to be loved and yet shied away from situations where there may have been recognition for my good deeds.

To this day I prefer the company of my solitude. It's not that I am a lonely person, it is that I am more *comfortable* alone or when I am in small groups. This is because I am happiest when I am in control of the situation, rather than letting the situation control me.

There are certain smells that instantly evoke tears. Sense memory is very strong for me. Similarly, I cannot tolerate anything being in my mouth for any sustained period of time. This makes trips to the dentist very upsetting for me. If I brush my teeth for a longer than normal time, I begin to gag—I have even thrown up from the feeling of having something in my mouth. This is a direct result of the abuse I endured.

I was so humiliated and ashamed of what had happened to me that I did not tell anyone the extent of the abuse. When I did finally tell people about the abuse in my community, my family was chastised for it. I was made fun of. People joked about me being raped as they had their morning coffee in the local donut shops. My parents lost friends over it. It was a joke to the community. People were more comfortable shunning me than realizing what was happening at the Catholic school.

I was the first person to publicly come out in my community about abuse at the school. I was mocked for it. I even had an aunt who made fun of me because I was abused and sent me a letter telling me, "You'll never amount to anything because you are a horrible child and deserve everything that happened."

Over the years, people have come to realize that the seemingly secluded incident of my claim was more prevalent. The exposure of systemic abuse by the clergy exploded a few years after my revelation. Now, thousands more victims are stepping into the light as a result of recent findings.

How many victims couldn't cope? How many have ended their own lives to escape the pain that is left behind after the abuse? I am sure the number is high, for many of us continue to neglect ourselves once the abuse stops. We continue to ignore our need for healing. Only through sharing our stories do we enable other victims to step forward. Sadly, people abused by priests are not alone. If you are reading this and are a victim of pedophile priests, thank you for reading. I am here for you. We are bonded through our baptism of blood and pain. You are my brother or sister. We need to stay together and share our voices if we want this to end.

On the outside I may appear whole; however, my soul was shattered in the aftermath of the abuse. Over time I have been able to piece together many parts of myself. It's a long process.

The Japanese have a practice called kintsugi—the art of repairing broken pottery. The idea is that by bonding the broken pieces of pottery back together with gold, the bond is made stronger, and the repaired item is more beautiful for having been broken. The lines of repair are visible, not hidden. I feel my soul is a bit like that—it was shattered, and over the years, I continue to forge it back together. It's not perfect, but it is beautiful for those who can see it. It is stronger, and its scars are ones I am not afraid to show, for my story of abuse is important to share. I need to speak out and up for those who have yet to find their voice.

Star Wars appealed to me as a child because of the Force. An energy field that binds us and surrounds us—it makes life grow. We come from it and return to it when we exit this physical plane. The Force is a powerful ally. It is my ally, for I am one with the Force, and the Force is with me.

It would be many years before I would come forward about the abuse by priests—and even then, as an adult, a small part of me worried that my confession would eventually lead to the destruction of my family. After all, I was an abomination and a disgrace to God. My abusers had been able to keep me silent as a child, but as an adult it is my directive to spread the word of abuse, abusers, and healing. I do this with the hope to bring about a world where abuse towards children is only read about as a part of history rather than as current events.

My heart goes out to all victims of abuse who have lost the light, for we are one with the Force. We must find the strength to carry on and to never let this happen again. Strengthening my soul, over time, is becoming a practice in the art of precious scars—for we are all deserving children of the Force.

18
MRS. REED

We're doomed.

— C3P0, *A New Hope*

Years passed. I was in fourth grade. The priests were not the only ones who were abusing me, and not all of the abuse was sexual in nature. Mrs. Reed was my fourth-grade teacher. She was devoutly Catholic. Her hair was dyed brown—an attempt to cling on to the youth that had inevitably slipped away as it does with us all. The lines of her brow accentuated her harsh bearing, as did her horn-rimmed glasses. I cannot recall her ever smiling. She was not a nun, but she was a teacher who was old school.

To maintain discipline in her class, Mrs. Reed used a foul mouth and her mastery of the kettle cord whip. This cord was not like a modern tea kettle cord. The prong was not a small plastic or rubberized bit; this kettle cord was made of Bakelite. It was hard, solid, and very big. We had to line up to enter and leave class, and if you were slow enough to be the last one in the door, then you were at her peril. Very quickly the faster, leaner boys would rush inside, leaving the slower, fatter children to be at the end. I was the slowest and the fattest. According to Mrs. Reed, I was a disgrace to God and to the school, and, as such, she took no mercy in striking my abomination of a body with her cord. We wore long pants and long-sleeved shirts in school, so the marks from her endeavours went unnoticed for a long time. I learned to live with the welts on my arms, legs, back, stomach—everywhere her improvised whip could strike. She took great pride in her prowess.

As recess nears its end, I begin to feel the dread inside me. I start to make my way towards the outside door near Mrs. Reed's class. The tension mounts as I can sense the bell about to ring. My heart starts racing, and my mouth becomes dry. I am getting close to the door when the sharp, shrill metal bell sounds, signalling the start of her class. As usual, the other kids rush past me as they jockey for a place in line, knocking me about in the process. One kid grabs me by the collar and tugs me back so he can save himself the upset of being last in line. I try to cut in the middle, but none of the other kids allow it. Once again, I am forced to take up the rear.

Mrs. Reed appears at the door and signals for us to enter. She holds her electric tea kettle in her left hand and the cord in her right. The kids in front of me rush to the door and purposely slow down once they pass Mrs. Reed, knowing they are safe from being whipped. I can hear them laughing as they escape the discipline that awaits the unfortunate stragglers at the end. As is the case most days, the straggler will be me.

"Last again," she sneers as I approach the door.

I start to tense my body in anticipation of what is to come.

"No slouching!" she bellows as I approach.

I know it's a trap. As soon as I uncoil to walk upright, I will be exposed, and it will begin.

It does.

Whap! Whap! Whap!

Mrs. Reed is quick with the cord. I am her favourite target. The heavy Bakelite prong strikes my arms and legs no less than fourteen times. The pain is intense. She purposely strikes me where clothes will conceal the marks left on my body. The kids ahead of me continue to take their time entering the class so that I will be whipped longer and harder. I can feel the parts of my body that have been hit swelling. There will be marks. Several marks.

10
MOM

Mom ... you said that the biggest problem in the universe is no one helps each other.

— Anakin Skywalker,
The Phantom Menace

Despite my mom's reaction to my ill-fitting pants, I know my mom loved me. I know this with all of my heart. As a parent myself, I now understand how much a parent can love their child. My children are my world, as I know I was my mom's.

My dad was often called away to work for weeks at a time. My mom spent her time working at the bank and keeping up our house. As a female bank executive, she was constantly having to take on more responsibilities to prove her worth in what was considered a man's profession. This resulted in longer and longer hours at work and less time at home. She would drive me to school on her way to work in the mornings, but after school it was up to me to either catch the school bus or walk home.

The school bus ride was a frightening experience. The driver, Phoebe, was a person of the most unpleasant demeanour. She would yell at us, swear, and smoke while she drove us to our individual stops. As she approached a designated stop, she would slow down. When we stood up and stepped into the aisle preparing to disembark, she would slam on the brakes causing us to fall down. Then she would yell at us to stay seated. It was her idea of a joke. It was not uncommon for children to exit the bus with bloody noses or, sometimes, missing teeth. Because of this, when the weather was cooperative, I would walk.

When I arrived at home, it was my responsibility to call my mom and let her know I had arrived safely. She would often ask me to peel potatoes or to do some other task to expedite dinner.

When my dad was away, my mom would sometimes treat me to an occasional dinner out. I loved going out with her. It seemed like she knew everyone in town. Our favourite place to eat was a popular local steakhouse called Mr. Steaks.

On weekends I devoted my time to homework and to assisting my mom with household tasks such as folding clothes, feeding our pets, washing dishes, and taking out the garbage. My aunt would sometimes drop in unannounced on the weekends. It always seemed that my mom went out of her way to make her sister happy.

My mom was six feet tall but was not obese. Aunt Agatha, however, was a large, unpleasant woman. She too was tall, but unlike my mom, she was rotund. She was loud, obnoxious, and took great delight in putting my mom and our family down.

Agatha was a woman of great wealth and took every opportunity to brag about her money to anyone who would listen. She was a landlord and made her money through taking advantage of her tenants' hardship. If rent was not paid to her on time, properties were seized, and tenants were evicted. She was not well liked in the town of Hopeless. People referred to my mom as "the good sister" when comparing the two siblings.

When Agatha arrived at our house, everything stopped, and my mother's focus became that of appeasement. It was not uncommon for Agatha to demand that my mom make her "flapper pie." Having grown up in Saskatchewan, my mom and her family were partial to flapper pie. I am sure that many of you reading this have no idea what flapper pie is. It's a dessert unique to Canada's prairie provinces. It is a graham cracker pie crust filled with creamy custard and topped with meringue. According to my mom, flapper pie was a family favourite when she was growing up, and it fell upon her to make this particular pie.

Agatha loved flapper pie but could not make it herself. So, almost every weekend when my dad was away, Agatha's visit consisted of her boasting about herself while my mom made fresh flapper pie to placate her. Visits between the two often concluded when my mom had upset Agatha by calling out her "bullshit" (as my mom eloquently put it), or when Agatha decided her belly was full of pie and coffee.

Because we never knew when Agatha might arrive, my mom and I would try to get as many chores as possible finished in the morning. We washed laundry in the house, but, whenever possible, we took it outside to dry on the laundry line. My mom would often bring out the portable radio while she hung laundry and listen to the radio broadcast of the CBC.

Sometimes she would tell me stories of her early years as a bank teller. The stories were fascinating, and I loved hearing about them. I remember her telling me how the police gave the tellers a seminar on how to remember facial features when dealing with customers in the event of a robbery. She had a good time in the seminar and listened attentively. Soon after the course was over, she had a pleasant conversation with a customer. When he had left, her manager asked her if she could recall any particulars. He was eager to see how well the identification training went. She remembered her customer's pleasantness, his brown hair, and his smile. However, the manager pointed out to her, after her vague description, that the customer also had no ears.

She also told me about carrying a gun at her wicket as a young bank teller. It was common practice at the time. Once her loan manager borrowed her gun to collect on an outstanding bank loan, returning some time later with the defaulted loan. Obviously, things have changed since she was a teller in the 1950s.

I hoped she was going to tell me that she still had the gun and show me where it was. I still believed that if I had that kind of protection at school, no one would touch me again. It wasn't that I wanted a gun for killing, but that brandishing one would prevent anyone from wanting to violate me. I felt the same way about dynamite from watching cartoons. Fortunately, I learned we had no live handguns or actual dynamite in our house.

It was a rather sunny and warm day in early March of 1977 that I remember as the most important laundry day of my life. The spring winds brought unusually warm weather, and it was almost summer-like as a result. Even so, I had chosen to wear a long-sleeved shirt and pants. My mom was so happy to finally see the end of winter that she asked me to put on shorts and a T-shirt instead. I was reluctant to comply with her request. The day before I had received a rather harsh whipping at the receiving end of Mrs. Reed's kettle cord. My arms and legs were covered in welts.

There was no way I was going to let my mom see them. I argued with her that I was rather comfortable in my long sleeves and pants, despite the sweat accumulating on my brow. My mom persisted. Her request turned into a demand.

"Now go and change, you silly monkey." She stood on the platform below the laundry line, seeming even taller and more imposing than usual.

I had no option but to comply. I turned and walked towards the house. Elton John and Kiki Dee's hit 'Don't Go Breaking my Heart' crackled away on the portable radio at my mom's feet as she resumed her laundry duties. I entered the house and walked slowly to my room. I felt sick.

As I took off my shirt, I looked into the mirror. Several deep blue and purple welts adorned my arms and chest. Next, my pants. Several more black and blue patches covered my legs. If we had lived in the jungle, I might have been mistaken for some sort of leopard-boy hybrid. The bruises were everywhere.

I took my time putting on my shorts and T-shirt. Spots were still visible. This was it. My mom would ask me what happened. If I told her, God would personally stop what he was doing in the universe and smite my family for what I was causing at school. I was about to seal the fate of my family. It was my fault and now I was going to get us all killed. It was not such a great day after all.

I hated myself more than ever in that moment. If only I had been faster. I looked in the mirror one last time before turning and exiting my room. The hall seemed unusually long. *Dead man walking*, I thought as I dragged my feet to face my mom and destroy my family with the imminent wrath of God.

I approached the laundry line as quietly as I could. The top-of-the hour CBC news was on. I grabbed some laundry in an attempt to hide as much of the evidence on my body as I could.

My mom was focused on hanging a bedsheet on the line. "You know, your dad will be back next week if all goes well. He's almost finished that pulp mill shutdown up north." She continued to struggle with the bedsheet. "He wanted me to tell you he misses you and can't wait to see us again. He also said—"

She turned to me with a smile but stopped speaking once she looked at me. My attempt at covering myself up with laundry was not successful. Her smile quickly faded into a shocked expression. She turned into inquisitor.

"What happened to you? Who did this?" she pleaded.

"I don't know."

I could hear desperation in her voice.

"You *must* tell me who did this to you. Did this happen at school?" She dropped her laundry and stepped off the platform as she knelt down before me.

My mind was racing. "I fell?" My answer was far from convincing. I was having a hard time convincing myself.

My mom persisted. "You must tell me who did this. I can make this stop."

I could feel the tears starting to well up inside. This was it. My last moments on Earth: shattering my mom's happiness and destroying us with the wickedness of my sins.

It was at that moment that I realized something rather important. I found a loophole in the warnings I had been getting from the priests. In that moment there was a ray of hope. I may not destroy my family after all. The priests had constantly warned me that if I were to tell on *them*, then that would bring destruction upon me—but they said nothing to me about people who were not priests. Mrs. Reed was neither a nun nor a priest, so it seemed logical to me that I could tell on her without the wrath of God raining down upon me. I tried to breathe. I could feel my heart pounding in my forehead. This was it. This was the moment. I looked down at the ground.

"It was Mrs. Reed, Mom."

"Mrs. Reed?" My mom rocked back in shock and horror before quickly regaining her composure as a mother to her hurt child. "How? When?" she queried.

"I'm too slow."

My mom looked both concerned and confused.

I continued to explain to her. "She makes us line up in class, and I'm too slow, so she whips me."

"She whips you?"

"Yes, with her electric kettle cord ... the big hard prongy end." I continued to look down and shuffle my feet. I was getting more uncomfortable. But nothing was happening. The skies were not clouding over, and there were no apparent signs of a forthcoming lightning strike. I breathed a little easier.

My mom looked carefully at my wounds.

"Turn around."

I turned on the spot.

"Your arms, your legs. You're covered."

I could see her disapproval. Was it with me?

"I'm sorry Mom. It's my fault. I'll try not to get hit next time. I promise I will try to not let the other kids push me out of line on Monday."

My comment snapped my mom out of her contemplation and shock. She looked right at me, taking my hands as she spoke.

"No." Her voice was firm yet somehow comforting to me. "No," she repeated, "you are not going back there."

I stood before her, frozen. *Could this be it? Could my time there be over? Would I really not be going back?* A tidal wave of emotions flooded over me. My fear, anger, and happiness collided. My mixed emotions were too much for my nine-year-old body to handle or process. I began to cry. My mom, ever the protector, looked at me. She began to cry—something I had never seen before. She opened her arms towards me.

"Come here, my poor little monkey."

I rushed into her arms. We held each other tightly. Not too tightly. It was more like the swaddling of a baby—comforting, reassuring, and protective. There I stood hugging her as she kneeled before me. Mother and son crying together. We had survived the wrath of God for the moment. Yet, as we clung together, I feared for us. If she or my father were ever to find out what the priests had done to me, or what I had "forced" the priests to do to me, then we would all be destroyed by God.

Thinking of this made my tears turn to sobs. She responded by hugging me tighter. Her constant touch was almost too much for me. Over the four years that I attended the Blessed Virgin of the Bleeding Heart Elementary, I had been constantly reminded how dirty I was and how I was an outcast in the eyes of the Church. If my family was to survive on this planet, then it would be up to me. At nine years old, I vowed to carry the burden of the rape and abuse bestowed upon me as my secret and mine alone. If I were to ever slip up, then it would be me who destroyed my family.

I honestly don't know how long we remained there at the laundry line hugging and crying. I remember the cool wind on the back of my neck and the feeling of my tears sliding down my cheeks. I remember that though I knew I would bear the secret of the extent of my abuse for years to come, I felt somehow lighter. A weight had been lifted.

I looked up to the sky on occasion to see if there were any signs of the possible wrath of God. No. Nothing had happened. The clouds were not darkening. The sky remained blue. I was safe for now.

The next morning my mom did not go to work. She stayed home with me. It was not long after breakfast that she asked me to watch television while she "attended to things." I put my dishes on the counter next to the sink and moved to the living room. I turned on the television to find Mr. Dressup taking Finnegan, Casey, and Beth Anne to an animal fare, and then returning to watch Finnegan perform his own kind of dog show in the garden.

The volume was low enough that I was able to hear my mom in the kitchen picking up the phone and placing a call. The phone lived in a cubbyhole in the wall between the kitchen and the living room. When my mom used the phone, she would take the phone from the cubby and place it on the table, sitting before she began dialling. It would still be a few years before speed dialling and touch tone phones became commonplace in the home.

That morning, she did not sit to make the call. She stood over the table, talking under her breath as she clutched the phone's receiver in her right hand and dialled the number with the index finger on her left hand. I knew who she was calling. I strained to make out what she was saying. I heard "God damned" and other expletives as she placed the call. Then silence that seemed to go on forever. Then I heard her speak determinedly into the phone.

"Yes, this is Pearl Harrison. I need to speak with Brother Ignatious immediately." More silence. Then suddenly she shouted into the phone, "No, right now!"

More silence followed. I heard her breathe heavily while she waited. After a moment, she began yelling into the phone with as much control as she could muster.

"Ignatious, this is Nicholas's mother, Pearl Harrison. What the hell is going on there?"

A Pause. Finnegan was doing some tricks for Casey on the television while Mr. Dressup applauded. The silence in the kitchen was again broken.

"Mrs. Reed has been whipping him in her class."

I can only imagine what may have been running through Ignatious's mind as he tried to speak with my mom.

My mom's voice became even louder. "He is *not* returning! My son is being abused by one of your teachers, and if you expect me to stand by and let your staff lay their hands on him, then you are sadly mistaken."

Another pause. This time it was much shorter.

"He is not coming back!"

It was at this point that my mom lost all composure as the stern banker and became the angry mother bear on the phone.

"You want *me* to keep him there for *four more months* so you can get your GOD-DAMNED GOVERNMENT FUNDING? Don't you realize that you should be thinking about the kids and not your GOD-DAMNED GOVERNMENT FUNDING? He is NOT coming back there you ... you ... EVIL SON-OF-A-BITCH!"

Slam!

I heard something breaking off the phone. *The Friendly Giant* was now beginning on the television. I looked out the big window in the living room. The sky was blue. Buds were starting to come out on the pussy willows outside. There were no signs of an apocalypse. God was not in the destroying mood. I let out a sigh of relief.

It was over. My days at that school were now over. I felt amazing relief. I had spent four and a half years of my life being abused. At nine years old, half of my life had been spent being secretly tortured and raped.

My mom was shocked that Brother Ignatious had pleaded with her to keep me at the school until the end of the year. Private schools received funding from the provincial government based on total enrolments. My withdrawal would decrease the amount of funding the school could claim at the end of the year, affecting their overall budgeting. By having me complete the school year at The Blessed Virgin of the Bleeding Heart, Ignatious could have taken steps to make sure I would never reveal to anyone what had been happening to me at the hands of the priests.

Only weeks before my mom found the welts on my body, Ignatious had attempted to kill me—at least that is what I believed he was trying to do. I described earlier the incident when he threw me down the stairs, cracking my jaw on the floor as I landed on the polished lino-leum. I knew I could not go back to that school, for if I did, I was sure my execution would have been inevitable. It would have been far safer for me to be dead, for dead men (or dead children, in this case) tell no tales. The grooming worked. I was terrified for anyone to find out my secret. The abuse was my fault and my fault alone.

While a part of me was relieved that I no longer had to pray or have any further private encounters with the priests, another part of me felt hollow. The four years of Catholic indoctrination had ended, and I didn't have any experience with religion other than what they had taught me. On one hand I had learned that God was supposed to be all-loving, and on the other I was violently abused by the pedophiles at the school who were entrusted with my care. As this was my spiritual education, I believed that all churches operated this way, and that if I ever revealed the secrets of my religious experience, I was sentencing my family to damnation. I felt that I could not risk telling anyone what had happened, and that the only way to resolve the psychological pain within me was through my own death.

20
NEW KID ON THE BLOCK

Confronting fear is the destiny of a Jedi.

— Luke Skywalker,
Rise of Skywalker

I spent a few more days at home while my mom arranged for my transfer to a local public school, South Hopeless Elementary. My mom and I met with the school's principal, Mr. Woodly. He seemed friendly enough, though I had no idea if I would be secretly subjected to the same kind of abuse by him as I was by the Catholic priests at my former school. I had difficulty trusting adult males who were not my dad. I was very relieved that Mr. Woodly did not wear black.

I was assigned to Mrs. Gray's class. She was a small, prudish woman with dyed black hair. She had a serious demeanour, though she was nothing like the nuns or teachers at the Blessed Virgin of the Bleeding Heart Elementary. Although she was strict, I could feel that she would not hit a child. First impressions are important.

Having spent four years in a regimented school, I did not transition well to public school life. I was branded as the odd kid out on my first day. Having no other experience to draw on, I wore my school uniform to class. I was laughed at for that. I also had a different approach to answering questions. In private school, students who raised their hand or who were called upon were expected to stand beside their desks. I quickly learned that there was no such regulation at my new public school. In fact, the new school seemed to be more like a chaotic cacophony of mayhem rather than an educational institution. If I was going to survive public school, I was going to have to adjust to the lax rules.

Because I was the new kid, I immediately found myself the outlander. I was not part of any cliques, as they had been formed long before my arrival. Recess and lunch were times I found myself falling back into my old routine of wandering the school grounds alone. There were no priests to watch over us, but instead volunteers and teachers who rotated duties as monitors.

It took several weeks for me to adjust to not having to wear a uniform. In fact, I remember how oddly cool it felt to wear T-shirts to school. And better yet, I could wear T-shirts with prints and logos. Amazing.

Being the new kid meant that I was also the new target of the school bullies. I am sure whoever had this role before me was quite happy to be stripped of being the victim once I arrived to take over. The duties of a new kid—for those who don't know—are to be excluded from lunch gatherings, to pay tribute to the bullies by means of giving up any and all worthy treats in their lunch, and to take a punch or two.

One of the bullies took great interest in tormenting me. His name was Daryl. Daryl was much smaller and shorter than I was. He began bullying me by making fun of my size and weight. (By this point I had eaten myself into the shape of a rather plump butterball turkey.)

Adding to my features of bully-ability was the fact that to save money, my mom had been taking me to a salon school for my haircuts. Student hair stylists were able to practise their weakest skills upon my locks, and my mom would get a reduced bill for my haircuts. Unfortunately, the school focused mainly on women's cuts. So, to add to the growing list of unfortunate events at the new school, being fat and a former private school student was further augmented by the sudden change in my hair from flat to "fabulous."

Daryl reminded me of my boyish hideousness on a daily basis. He would punch me, and I would take it. I would go home later and cry—openly now, since Daryl wasn't a priest. My mom and dad were concerned that I did not fight back. After a while I even told my parents that I didn't want to go to school anymore. My mom took me to meet the principal once more.

Mr. Woodly sat down across from us as my mom told him what had been happening. He seemed to be genuinely concerned with my transition to his school. He asked me if there was anything he could do for me, but I found it hard to put trust in him due to having been exposed to such extreme abuse at the hands of my former headmaster. I told him not to do anything. I knew I could take whatever any student could do to me. The punches and kicks from Daryl and the other bullies were not nearly as painful as the full-handed slaps, strikes, strappings, and rapes at the hands of my former adult abusers. I could take it.

Mr. Woodly told my mom and me that nothing would change unless I fought back. He said that the students would continue to single me out unless I proved to them that I was not going to let them bully me.

I couldn't believe what I was hearing. He was wanting me to fight back. In his office, in front of my mom, he gave me permission to strike my bullies back. Later at home, my mom encouraged me further. She told me that she would give me twenty dollars for every phone call she received from a child's mother who called to complain that I had hit their son. I couldn't believe what I was hearing. I was now being encouraged to fight. It didn't feel right, yet at the same time I felt excitement that I had carte blanche to strike out.

My dad purchased a set of boxing gloves and a bag for me to practise on. He set up the bag in the garage and began teaching me how to jab, duck, block, and weave. After a few weeks of lessons, I was getting more into it. I would go into the garage after dinner and put a record on the record player while I practised my moves.

I still was letting Daryl and the others hit me at school, but the time was coming when I would strike back.

Then one day it finally happened. It was a rainy spring day. Daryl had punched me twice in the school yard because I didn't have any good snacks for him to take from my lunch. I felt something stirring deep inside, and I turned to go into the school to get away from him. Daryl followed close behind, shoving me and shouting obscenities in my ear as I moved towards the entrance to the coat room. I opened the blue steel door and was shoved hard from behind.

I cannot explain exactly how things progressed from that point. I remember the feeling of being jarred from real-time into a realm of slow motion. I stopped in the middle of the coat room and turned to face Daryl. He was yelling in my face, calling me the usual list of names: fat-ass, asshole, lard-ass, dumb-fuck, stupid fat-ass, and so on. He pushed me with both arms, but instead of falling back, I held my ground. He tried pushing me again. I didn't move. My arms were at my sides, and Daryl continued to get into my face, shouting at me. He was unaware that my right hand, seemingly of its own accord, had begun to clench into a fist, each finger slowly curling inward. I stared at Daryl, unemotional. I remember him taking a step back and rolling up his sleeves while he continued to yell at me. At this point I had no idea what he was shouting—it was a blur. My right arm swung back and then I took a step forward with my right foot, landing the foot at the same time my right fist connected with Daryl's face. His angry expression turned to a look of shock and he (at least in my memory) flew backwards, hitting the bar of the blue doors as he flew out of the school and onto the ground outside.

Mrs. Gray, who had witnessed me punching Daryl but had not seen what had led up to my outburst, grabbed me by the collar of my Snoopy T-shirt and yanked me back towards her.

"You're coming to the office, now!"

She walked with me, forcibly hanging on to my collar as if I would, at any minute, attempt to flee from her grip. I walked with her, crying as we went—not because I was sad, but from the overload of emotions I was feeling. I had actually struck someone. It was the first time I had done so. I was overwhelmed with anger, delight, and a surging sense of power having watched Daryl fly through the air as a result of my fist in his face.

"You will sit here and think about what you did to that poor boy," she said as she left me on the row of chairs outside Mr. Woodly's office. She went into his office and slammed the door. She exited his office moments later, glaring at me as she went back to class.

Mr. Woodly opened the door. "Come in, Nicholas."

I stood up, wiping the tears from my face with the sleeve of my Snoopy T-shirt.

"Sit down," he said calmly.

I sat. Mr. Woodly looked at me. I looked at him, then the floor, the ceiling, and what appeared to be a framed photo of lumber on the wall behind him.

This is it, I thought. *This is when it starts with him.*

"Well done."

What the hell?

Mr. Woodly congratulated me on punching Daryl. He told me he was waiting for that moment to come and was glad it happened. I was more than a little surprised. He assured me that I would not be punished and then sent me on my way back to class. He told me not to apologize to Daryl. He told me he was proud of me.

I know this is the kind of scene people see in movies. It's the pivotal moment when the bullied victim becomes the hero. All becomes right and the world changes before them.

Having lived this moment, I can state that it's kind of like that, but not really. Daryl never bothered me again. In fact, he began to work hard to make me laugh. He tried to befriend me. He wanted to stay on my good side after that. It was like a *Looney Tunes* cartoon I had watched. You may remember it. There were two dogs. The small dog was bossing the big dog around. The big dog kept trying to please the small dog, but the small dog would have none of it. "Awww shaddup," he'd say and slap the big dog into submission. Eventually things changed and the small dog tried to keep pleasing the big dog. Remember that cartoon? That's how it felt with Daryl and me.

21
FEED ME

You look absolutely beautiful.

— Lando Calrissian,
The Empire Strikes Back

Though my trials and tribulations with Daryl were behind me, I found myself encountering more bullies. I was in freefall—released from the oppression of the Catholic colonization, I found myself desperately seeking redefinition. Shedding the dark blues of my school uniform, I looked for more colourful expression. I grew out my hair. I tried to become "cool" in an attempt to fit in.

My mother was doing her best to balance her executive bank job as well as taking care of the family. My dad was often away on factory shutdowns, so most of the time there was an air of loneliness around our home. Money was in short supply, as most of what was earned between my parents went to pay for my dad's other children from his previous marriage. If there was a way to save on the little things, my mother did so. This is why she took me to the salon school for my haircuts. I once discovered, only after I was settled into the chair, that I was the test subject for students practising giving permanents. After a couple hours of being subjected to harsh chemical smells and a slight burning sensation on my scalp, my longer hair was transformed into a tight ball of curls. I found myself having to explain to my peers why I suddenly looked like an extra on *Welcome Back, Kotter*. I was not impressed. Sure enough, the new hairstyle proved to be yet another sticking point for the endless taunting in the schoolyard during recess and lunch.

I would walk home for lunch, and it was in our quiet kitchen that I could fill the sadness and the shame with bowls of mint ice cream, Captain Crunch, and Wagon Wheels covered in peanut butter. Since I was alone in the house, the portions were not small. I once again indulged in the sweet taste of burying my shame. The sweetness masked the bitterness swelling inside. My old companions were back to comfort me.

Worthless.
Wigwam, Aero, Kit Kat!
That's it!
Feed the pain. Feed the shame.
Worthless.
   Piece.
     Of.
     Shit!

22
OF BRONCOS AND EAGLES

Get your head out of your cockpit.

— General Leia Organa,
The Last Jedi

Despite my tumultuous start at the public school, I was gradually able to make a few friends. One of my friends lived only a few houses down from me. His name was Guy. We got along well enough—so well that he invited me to his birthday party. A real, actual birthday party that was not simply a family event. I was pretty excited. I had never been to another kid's party before.

A handful of kids gathered at Guy's house for cake and soda and were then shuttled to the local cinema to see a movie. I was driven to the theatre with another boy, Wade.

Wade's dad was a small-town kind of guy. I have no idea what he did for a living. His pride was his 1977 Ford King Cab truck. It was sky blue. Wade's dad wore a blue and white ball cap, blue jeans, cowboy boots, and a button up jean shirt that he tucked into his pants. He also had the largest brass belt buckle I have ever seen. To complete the look, he had a handlebar moustache that extended from the top of his upper lip to the bottom of his jaw. He was definitely a guy who enjoyed working with his hands. I remember reading the bumper sticker on the back of his truck: "Ass, Gas, or Grass. No one rides for free." Of course,

I really didn't know what that meant, but I thought it was funny to see "ass" written on a bumper sticker.

We settled into the truck—Wade and I sat across from each other in the back of the cab. As we started towards the movie theatre, his dad rolled down the window and spat out some chewing tobacco, a small drip of brown spit remained on his chin as he turned on the radio. He casually wiped it off with his hand as he turned to us. He attempted a conversation with the two of us while KC and the Sunshine Band's hit 'Shake your Booty' played over the radio.

"Hey kids, if you could be anything you wanted to be, what would you be?"

Wade's answer was immediate—it was obviously a game they loved to play in their family.

"An eagle. They can fly and they are the strongest bird in the world!"

I thought about this answer. *An eagle? Really?* I remembered my dad telling me a story about how he had watched an eagle drown while attempting to pull a salmon out of the waters of Ootsa Lake. It was a struggle that lasted well over twenty minutes until the eagle, exhausted, was pulled beneath the water and died. *Screw being an eagle*, I thought.

Wade's dad turned his attention to me. "What about you? Nic, is it? What would *you* be?"

My answer was simple. I knew what I wanted to be more than anything.

"Mighty Mouse."

"What the fuck is a mighty mouse?" Wade's dad was equally confused and intrigued at the same time. It was obvious that he had no idea who or what Mighty Mouse was. Fortunately, we arrived at the movie theatre avoiding an in-depth conversation about the heroics of my favourite superhero.

Pulling up and over the curb outside the theatre, Wade's dad again spat out some chaw before turning to us.

"Here you are, boys. Have fun!" he said as he wiped the brown goop off his chin again. We were barely out of the Bronco before Wade's dad sped off "burning rubber" as Wade called it.

ᕲᕴ
SMOKEY AND THE
TRASH CAN

*This is not going to go
the way you think.*

— Luke Skywalker, *The Last Jedi*

The birthday party regrouped outside the local cinema. Guy's dad purchased tickets for us to see Burt Reynolds in *Smokey and the Bandit*. He told us to wait outside the theatre after the movie to get picked up and returned to our homes. Guy took the movie tickets from his dad and handed them out to us.

As we made our way inside the theatre lobby, I walked past a large movie poster. It had no images, just large text. The script read, "A long time ago in a galaxy far, far away ... STAR WARS." Those two words stood out bolder than the rest. I began to wonder *What were the Star Wars*? A war in the stars obviously. *But how? What?* I began to feel excited.

Mere moments after the birthday group settled into the theatre playing *Smokey and the Bandit*, I excused myself to use the restroom. I really was not into Trans Ams and cowboys who laugh funny and who have contests for beer. I am sure I was likely an exception in the town of Hopeless. It appeared to be the kind of film that would appeal to someone like Wade's dad.

I exited the cinema and headed straight for the concession. Junk food helped ease my anxiety. I ordered a package of Twizzlers and a Dr. Pepper. This was always a tasty, winning combination for me—I would bite off each end of an individual Twizzler and use the licorice as a makeshift straw as I drank from the cup of soda. Gradually I would eat each straw as I sipped away the Dr. Pepper.

I prepared my first straw at the side of the counter and turned to head back to join the rest of the birthday crew. I took a few steps towards the cinema that I had previously been in, but then I stopped. The poster of *Star Wars* again caught my attention. Before me was the cinema playing this movie.

It felt as though a tractor beam was pulling me into that theatre. I stood still for several more moments before allowing the allure of the space movie to take over and change my life forever.

⤴4
A LONG TIME AGO

That's good. You have taken your first step into a larger world.

— Obi-Wan Kenobi, *A New Hope*

I pulled on the purple door to the cinema and stepped into the darkness. The door closed behind me as I looked towards the screen. A gold-coloured robot was speaking to some sort of moving garbage can as they moved through a vast desert. The gold robot spoke: "We seem to be made to suffer. It's our lot in life." I related to that comment immediately. Those words echoed inside me. That was exactly how I was feeling. I was made to suffer. It was all I had known.

This movie was already speaking to me, and I found myself torn between my obligation to the birthday group and my desire to watch this space story unfold. I decided that it would be best if I were to move back and forth between the two screens.

My time split between the two theatres created some suspicion with the birthday group. I told them I was not feeling well and had to keep using the restroom. Each time I entered the theatre playing *Star Wars,* I found it harder to leave. My sessions in that theatre were getting longer and longer until I forgot about needing to keep up with the other group.

The story was so much more appealing to me than a race for beer. There was this boy who was all alone—Luke. He was a farmer from a planet made entirely of sand. He had an older friend—a Jedi Knight named Ben. There was a space pirate, Han, and his huge furry friend, Chewie. They were trying to help a rebellion against the Empire. The Empire was controlled by the villain, Darth Vader.

Vader was the embodiment of evil. He was covered in black, and his face was covered by a terrifying mask. He could not breathe on his own—instead, whenever he appeared, the mechanical breathing apparatus of his suit made me feel that he was more monster than human being. Vader wore long, black robes. The Death Star, a giant space station that looked like some kind of mechanical moon, was grey and black, and the interior looked cold and unforgiving. My connections were already being made.

Darth Vader was a Catholic Priest.

My young brain was rapidly making associations with the movie and the relationships between the Church, the Rebellion, and of course good and evil. Darth Vader was frightening. He was taller than everyone, and when he spoke, I felt someone was going to be killed or punished. Vader reminded me of the priests I had been victimized by at the Catholic school. He commanded respect through fear and intimidation.

Luke was like me—he was from nowhere. He was insignificant. He was unimportant. Yet, at the same time, he was not. It appeared as though Luke was going to be very important. The old man, Ben, told Luke that there was a Force, and that it was in all living things.

The Force was going to become my version of God. The Force wasn't scary. It was something that gave life, took life, and repeated the cycle.

The final words that I heard in the movie that night were from Ben, or Obi-Wan Kenobi as he was known to Vader. He confronted Darth Vader in the Death Star. Wielding his laser sword, Obi-Wan stated, "If you strike me down, I shall become more powerful than you can possibly imagine."

There he was, a frail old man squaring off against some sort of robot man who was much more powerful and stronger than himself. The image of the two and the devotion of Obi-Wan to his statement made me so happy. So happy indeed.

Suddenly there was a hand on my shoulder. It was Guy.

"We're going now, come on!"

I had no idea that the movies were staggered, and that *Smokey and the Bandit* was a much shorter film. The birthday crew had been looking for me for a while before coming into the other cinema. Guy was mad that I was watching "some dumb space movie." I was embarrassed at being caught, but I felt an anger towards Guy and his friends for pulling me out of the one thing that I loved watching more than anything else I had seen before.

I was escorted out of the theatre surrounded by the birthday group. I remember them chastising me, but I really couldn't make out what they were saying. I was in thought. Deep thought. *What had I just witnessed?* It was some sort of space odyssey. It was not like anything I had seen that was set in space before. It didn't have that pristine clean look that many of the space movies had at the time. It was dirty. The robots didn't shine. Everything I had seen (albeit in starts and rather briefly) looked well used and lived in. The spaceships were mostly beat up. An old man in tattered robes, Ben Kenobi, was mentor to no hero but to a farm boy. A *farm boy*. He had nothing going for him, yet in some way he was to play a part in this unfolding journey. *But what?* My head was spinning. *How could this possibly all end?*

Those words from Ben Kenobi sparked something deep within me. My stomach was fluttering. It may have been the popcorn and Dr. Pepper, or the Twizzlers, but I was sure it was something else. Something within me was being awakened. What was this feeling? Excitement?

We exited the theatre and were again sorted back to the awaiting convoy of vehicles. I was soon in the back seat of the Bronco alongside Wade as his dad drove us home. I was still reflecting upon those words: "If you strike me down, I shall become more powerful than you can possibly imagine." I had been struck down many times. I was given the burden of carrying the secret of rape and abuse around with me. My pain and guilt were weighing me down. But to imagine that power could come from powerlessness gave me such hope. Maybe I could rise up. Maybe I could speak my truth. Maybe I was a child of the Force after all.

My first step into this larger world was going to have to be actually seeing the movie in its entirety. But how and when? I felt the urgency to go back and see the movie.

The silence of the drive back was broken by Wade's dad. He smelled slightly of hops and barley.

"Movie any good?"

Wade answered enthusiastically, "It was great, Dad. There were cars, trucks, and a Trans-Am, and there was a cowboy and a contest for beer."

Wade's dad perked up. "That sounds really cool. I hope the Trans Am was black."

"Yeah, it was. And there were these funny cops who couldn't catch them."

"That's cool. What about you Nic, what did you think about the movie?"

Before I could respond, Wade jumped in. "He didn't see much of the movie, Dad. He kept sneaking into another theatre and then, when our movie ended, *we* had to go and *find him.*" Wade gestured emphatically as he shared this information.

Wade's dad seemed to be curious. "What kind of movie? Was it a girlie film, eh?" he laughed, and the smell of hops and barley became stronger.

"No," I responded. "It was *Star Wars.*"

Wade's dad seemed confused. There was a bit of a pause as he took in those words. The silence was short lived as he abruptly changed the subject. "If you could be anything you wanted to be ... what would you be?"

Wade shouted with an exuberance that frightened me, "A ... a ... an eagle!"

Here we go again, I thought to myself.

Wade continued, "... or ... or ... or a cowboy with a Trans-Am!"

Wade's dad seemed to really like that answer. He joined in, "That would be so cool ... A Trans-Am ..."

As he smiled his face seemed to freeze with a somewhat empty look. It's hard to explain. There is an expression that appears on Wile E. Coyote's face every time the Road Runner hits him with a frying pan, or an anvil, or any heavy object. Coyote's eyes become half closed and his mouth opens into a smile just before his teeth fall out. That's the look that crossed his face. It stayed that way for a few moments as he drove through the four-way stop, nearly side-swiping a Datsun compact as we drove on.

He then focused on me.

"What about you ... er ... Rick, no ... Nic ... what would you be? You still want to be that creepy rat thing?"

"No."

Wade jumped in. "An Eagle?"

"No."

"A Trans-Am?"

"No."

Wade's dad thought he had the answer. "A cowboy *with* a Trans-Am!"

"No." My heart swelled. I knew what I wanted to be, even if I didn't know what it really was exactly.

"A Jedi."

25
A WHOLE NEW WORLD

Something inside of me has always been there. And now it's awake.

— Rey, *The Last Jedi*

All I could think of when I went home were the fractured bits and pieces of the movie that I had been fortunate enough to see—or was it that I was *destined* to see? I needed to go back and see the whole movie. But how? It was not common (at least for my family) to go back and watch a movie a second time—especially some "space film."

I was determined to see it. I presented the situation to my parents and explained what had happened at the birthday party. My dad agreed to take me back to the theatre and watch the movie together. The days leading up to the weekend dragged on, but finally Friday came and my dad, true to his word, took me to see *Star Wars*.

I ordered my usual—a Dr. Pepper, a package of Twizzlers, and some popcorn—and then my dad and I entered the cinema and found the perfect place to sit down, centre screen. It was only a couple of minutes until the lights in the cinema dimmed and we heard the whirring of the projector in the booth as the movie started. In those days there were no previews.

The movie began, and my whole world was about to change.

Darkness. Drumroll ... the 20th Century Fox logo appeared momentous on the screen. Then silence. And then ... in the brief cesura of the music, words flashed on the screen.

A long time ago in a galaxy far, far away ...

My heart skipped a beat. It was the beginning of a space fairy tale. Even now, writing this, I can feel the exuberance of that moment in my young, wounded soul. *Hope.* Then, a blast of trumpets as the opening music accompanied the scrawl, bringing the audience up to date as to where we were in this story. The words *STAR WARS* filled the screen, slowly fading away as I read that this was a period of civil war. There were rebels striking from a hidden base who had won their first victory against the evil Galactic Empire. Plans to an ultimate weapon, known as the Death Star, that could destroy an entire planet, had been stolen. A princess was being pursued by the Empire and had the plans in hand.

I was hooked.

My dad and I sat in silence watching the film—side by side, together in the solitude of the story unravelling before us. It was all making sense to me. A giant organization was doing all it could to impose its will on everyone in the galaxy. A small group of rebels—made up of a princess, a smuggler, a farm boy, a Wookiee, an old man, and two droids—would take on this vast organization by themselves because they needed to do what was right. The princess survived torture but was resolved to keep the secret of where her base was hidden. The farm boy saw his aunt and uncle burned to death at the hands of the Empire who were looking for the plans placed in the droids. The old man sacrificed himself for the cause. The smuggler and the Wookiee were in it for the money, but they ended up doing the right thing. The right thing. They stood up against evil.

Much more important to my young soul was that they survived. The years that I had endured the constant abuse and repeated rape from the priests at my school still consumed me. It would be years before I would speak out about what had happened. I was still hiding this horrible secret because I was warned that I would be forever punished if I shared the truth of the abuse. Worse still, I would take my own family down if I dared speak out against this "Empire" who was able to continue to suppress me.

This movie gave me the feeling of hope for something better for the first time.

I sat in that theatre with my dad beside me. I felt a happiness that was similar to the happiness I felt as a younger boy watching my dad build me my own log cabin, the Trapper John. My mom and dad were my heroes, and yet I knew I had to protect them from the reach of the Catholic Empire.

In the final moments of the movie, I was on the edge of my seat. The future of the Rebellion relied upon the success of a very few starfighters. It was down to Luke, the farm boy, to destroy the Empire. Luke's droid, R2-D2, was shot by Darth Vader, and just when I believed the movie would end with the destruction of the Rebellion, Han Solo shot Vader's ship, sending Vader spinning in space and clearing the way for Luke to take his shot. As they flew off, the Death Star exploded behind them.

I cheered out loud. I was so happy. Tears were actually running down my cheeks, and my brow was covered in sweat. My dad turned to me and asked if I was okay. I assured him I was fine. In fact, despite the secret I was hiding, I felt more alive than I had in years.

We exited the theatre. It was at this moment I knew *Star Wars* was going to be part of my life forever. I also wanted desperately to find out more about the Jedi and their power. If only *I* could have that kind of power. If only I could have the ability to destroy the school I attended, the way Luke had destroyed the Death Star ... maybe I could help other children who shared my fate.

It was that Christmas I remember asking my dad if he could secure me hand grenades. He and my mother laughed about this request, not knowing the real reason I wanted them. I fantasized about being able to destroy the den of despair I had attended during my early formative years. If Luke could do it, then so could I. It was my destiny to become a Jedi no matter what the cost.

I had stumbled upon a method of therapy without even knowing it. My spirit was in need of nourishment, and I found great comfort, guidance, and a sense of belonging in *Star Wars*.

My personal boundaries had been destroyed by the priests and teachers at the Blessed Virgin of the Bleeding Heart Elementary. The balance of good and evil was askew within me. The priests who were charged to feed my soul and educate me had instead violated and terrorized me. In the dark theatre, although I was surrounded by others, I was comfortable in my solitude. John Williams's musical score filled me with a sense of hope and life. With only hearing the first few bars of music, I was intensely and emotionally charged. His music was another character in the film, much like a narrator, guiding my thoughts and feelings through the melodies that accompanied the action. I wanted to believe that good could overcome evil. I hated Darth Vader. He was manipulative, all-powerful, and a destroyer. He frightened me.

Vader's abuse of power and regard for the lives of others further reminded me of my tormentors. I had been grabbed by the neck and orally raped in Ignatious's office. My neck ached, and the violent, disgusting act not only humiliated me, but terrified me as well. The scene in the Rebel blockade runner (the Tantive IV) when Vader crushes Captain Antilles's neck and tosses his lifeless body against the wall reminded me instantly of Ignatious throwing me down the stairs in his attempt to kill me.

I was creating a relationship with the characters on screen. Darth Vader was Ignatious, and I became the various Rebels throughout the movie as it progressed. I was inspired to learn of such a thing as rebellion. The Rebels in the movie fascinated me. Though smaller in number, the Rebels united against the tyranny of the Empire despite overwhelming odds. They did what they had to do because they had no doubt that they were right to do so. The Death Star, like the Church for me, represented a loss of humanity. It was a cold, technical, killing machine.

Perhaps the most exciting element of *A New Hope* was that it introduced me to a whole new spirituality—the Force. As it was new to Luke Skywalker, it was new to me. It became *my* new spirituality. I wanted to be a guardian of peace and use the Force to protect my family and myself.

In that small theatre in Hopeless, my path to a much larger world had begun.

25
DROID STORY

Be-boop.

— R2-D2, Every Star Wars film

As I continued to adjust to public school, I began to slowly make some friends, but my distrust for others prevented me from opening myself up to the other students. It was that fall that the bullying and the physical threats from the other children escalated. The ritualistic abuses from the priests were finally behind me, but the torment by my peers was only intensifying. My physical size and quiet demeanour at South Hopeless Elementary brought a different type of victimization. The bullies I encountered now were much closer in age to myself. Though I had stood up to Daryl, the stronger and increasing number of bullies made sure I was kept in my place amongst the elementary school hierarchy.

As a result of my previous abuse, I refused to wear anything "revealing." I wanted to hide myself away and insisted that if I were to wear shorts, I would cut them to a length I was comfortable with. I was only willing to expose my ankles and a little bit of my calves. I was still afraid of provoking someone to sexually attack me because I inadvertently may have enticed them to do so. There is no doubt that my look contributed to the torment from my peers.

One rather foggy Saturday morning in October, my mom took me with her as she ran her errands. We had stopped in a few different shops that morning. Low-lying fog covered the ground, and as we drove it looked to me as though all the cars were floating on clouds as we passed by. Honestly, it could have also been the pollution from the several pulp mills that surrounded Hopeless. The leaves on the trees were turning from red to yellow and had started to litter the streets and parks with the autumn blanket, preparing the ground for the eventual snow that would bury it for several months. It was a typical October morning in this small northern town. One of the final stops was Stephen's Pharmacy on Main Street.

It was a different time back then for small businesses. Computerization was on the way in, but many things were still done by hand. Clerks actually were able to earn a living wage; and, upon reflection, people that worked in shops must have been genuinely happier, and as a result customer service was much more personal and pleasant than today.

I had been in Stephen's so many times I knew my way around. Once we were in the door, I departed from my mom's side and snaked my way through the aisles to look at the latest tensor bandages. I had come to the conclusion that Luke Skywalker's legs were wrapped up in tensor bandages and that the Sand People, too, had their heads completely wrapped up in them. I was also pretty sure the eyes of the Tusken Raiders were based on welding goggles. I thought over how I could wrap my head in bandages while wearing my dad's goggles, completely unaware of the possibility that I could accidentally asphyxiate myself in the process. I was hoping that my mother would buy a large stock of tensor bandages so I could attempt my own Tusken Raider look. Luckily, we never had such a need.

The final stop on my rounds was the small selection of toys, right next to the birth control products. It didn't dawn on me (being a child and all) the irony of having toys and birth control sharing shelf space. It was that October morning that I spotted my very first Star Wars toy. The movie had been out for months, but for some reason, the toys took a lot longer to hit the shelves—unlike today when you can find the toys for sale months before the movie even comes out. Mass film marketing was in its infancy back then, and George Lucas was pioneering that field as well.

I stood there, in front of the small selection of toys, staring at the Kenner action figure of R2-D2. I immediately picked it up and held onto it. My mother was not one to give in to impulse purchases, but when I showed her the toy, she agreed to buy it for me. I had it out of the packaging before we were even back in the car.

As we drove home, I looked at my very own mini R2. Its head clicked when you twisted it. There was a little blue telescope you could pull up, and it had two legs to stand on. As far as an action figure goes, it really wasn't that exciting, I suppose, but to me it was amazing. I played with that figure for a long time—my very own personal astromech. A small part of the Star Wars universe was mine.

27
CONGRATULATIONS

Great kid! Don't get cocky.

— Han Solo, *A New Hope*

A contest was announced on the local radio station for the chance to win a new bike from Mulligan's Bike Shop. One lucky person was going to win a green ten-speed—an *Apollo* 10 Speed. The entry requirement was easy—you just had to fill out a contest ballot. There was no purchase necessary, and the ballots could be found at several locations around the town. My mom brought home several entry ballots for me. I remember filling them all out. I was determined to win that bike. I don't know why, but I became obsessive about winning it. It was as if there was a need for redemption—a need to feel special somehow. I had an urge to be noticed by the town.

The draw was going to take place on Halloween night. I had made a few acquaintances at the school by this time, and they invited me to go trick-or-treating with them. This was the first time I would go out on my own, and I was excited to have this kind of freedom.

I was only out for a short while before coming back home. I had gotten into a fight with the other kids because we had been talking about the draw. It was a big deal in the small town; everyone at school had entered to win the bike. For some reason I insisted that I was going to win. I didn't do this out of malice, nor to be argumentative. I really did think that I was going to win. I could feel it. Of course, my resolute attitude deeply offended the other kids—so much so that I was physically shoved to the ground, candy confiscated, and left behind.

I returned home with my empty pillowcase, and again the tears rolled down my face. I told my mother what had happened, and she became upset that I had been argumentative and belligerent with the other kids. I insisted to her that I *was* going to win the bike, and that they would soon find out.

I felt that I was going to win. I somehow knew. My mother, at her wits end to be dealing with such an indignant child, sent me to my room.

"Go to bed!" she shouted at me.

As I departed the kitchen for the back rooms, I defiantly announced for them to wake me up when I won.

It wasn't long before I was in my pyjamas, alone, waiting in my room. I still believed that I was going to win the bike. I was so sure that I began to cry about it. I not only was going to win, I *had* to win. For once, I had to be a winner. I pulled the covers over my head and drifted off to sleep.

I have no idea how long it was before I was woken up by the shouts of my parents in the kitchen.

"Jesus Christ, I can't believe it!"

A moment later my door was jarred open.

"Get up! You won that goddamned bike!"

The radio station called, and I was interviewed. My parents did not know how I could have been so sure of myself. To this day I really do feel it was as if I was able to see and feel the outcome of that contest—that and the fact I must have filled out dozens of entry forms.

I loved that bike. So much.

28
BROKEN

That's not how the Force works.

— Han Solo, *The Force Awakens*

In the spring, the snow had melted, and I was finally able to show off my bike in all its glory. I was signed up for a softball team and rode the bike to my first practice. As I peddled towards the field, I pretended I was flying my T-65 starfighter through space. The ride was smooth, and I was proud of my win.

I loved softball and was a fairly good hitter. The coach of the team was not overly enthusiastic to coach us. He kept his eye on his watch and our practice finished exactly on time. He grabbed his equipment and left. I went over to my bike and was followed by the rest of the team. I had a bad feeling about what was going on.

"So, this is the bike you won?"

Guy and three other kids from the team—Harley, Keith, and Rob—surrounded me.

"You didn't win this bike. It was a setup. You got your mom to buy it and they just pretended to give it away," Guy barked, with the others in agreement.

"No. I won it," I said, feeling defensive.

I got on my bike and attempted to ride off, but it was no use. Harley knocked me over. Once I was off the bike, they wasted no time partaking in its destruction. They used their aluminum softball bats to smash the wheels. They laughed as I cried, watching my prize being rendered unusable before my eyes. Harley pinned me down as childhood angst was unleashed on my bike.

Once satisfied with their handiwork, I was released, and the mob abandoned me and the bike on the field. I picked up the bike and attempted to walk it home, but the wheels were too bent. I ended up dragging it and crying as I walked down the street. My precious starfighter had been shot down, and again I blamed myself for it. It was my fault, and I didn't deserve nice things.

It was at this point in my life that I vowed never to brag about anything. Anger swelled inside me. I was learning hate in silence. I hated the other kids. I hated me. I hated the priests who had ruined everything. I hated my silence. My time soaring through space on my ten-speed bike was over, and I hated that I was stuck on the ground. I was sliding deeper down the path to the dark side of the Force.

20
SICKNESS

I have a very bad feeling about this.

— Han Solo, *A New Hope*

My mom worked hard and did her best to maintain the house and her job while my father continued to be called away for work across Western Canada and the United States. The stress played upon her, especially since she often had to deal with my half sister running away.

You'll notice that I don't write much about my half sister, Melissa. She was five years my senior, and since both my parents worked, she was often charged with looking after me. She was already in school when I was born and had already endured years of abuse at Blessed Virgin of the Bleeding Heart Elementary by the time I started. To this day, she lives in fear of the Catholic Church and her former abusers. She attended the Catholic school until she dropped out when she was fourteen, and she hated me for being taken out of the school when I was only in grade four. Her way of coping was drugs, gangs, alcohol, and running away. There is always a part of us that believes new locations can provide fresh starts.

My mother once intercepted a letter Melissa had written to a gang in California, when she was only fourteen, in which she offered to kill her little brother as a sign of her devotion to them. Thankfully (for me) that never happened.

Each time she ran away, my parents discovered more troubling things in her room—bongs, switchblades, pipes, and other drug paraphernalia. My mother must have been shattered, but still she soldiered on. She worked hard. She did the best she could with everything unravelling around her. Regardless, Melissa was not going to alter from her path to self-destruction.

I remember my parents getting calls from law enforcement across the United States asking for dental records whenever they discovered a body matching her description. It must have been horrible for my mother to never know where her youngest daughter was or if she remained alive during her times of running away.

The stress eventually got the best of my mother. The fall that I entered grade seven, my mother became ill. I did my best to help her when I was home. My dad was worried about her and asked me to stay near her when he was at work.

One Saturday, my mom was laying on the sofa in the living room. She asked me to go to the store and get her some ginger ale to help ease her stomach. I grabbed my bike and peddled to the nearby corner store. I was happy to be out of the house. The fresh air was a welcome change from the foul air in the living room as my mom lay in pain. On the way home, I stopped to chat with one of the neighbourhood girls, Kim, who was always kind to me. I told her why I was getting ginger ale, and I made fun of my mom's condition. Taking my time to return home, as children do, I entered the house and went to the living room to give her what she had asked for. She was gone. I checked the bathroom. She was not there. Her bedroom. Nothing. I panicked. Where was my mom? I returned to the kitchen and saw the note on the table. It was written in pencil in my dad's handwriting. *I had to take your mother to the hospital. I will call you when I can. Love you, Dad.*

I started to cry. I again felt that this could be my fault—that maybe by taking my time I had somehow caused whatever it was that prompted my dad to take her to the hospital. Maybe the ginger ale was in fact what she needed to heal. I had joked about her to Kim on the way home. I didn't know what to do next. I stood in the kitchen for several moments. I was now twelve years old. I opened the freezer door and grabbed a two-litre box of mint chocolate ice cream. It was half empty, so I forwent the custom of scooping the contents into a bowl and simply stood there with a soup spoon, feeding my fear, my shame. After finishing the box, I locked the door and went to my room to lay down.

My R2-D2 was sitting on the nightstand next to my bed. I picked him up and held him close to me. This gift from my mother just a few years prior made me feel close to her at that moment. I held R2 in my hand and looked at him, thinking about how my mom bought him for me because I wanted it. I wanted my mom back home. I was alone again, with only my toys to comfort me. I fell asleep clutching R2.

The next morning, I woke up to the smell of pancakes. Maybe my mom was all better. The radio in the kitchen was tuned to the CBC, and at the stove stood my father making me breakfast. It was a foggy October Sunday morning.

"Hi, Son. Hope you were able to get some sleep," my father said as he tended to the pancakes frying in the cast iron pan. I didn't know what to say. He was unshaven and still in his work clothes. It looked like he did not get any sleep.

"Is Mom ..." I couldn't find the words. I didn't know how to ask if she was going to be okay.

"She's going to be at the hospital a while."

"Is she ..."

"... she's not well, Son. It's her gallbladder."

I didn't know what exactly that meant, but my father's tone was such that I knew it was more than a cold or the flu.

"Will she ..."

"It's going to be fine. It will," my dad's attempt at reassurance was not entirely convincing.

"When can I ..."

"She's going to have surgery later today. I'm going to go back to the hospital in a little while. It's best that you stay home in case there's any news about your sister. I need you to help me, Son. Your mom needs us to be strong."

Again, I would have to be strong for my parents. I thought back to the new Star Wars movie I had seen only months before, *The Empire Strikes Back.* So many things went wrong for the heroes in the film. Luke lost his hand, Han was frozen in carbonite, and Darth Vader said he was Luke's father! By the end of the film everyone was in disarray.

I was allowed to go to the hospital a few days later as my mom was healing after the operation. My dad brought me up to her room. She was surrounded by flowers. She was hooked up to machines, and tubes were attached to her arms. The room was white. I started to cry.

My mom turned her head to see me. "It's okay honey," she said as she smiled. She was noticeably weak but happy to see me.

I was filled with so many mixed emotions. I was so happy to see her alive but felt this was all my fault.

"I have your ginger ale," I told her through my tears. She held out her hand to me, begging me closer. I moved closer to her, wanting to hug her but afraid I might disconnect some of the tubes attached to her.

"Come here, monkey," she said, smiling. "They have lots of ginger ale here. It's ok. I know I must look terrible."

"No ..."

"It's okay. I love you."

"I love you, Mom." The tears ran down my face.

Though I loved my mom, I wanted to get out of that room. Somehow, I felt I had caused her to be there.

She saw how uncomfortable I was. "Honey, I would love to visit with your dad. Do you think you would be okay waiting downstairs for him? John, can you give him some money so he can have a snack while he waits?"

My dad handed me some money, and I made my way down to the waiting area where I bought myself a package of barbecue chips and a can of Dr. Pepper, found a seat, and waited for my dad.

It wasn't long after settling into my seat that I could sense three figures approaching. I looked up to see the dreaded Aunt Agatha and my grandparents before me. Agatha wasted no time.

"Look at you, you fat little blowfly. You're stuffing your face while your mom is upstairs dying. She's going to die soon, and this is where you are. You little son of a bitch."

I immediately started to cry. My grandparents glared at me. Agatha, in her fur coat, satisfied with her attack, turned and walked towards my mom's ward, my grandparents in tow. The people around me who witnessed the outburst returned to their business now that the show was over. I remained seated and crying, only stopping between sobs to finish my chips.

It was not much longer before my dad came out to find me. He could see that I had been crying. He didn't have to ask me what happened—he knew how mean Agatha could be. We drove home in silence, but at least we were together.

Thanksgiving was only a few days away. Normally the holiday consisted of my mom cooking all the food, preparing the house, and making sure there was enough alcohol for Agatha and whoever else might show up. Our house was like that. People would show up unannounced from time to time, and my mom never turned anyone away when there was food to be had. This Thanksgiving was different. The "family dinner" was held at Agatha's house. Friends of her family, cousins, and my grandparents were invited to attend, but my father and I were not given an invitation. I suspect that my dad would not have accepted anyway.

Thanksgiving came, and my dad and I went to visit my mom. It was not clear how long my mom would need to stay in the hospital, and that uncertainty played upon my dad. He would become silent when he was upset or worried. It felt odd to be in the front seat as we drove; the front was reserved for my mom. I wanted to hold my dad, to let him know that this was my fault, but I could not do it. God was angry with me, and my mother was possibly the first victim of his wrath against me for what I had caused the priests to do to me.

We arrived at the hospital and stayed for visiting hours. My mom looked weak and withered. It was frightening to see her like that. When it was time to go, I carefully hugged her so as not to disturb the various hoses and wires around her. My dad and I went to the car and started to drive home.

"Happy Thanksgiving, Son", my father said. "Let's get something to eat. You hungry?"

That was a silly question. Years of shame eating had made me always hungry. I nodded, and before long we found ourselves at the local Burger King. Our Thanksgiving dinner was quiet and reflective. I noticed that there was an offer for *The Empire Strikes Back* collector glasses. He saw what I was looking at, and shortly thereafter one of the glasses was on our table. It was a Thanksgiving present for me—something to remember our night together. I still have it displayed in one of my kitchen cabinets: *The Empire Strikes Back* Darth Vader glass tumbler. That Thanksgiving I learned who my entire family was—whom I could count on. My family was my mom and dad.

I cried a lot at home. My dad remained strong, or at least he seemed so to me. He did what he could. I was expected to get to school on my own, as he had to work early each day at the mill. I had to pack my own lunches—often I would come home at lunch and just eat ice cream or cereal instead. My favourite lunch combination was mint chocolate chip ice cream topped with Captain Crunch cereal. My lunchtimes at home became longer and longer as I began to hate school. The teachers were aware of what was going on at home and all distanced themselves from me.

⊐⊙
TEMPTATION

I sense great fear in you, Skywalker.
You have hate. You have anger.
But you don't use them.

— Count Dooku,
Revenge of the Sith

The dark side of the Force was growing within me. Without my mom at home to help me, I found myself tempted to do nothing. Homework was often neglected, and I became even more isolated from other children.

One day I woke up and had no desire to go to school. I had twenty dollars in my drawer. I walked to school that morning and told the teacher, Mrs. Patterson, I had to stay home, and I cried in front of her. She gave me an awkward hug and sent me home.

I didn't go home. I went to the mall. Scotch Pine Mall. For the first time ever, I played hooky. Not only did I play hooky, but I also did something else to set me further on the path to the dark side. I found an amazing toy I wanted. It was the Kenner Snowspeeder from *The Empire Strikes Back.* I remember looking at it and wanting it. It looked amazing and would be a great distraction from the pain and the guilt I was feeling from my mother's illness.

It was slightly more than I could afford. I noticed, however, there was also a die-cast version of the same toy that cost significantly less.

I knew that the computer till at that Sears would only list the name of the item and the price. I carefully peeled the price tag off the die-cast toy and placed it on the full-sized version. I hoped my efforts would be rewarded as I approached the till. The white-haired woman who was working the till scanned the item. It came up *SNOWSPEEDER*. She looked at the box and then back at the till. She looked at the box again, albeit a bit hesitantly. She commented that it was a good price. She bagged it, took my money, and I got a lot of change back—so much that I could afford lunch out.

I took the bus to the downtown core. There was a cafeteria in the bottom of The Bay where my mom and I would eat together when I had a free school day. Sitting in the wooden chair at The Bay with my onion rings and Jell-O reminded me of my lunches with Mom. It was turning out to be a great day, at least until I got home.

Something didn't feel right. Something was wrong. My half sister was a drop-out. She was a shoplifter. A drug user. I skipped a day of school. I swapped price tags to afford a toy I couldn't otherwise afford. I didn't want that. I didn't want to become that kind of person. My mom would have killed me if she knew what I had done. I was doing this to fill a growing hole inside me—nothing was working. Again, I knew that I couldn't do this to my mom and dad.

This day off I took (and maybe it was needed) was the last day off I would take. It was the last time I would do those things, but it wouldn't be the last time I would cry about my mom and the fear I had inside. Unfortunately, the hate and shame within me only continued to grow.

Thankfully, my mom eventually recovered. Maybe God saw that I needed her and her love. Maybe God saw that the only two people who really loved me were my parents. Maybe God wasn't going to destroy us after all. Maybe, just maybe, there was something worthy inside my messed-up childhood self—something worthy within me that should live. In many ways, I think of that particular fall as my experience in the Cave of Evil. I had a choice to make between following my half sister's path into a deception of theft, drugs, and dropping out, or to take a more solitary path towards my own inner discovery. Unfortunately, this path was still fraught with attempts to bury my past along with the shame and anger for what I had done and what I had caused to my family.

Decades have passed, yet I am still untangling the past, one strand at a time. Along the way, Star Wars has provided me a new hope. If you ever come over to visit, be sure to ask me about my Darth Vader glass. As each Thanksgiving approaches, that glass serves as my yearly reminder of my father's love for me during a time when family failed us in our time of need. It is a reminder of the year I almost lost my mom and almost turned a corner into a life I don't even want to imagine. I will never forget the Thanksgiving my father and I were excluded from the rest of the family's dinner. Ask any of my in-laws what I do, to this day, on Thanksgiving. Our house may be full of people, but every year I politely slip away and end up watching television with my arms around my kids.

Maxima debeteur puero reverentia.

We owe the greatest respect to the children.

My mother returned home shortly after that fateful Thanksgiving and received daily visits from a home nurse who changed her bandages and monitored her recovery. It would not be until the end of November that she was able to return to work and to a somewhat normal life at home.

Э1
RETURN OF THE WINTER

There isn't enough life on this ice cube to fill a space cruiser.

— Han Solo,
The Empire Strikes Back

The winter snow arrived by late November. By early December, the snow was easily four feet high. The temperature at that time of year created ideal conditions for fluffy snowflakes that were perfect for snowball making, sledding, and skiing. It was a northern kid's paradise.

It had now been almost four years that I had been free from the tormentors of my Catholic school prison, and though Guy had unfriended me soon after the *Smokey and the Bandit* experience, three other kids soon befriended me: Joshua, Derek, and Seth. We shared a love of Star Wars and, in fact, bonded over it. Joshua introduced me to the fun (and possibly quite dangerous) activity of setting up small plastic action figures in the forested area at the side of the school. "Cowboy and Indian" figurines would be placed on the ground in carefully staged settings. Once in place, Joshua would take out his can of WD-40 and a disposable lighter. He would start to spray the figures with the contents of the can and then hold the lit lighter underneath the stream. This immediately became a four-foot flame scorching the earth, quickly melting the figurines. The three of us would bring plastic items to melt under Joshua's improvised flame thrower. We had a lot of fun melting and disfiguring the toys, and there was a sense of power in the act of the burning. Looking back now, it's hard to believe we didn't burn the whole schoolyard with our antics. We had fun, though.

Derek's dad was an angry man, and we were never allowed to go to his house. His dad had an injury that prevented him from returning to work at the mill, but the compensation he received managed to cover his drinking costs. It was not uncommon to see Derek with a black eye or with his wrist wrapped in a tensor bandage. His dad was prone to fits of violence against Derek and his mother when he was in one of his moods. Sometimes Derek would tell Seth and me how he was going to kill his dad someday. I believed he would.

Seth was the craziest of us all. He loved mischief and had an eye for detail. One Halloween the three of us took a pair of coveralls, an old pair of boots, a Styrofoam wig head, and a baseball hat and created a life-size dummy. We hung it from the basketball hoop on my garage. We were very proud of it. Later that night, once the novelty of trick-or-treating wore off, Seth had the brilliant idea that we should remove the dummy and place it on the road outside my house, just around the blind corner at the top of the hill. We all agreed this would be great fun. We removed the dummy from the hoop and set it on the road. Seth thought it would be better if we put a trick-or-treat bag near one of the arms, and even have some molasses candies around it—to create the illusion that this body on the road had been trick-or-treating. While Derek, Joshua, and I waited in the bushes at the side of the road, Seth obsessed with the placement of the candies to make it look as realistic as he could. We could hear a vehicle racing towards the blind corner in the distance. Seth casually walked across the street just as a giant truck sped around the corner and ran over the dummy on the road. Tires screeched as the truck came to an immediate stop, and the driver rushed out of the truck screaming, "Oh God!" as he ran to the body on the road. Once he noticed that it was only a stuffed suit of leaves, he turned towards Seth. The chase was on and as he sprinted towards us, we dispersed through several paths at the side of the road.

This was my group of friends. They were my only friends at that time. All of us were misfits. All of us were Rebels.

We were all obsessed with the two Star Wars films, and we watched them over and over. For me, watching these films became my Sunday Mass. I learned from them. I wanted to be a Jedi so badly but had no idea how to start. I did think that it would be amazing to carry a fully functional lightsaber and be able to Force-choke people at will. Those things would come in handy in a town like Hopeless.

It was the fourteenth of December. Hopeless was covered by a deep blanket of snow. My friends and I thought of the town as Hoth, the ice planet in *The Empire Strikes Back*. It was dark out but not too cold that night—at least not as cold as Hoth would be. After all, the odds of surviving a night on Hoth were 725 to 1 as we all knew from C3P0's warning in *The Empire Strikes Back*. The snow clouds blanketed the night sky. Derek, Seth, Joshua, and I had been skating that evening in the tennis court at the school, which doubled as a makeshift rink in the winter. It was getting close to eight o'clock, and the four of us were sitting in the piled-up snow beside the rink. The snow began to fall from the sky, and we laid back, catching snowflakes on our tongues and feeling the flakes gently land upon our faces.

Eventually, Seth and I excused ourselves from the others and began our walk home. We decided to cut down an alley just a block away from the school. The snowplows had carved a path through the alley, forming snowbanks on each side at least six feet high. We both thought the alley could easily function as a trench for the Rebels to defend themselves against an AT-AT attack. Midway through the alley, two silhouetted figures jumped over the picket fence to our right and landed in front of us. They were both dressed in similar clothes: black and red buffalo plaid jackets, black jeans, and hiking boots. Seth and I stepped back, both of us startled by the sudden arrival of the pair. The taller figure was Alex Glum. Alex was fourteen years old. He had been held back for a few years at the school. Everyone at school knew he was trouble. It even seemed the teachers at the school did not want to get in his way. He stood before me and Seth, blocking the way home.

Alex appeared quite happy to see us in the alley—much the way a cat enjoys toying with a mouse before it pounces and rips it apart alive.

"Well, well, well ... It looks like it's not your night," Alex pronounced. He turned his attention towards Seth. "You, get lost ... and you better not tell anyone about this!"

Seth looked at me, his eyes wide as if to say, *Well, better you than me, buddy.*

Alex stepped aside, clearing an exit opportunity for Seth, and Seth wasted no time in taking it. I watched him run off, skates around his neck, the legs of his snowsuit rubbing together as he disappeared into the night. He did not look back, and I did not blame him for getting out of there. I would have done the same thing. After all, while the four of us were Rebels and spoke confidently to each other of how we were unified, deep down we all knew that each one of us was cowardly. We were all just terrified kids in a poor neighbourhood trying to keep our heads down and exist. Seth had been granted a pass that night, and he took it.

I started to have a bad feeling about the sudden turn the night was taking. I took a couple of steps back, but Alex's little buddy quickly ran behind me, blocking a potential escape route.

"Where the hell do you think you're going?" Alex barked.

I looked down, making a desperate effort to avoid eye contact.

"Look at me when I am taking to you," he continued, "Do you think you are better than us because you like to stand up when you answer the teacher's questions?"

I always tried to stay seated, but the ingrained fear of repercussions from the teachers forced me to continue with that private school practice.

Alex's grilling continued. "You pathetic fat twerp, you're not so tough."

"I know." I blurted out.

Alex, not used to having a victim speak out, became even more agitated. "Oh, you think you're funny?"

"No ..."

He inched closer to me. His eyes narrowed. "You're not going anywhere."

My heart pounded so hard I could feel it in the back of my throat. I couldn't breathe. I desperately wanted to run, but I could not. Alex was inches away from me, and his small friend was immediately behind me blocking all means of escape.

Yoda, the Jedi Master Luke meets and trains with in *The Empire Strikes Back,* warned Luke to beware that fear, anger, and aggression were paths to the dark side. *Fear.* I was so afraid in that moment. I tried to breathe, but tears streamed down my face instead. I had a bad feeling about all of this.

Alex, content with the result he was getting from his fear tactics, pressed on sarcastically.

"Ohhhh, is the fat little baby going to cry now?"

I just stood there, looking down, my crying quickly turned to sobbing. Alex became even more agitated. Whatever it was he was wanting to do, it was going to happen soon.

"C'mon lard-ass, let's see what you've got!"

Alex shoved me hard and fast. His friend had gotten on his hands and knees behind me, creating a barrier for me to fall over backwards. I landed hard on my back; the night sky stretched out before me. I immediately did what we were all told to do when facing a bear attack—lie perfectly still and pretend to be dead. I closed my eyes. I could hear the two of them getting closer as their boots scrunched on the snow beneath them. I opened my eyes to see both Alex and his friend looking down upon me. They started kicking me with their steel-toed hiking boots, swiftly and relentlessly. I remained as still as I could throughout the beating—occasionally the cracking of a rib vibrated within my body.

After a few moments that seemed like an eternity, there was an eerie pause to their sadistic exercise. It became quiet. Too quiet. I opened my eyes and saw Alex fumbling with the pockets of his buffalo plaid jacket. He pulled out a knife. I can still recall it vividly. It was a Buck brand Ranger model folding-lock blade knife. The body of the knife was wood, accentuated with brass fittings on either end. He snapped it open, and the blade made a loud sound as it locked in place.

Click.

With a sudden downward motion, Alex forced the small blade into my stomach. The blade pierced through my snowsuit and entered my side. The cold blade felt like burning metal as it penetrated me. As Alex pulled the knife out, I turned to my side and curled up into a ball. Blood—*my blood!*—oozed out and I could see the dark crimson stream upon the white snow surrounding me. The pain was so intense that I could not even scream as I grasped for air, terror and pain shooting through me. Blood continued to stain the snow as Alex and his friend disappeared into the night. I could not even lift my head to watch them leave. I tried to scream out for help, but my eyes started to shut. I could feel life leaving my body. I tried to drag myself towards home. The pain intensified and my eyes closed. My heartbeat slowed. I was dying.

The sensation of being stabbed is a difficult pain to describe. The best way for me to describe it is this: Imagine you suddenly find yourself floating on a sea in complete darkness surrounded by triangles that both burn and freeze at the same time. The triangles are everywhere and are of all colours imaginable. They spin, float, and fall all around as the burning freeze intensifies. The feeling is more painful and jarring than sticking your tongue on a nine-volt battery. This is the only way I can describe the pain I felt in that moment as I fell unconscious.

I started to dream. I was suddenly Luke on Hoth, laying in the snow, desperately trying to drag myself to shelter. Obi-Wan Kenobi appeared before me, sparkling blue light surrounding his ghostly form.

You will go to the Dagobah System ...

... Dagobah System ...

There you will learn from Yoda, the Jedi Master who instructed me ...

... Dagobah System ... Ben? ... Ben!

The ghost of Obi-Wan disappeared and was then replaced by Yoda.

Always in motion is the Force. Past, present and future together ... Do not give power to the fear you have or destroy you it will ...

Then I heard the sound of Vader's mechanical breathing, and he appeared before me. His message was simple and direct.

Turn to the dark side. Do not underestimate the power of the dark side.

Yoda took immediate issue with Vader's command.

To him you must listen not. Luminous beings are we, connected by the Force. Only through balance will you at rest be ...

Vader's retort was direct.

Bad will always triumph over good because good is dumb.

The next thing that I remember was waking up in the hospital. I had no idea how I made it there since the last thing I remembered was laying in the alley at night. The building that overlooked the alley was a two-storey home that had been turned into four different apartments. The second-floor apartment was rented by a police officer. I learned that this officer had returned home that night, went into the kitchen, and started to prepare dinner. Something made him look out into the alley below, and he spotted me, curled up in the snow. Lifeless. He had rushed me to the hospital after coming out to take a closer look. The cold had slowed my bleeding. My life was saved.

The officer tried to find out what had happened—who had stabbed and beaten me in the alley. I refused to give up Alex's name, telling him I didn't know who my attackers were. I was strictly following the rules of the schoolyard: if I told, I would get it worse.

I later learned that Alex and his family had left Hopeless the same night he attacked me. They were basically a transient family, and I would later hear a rumour that Alex spent his life in and out of jail before finally dying there years later.

At least I had survived. I was still alive, and the Force was with me.

32
THE HAPPIEST
PLACE ON EARTH

*I'm just a simple man trying to
make my way in the universe.*

— Jango Fett,
Attack of the Clones

As I recovered from the stabbing, I thought more and more about the time I spent at Catholic school. I thought the stabbing was a warning to me from God. He was warning me to stay quiet, and he was sending me this warning by keeping me alive.

I was now entering puberty and my natural development of sexual awareness was impeded by the shame of my past. I began to feel even dirtier and more ashamed of what had happened. I was attracted to girls yet felt that no one would bother to get close to me because I had been sodomized by old men—men who had direct communication with God.

I still believed that the pleasure my abusers obtained through raping and beating me was entirely my fault. I had tempted them, and, as a result, I needed to make my body so physically unattractive and my presence so small as to not be noticed. Hopeless was very much a Catholic town, and there was no way I would ever be able to wash those sins off of me. I accepted the bad that happened to me as penance for my earlier childhood sins. Yet there was an underlying anger and resentment I was nursing deep inside me.

Once I had healed from the attack in the snow, my mother and father enrolled me in a private karate class. I was reluctant to attend an open class, and my parents respected my apprehension of learning martial arts alongside my peer group. I have no idea how much they spent on private lessons, but three times a week I was taken to the local freestyle karate club where I was taught one-on-one by the head instructor, my sensei, who owned the school. I was forced to run, punch wood blocks with my bare hands, and meditate. I learned the best places to strike someone when attacked. Initially I was terrible with my self-defence training. Over time I gradually became better. Every week I became a little less clumsy, a little stronger, and slightly more confident. Sometimes I would pretend my six-foot instructor was Yoda and I was Luke. The mats on the floor became the marsh lands of Dagobah, and I was on the path to becoming a Jedi. There were a few differences, though: Luke never had to sweep the floor of Dagobah; Yoda was not six feet tall or a ginger-headed middle-aged man; I couldn't levitate no matter how hard I tried; and despite the warnings Yoda professed to Luke, I was nurturing hatred deep within. It was deep, but it was growing nonetheless.

That spring break, my parents decided to take a vacation away from Hopeless. The trip included my parents, my grandparents, my half sister Melissa (who had just returned from another runaway trip), and myself. All six of us travelled in my parents' motorhome. My mother and father chose stops along the way with me, specifically, in mind.

The first stop on our journey was the popular eighties attraction, Bedrock City, in southern British Columbia. I remember that it was raining on the day we arrived, and the park was not the greatest. I had never been to a theme park (or in this case what was attempting to pass as a theme park) before. As I recall, we spent most of the time in the gift shop, and my grandparents complained to my parents about making such an unnecessary stop for me. Melissa went off on her own, and I was self-conscious that everyone was waiting on me to leave. Bedrock City was not a place where I remember having a good time—or a *yabba-dabba-doo* time.

Once the final ashtrays were purchased at the gift shop and Melissa was located, we headed out on the road once more. At the end of each road day, we stopped at a campground along the route. My mom made sure we found campgrounds that included waterslides—again keeping me on the top of her mind. I loved exploring the waterslides, and the thrill of sliding down them reminded me of Luke sliding through the air vents within Bespin. I know Luke was not having fun when he was sliding through them, but I pretended I was on a mission to save him and get him back to the Rebel base. Each trip down the slide, I concluded he was just out of reach, and I needed to keep on trying. I spent hours on the slides, dunking in the water, feeling that odd combination of fatigue and adrenalin.

I don't recall too many other specific stops along the way, but I do remember Reno, Nevada; Anaheim, California; and Tijuana, Mexico. In Reno we spent time at a casino called Circus Circus, and I found great pleasure in the gambling training games for children where I could win stuffed animals. My father had trained me to shoot when I was younger, and it was evident that I had become a good shot under his tutelage. My testing grounds were the target games at Circus Circus. I pretended that the rifles were blasters and that my mission was to shoot the Imperials down to save Leia and Luke from their advances. Sometimes, the targets became the faces of my abusers, at other times, the targets were their genitalia. During one game, I began to cry as the visualization became realistic, and I could picture the heads of the pedophile priests exploding with every target I eviscerated. After winning twelve stuffed animals in a row at the target range, the game supervisor came over and prevented me from playing any further. He claimed there was a problem with the game and that they needed to shut it down. My winning streak was brought to an abrupt end.

I hauled out my stuffed animal kill in a clear plastic bag. It seemed that my haul did not please my grandparents with the space the menagerie took up in our cramped mobile living conditions. I, however, was very pleased with myself and pleased that my father's training in teaching me to shoot had paid off quite well. I was even more pleased that in my mind I had destroyed my abusers several times over.

Once banned from the family games, I roamed the casino to pass the time. I was bored. Children were not allowed in the gambling area, so I had to stay on the walkways of the casino. I spent a lot of time standing on the walkway watching my mom and my grandparents playing the nickel slots. They had buckets to collect the coins they won. I wanted to play, but there was no way I could get close. I asked my dad if he could find me a fake moustache, convinced that if I had a realistic one, no one would question my age, and I would have full access to all sorts of casino games. My dad played along, humouring me that we may be able to find something, but it wasn't long after that we were back in the motorhome on our way south once more.

Our next stop was Tijuana, and it was exciting. It was my first time to a "foreign" country, and it is where I had my first taste of avocado. I loved it. It was the start of my lifelong love affair with the green fruit. Outside the restaurant, my grandparents found what they thought to be an excellent deal. They bought a street vendors' entire stock of lanterns at a great price—"a steal," they said. They were boasting throughout the day and dinner about what a great deal they had found, purchasing his last ten lanterns, and how these lanterns were so beautiful. Because they could not compact, they would be difficult to store; I observed that their lanterns took up much more space than my stuffed animal win, but that didn't seem to bother them at all. After dinner (and more avocado for me) we walked around the corner only to see the same vendor with a fully replenished stock of his rare lanterns. After the trip, my grandparents never even put them to use, and I remember only a few years ago helping my mother with a garage sale where we had six of these former bargains up for grabs at fifty cents each.

The greatest thing about the trip was that it was my first visit to Disneyland. I had no idea what to expect. We had spent a day at Knott's Berry Farm, where my father became my ride companion, riding Montezuma's Revenge at least five times. The rides were much better than those at Bedrock City, but nothing prepared me for the experience of visiting Disneyland for the first time.

People often ask me what the lure of Disneyland continues to be for me. Many people who know me understand that I am a big kid—and those who know me well, know why. Disney's slogan "the Happiest Place on Earth" really sums it up for me. From kindergarten through fourth grade, I had endured the most severe physical, sexual, and emotional abuse. I had my innocence ripped away from me. I never felt comfortable playing with others since I really never had done so. I was too afraid and distrustful of people other than my parents. The day we arrived at Disneyland was truly one of the first days I can remember fully enjoying myself. There is a particular smell I encounter each time I visit the park—I can smell it near the flower fountain by the Sunglass Hut kiosk near the Downtown Disney security checkpoint and in front of the LeBrea Bakery. It is a combination of three distinct smells: asphalt, plastic, and chlorination. I love that smell. Yes, it's weird, but it reminds me of that first experience arriving there. To this day, each time I visit the park and smell this, I cry. I really do. Just a tear or two as I take in the smell. I know it sounds crazy, but that is the same smell that I encountered visiting the park for the first time when I was a child. The power of that smell brings me back to that time and that day, when I truly experienced the innocence of youth for the first time. It was the first place I felt genuinely safe after the years of abuse at the Catholic school in Hopeless. My children and friends have seen the tears when I pass by this particular place. It happens only once per visit—it is my olfactory reminder that I am coming back to the place that demonstrated that the power of being a child had merit.

My dad was incredible with me in Disneyland. He was my ride buddy and my roller coaster partner. He waited in line with me, and I will never forget the overwhelming feeling of love for him I had as he endured ride after ride with me. Together we rode the coasters, and together we experienced Space Mountain. Space Mountain to me was a place where I was imagining being put through Jedi training. I imagined the coaster to be an X-wing simulator, and I was preparing for the day I would join the Rebellion. The darkness of the ride and the feeling of soaring through space reinforced my imagination and made it seem all the more real.

The Haunted Mansion became the tree on Dagobah, and I searched the ride for Vader who could pop out at any minute. Pirates of the Caribbean was the Mos Eisley area with a number of characters that needed to be watched. It didn't matter that I was on a water ride believing that I was in the middle of a desert planet, for my imagination was in overdrive and everything was turned into a Star Wars experience. It's a Small World became the place where the Ugnaughts had tossed around C3P0's head. Even the song on that ride couldn't shake my Star Wars fantasy.

Disneyland was incredible—unlike anything I had ever experienced before. In fact, it has spoiled my amusement park expectations everywhere. I still find myself looking forward to every pilgrimage I can make.

I remember walking through Frontierland and, like most park guests, rushing to look for treasures in the gift shop inside the fort. I picked out a toy musket and a hat. It was no ordinary hat. I had never seen that kind of hat before. I thought it looked really cool. It had crossed swords on the front and a short black visor. It slouched down in the front and was taller in the back. It had a screen-printed fabric sticker on top of a red and white flag in a cross formation—just like the flag on the car in one of my favourite TV series, *The Dukes of Hazard*. It was grey. I was innocent and ignorant of the events of the Civil War and the meaning of the Confederacy. I just knew the hat was unique and that I had to have it.

My parents acquiesced and allowed me to purchase the hat. It was no big deal, or so I thought. I sported my grey cap throughout the park. I thought it looked cool. I received compliments from the Disneyland cast members and had no idea what kind of message I was broadcasting.

My family had lunch at the Blue Bayou in Disneyland that afternoon. As we were sitting and enjoying our meals, I noticed my hat drew the attention of a middle-aged man at the table next to us. He kept looking over at the hat and at me. I thought he must have been admiring my ultra-cool look. After a while, he leaned over to make pleasant conversation with us. The first thing he asked us was where we were from. We told him we were from Canada. He turned back and said something to the others at his table, and then he spoke to me.

"That's a mighty fine hat you are wearing."

I thanked him.

"Do you know about the history of that hat?" he asked.

I told him that it was a soldier's hat but that that's all I knew.

"Do you know anything about that flag on the top of your hat?"

I told him it was the same flag the Dukes of Hazard had on their car.

He then said, "You know, that hat would look a lot better without that flag. They didn't used to have those flags on them."

I looked at my hat and thought he may be right. Perhaps my hat would look better without that flag.

"Do you like grey?"

I told him I thought it was okay.

"I prefer blue," he said. With that he turned back to his table and continued his meal. We finished our meals and said goodbye to the people we were sitting next to. They wished us a safe and fun stay. Before we left, he told me that blue would be a really nice colour for that kind of hat.

As we roamed around the park that afternoon, I began to take notice of the looks I was getting. They were mostly pleasant, but I started to notice that the people who were like the man at the restaurant gave me more studied looks. Perhaps the man was right—the flag on top of my hat did not look as cool as I thought. We sat down later that day for a snack and a break, and I took my hat off and looked at it. I started to pick at the sticker. It pulled off rather easily. I discarded it in the trash and believed the hat did look better without it. I thought it would look even better with a Star Wars Rebel symbol on it. But where would I find that?

Decades have passed since that first trip to Disneyland. The escalation of racial disparities and violence remind me of that time and that man. Upon reflection of that memory, I can understand his initial hesitation when asking my family where we were from and his relief to hear we were from the North. His short conversation with us that day was bold. He planted the seed for me to look into the deeper meaning of the colours of the hat and why he had subtly told me that blue was a good colour. It was a few years later that I began to learn about the Civil War and really began to understand what the man at that table, the Black man, was telling me. My grey hat eventually found its way to the trash, and I came to agree that blue was a much better colour for me.

I wish I could find that man and thank him for his lesson all those years ago. It was not a lecture, and it was not provoked by anger. I was ignorant to the facts, and he offered me an opportunity to educate myself on a matter I had known nothing about. I can't assume anything about that man's history, but I can imagine how the image of a Confederate flag might feel to some people. I had thought it looked cool. I was ignorantly innocent. I can only imagine how blind acceptance of hate symbols in our society can humiliate and intimidate some of us within our multi-faceted world.

This was the first of many pilgrimages I have taken to Disneyland over the years. Perhaps I have visited it too many times. It has become a place where I visit for fun and for work, and where I have met some very important people—it's a place where I can really enjoy mixing business and pleasure. Though I have been down there at times by myself, I really have enjoyed it so much more when I go with my own children. Seeing how they enjoy the experience is so much more rewarding. It reminds me of the patience my mother and father had with me when we went there. I know my mom made sure we would stop there as a way of telling me she loved me. I am sure she put up with complaints from my grandparents about the frivolity of visiting theme parks on that trip, but I am so grateful that she put Disneyland on the itinerary. She will never know how important that trip was to me—that one day in the park. Each visit to Disneyland brings tears to me. It's the place where I am allowed to be a child, however briefly, over and over. It's something I hope to pass on to my grandchildren one day—the power of play and the seriousness of childlike abandon. I also hope to pass on a little magic to everyone I have the blessing of interacting with, for we are not complete if we cannot keep the magic alive in our own special way.

ƎƎ
EMERGENCY 911

That is why you fail ...

— Yoda,
The Empire Strikes Back

It was only a few days after we returned home from Disneyland that Melissa ran away again. I had no idea how long she would be gone for, or if she would even return. My parents must have anticipated her to be away for a much longer time, because they moved me from my smaller room into her room. I was excited to have more space for my collection of Star Wars toys.

My martial arts training continued. Although you might think that it would put an end to the bullying, it did not. I was not a typical kid. I was quiet and awkward. It wouldn't be until I was in eleventh grade that I would grow taller. I was still short, round, and quiet. The attack in the winter of 1980 had given me more reason to withdraw into my shell. Derek, Seth, Joshua, and I were still friends, but we were not as close as we had been. This was largely due to the fact that I felt I had been abandoned by Seth in the alley the night I was stabbed. I didn't trust them. I am sure they could feel it.

When I finally finished elementary school, I believed that the worst times were finally behind me. Junior high was a chance for me to reinvent myself. The scars from my emotional wounds were starting to set, and I thought I would be able to finally see who I could grow into

147

being. I was getting heavier as a result of the continued stress eating that kept my inner demons well hidden. My exterior shell was a fortress of ugliness that prevented people from wanting to get too close to me. If anyone was going to get close, it would be on my terms.

My first week of high school was not what I expected. There were many more students than at South Hopeless Elementary, and I had five teachers instead of one. In physical education my teacher was Mr. Willfun. He was a small, ball-headed man and had been teaching physical education his entire career. The group of new students waited in the gymnasium for him to come out of his office. I didn't know any of my new classmates. I felt a bit uneasy. He took attendance and then announced that during our following class, he would be administering our physical fitness testing. There was going to be a host of activities that we would be rated on. There were things like how many chin-ups you could do in one minute, how high you could rope climb, the highest you could jump, the farthest you could jump, how many push-ups you could do in one minute, how far you could run in ten minutes, and so on. I felt like I had been conscripted into the army. I knew then that this would not be my favourite class. Willfun saved the most humiliating activity for last. He was going to give us all a fat calliper test. He had a tool that looked like a giant clamp with a dial on it. The wider the calliper opened, the fatter you were. Such joy for an eighth-grade fat kid. Some of the kids looked over at me and started to laugh amongst themselves. I can't remember what the rest of the day was like as I became fixated on how I could get out of the predicament. I had two days until I needed a foolproof plan.

I became obsessed with planning my exit strategy. I attempted the sick test with my mom that night. I looked as sad as I could and picked at my food. I threw in some coughing fits and a couple well-timed bouts of sneezing for good measure. My endeavours appeared to go unnoticed. I had to take things up a level if I was going to have any success in getting out of the fat test. I mentioned casually, probably about six times, that I didn't feel well. My mother felt my forehead and told me I was fine. She wasn't falling for it. So much for that plan.

The two days passed rather quickly, and I found myself pacing the field near the school on the morning of the dreaded test. What was I going to do? Maybe if I closed my eyes and used the Force it would guide me to a stellar plan. I found a place near the field where I could sit, like Luke did, to meditate. I could feel it working as I concentrated on my breath. I breathed deeply as my foolproof plan formulated in my mind's eye. It was perfect and iron clad, though possibly excessive. But it would have to do, as I only had forty-five minutes before I was to be humiliated in front of everyone with the fat test.

There was a long cement staircase at the back of the field that led to the road below. Students would traverse the stairs down the cutbank on their way to Scotch Pine Mall across the street or to the local McDonalds just up the street. I walked down the first few steps and my heart began beating faster as I decisively took action. I had no time to lose. I looked around, making sure there were no witnesses to what I was about to do. Just in case, though, I put some effort into making what I was about to do somewhat realistic. I carefully "fell" down the cement stairs making sure to not actually hurt myself in the process. Once settled into a somewhat believable position, I clutched my right ankle and began to cry as best as I could. It was probably my first attempt at performance art. The first five "audience members" who witnessed my dramatic scene didn't stop to take part in my scheme, but rather continued to step past (or over) me as they returned to, or left, the school. I was determined for this to work, though it looked like I was going to have to stay on the stairs for the rest of the day. So be it. I was dedicated to my performance. I faithfully clutched my "hurt" ankle and carried on.

Then it all came together rather nicely. A school senior walked up the stairs, face in her book. I let out a yelp and she looked up, closed the book, and ran up the stairs towards me. She was genuinely concerned. Maybe my acting was good.

"Are you okay?" she asked.

"No, it's my leg. I can't get up."

She looked around, not knowing what to do. At this point neither did I. I hadn't thought much past laying on the stairs clutching my leg.

"Stay here, I'm going to get the principal!"

"What? No! I think I can—"

"No. Don't put any pressure on it. I will be right back with the principal." She ran off, on a mission to save me.

Crap! What was I going to do next? I hadn't thought about the possible scenarios that might unfold after my initial act was discovered. My acting was obviously stellar. *Damn my brilliant conviction!* Maybe I could get up and move away, but if anyone saw me ...

Too late. The girl was back with Mr. Flemming in tow. *What had I done?* It was too late to back out now. Maybe they'd help me back to the office, let me lay down for a while, and that would be that.

"Here he is, Mr. Flemming."

"Thanks, Nancy. I've got it from here," he said as he rushed down the stairs.

"What's your name?" he asked.

I gave him all my details and then he dropped the bombshell.

"The ambulance will be here shortly."

Ambulance?

Damn my Academy-Award-level acting skills. Maybe I laid on the pain too much. I didn't gauge my audience. I was really into it. I could hear sirens in the distance. My heart was racing. I was going to have to keep this up. Mr. Flemming went down the rest of the stairs to greet the ambulance crew. Three paramedics jumped out, grabbed a stretcher, and came up the stairs to me. A group of students had assembled on the hill above the stairs. They were obviously enjoying the show.

I was asked where my leg hurt. I had to remember which leg it was before I responded. They isolated my leg and then placed me on a packboard before putting me on the stretcher and locking me in. There was no way I was going to get out of there.

Just as they were closing the doors, Mr. Flemming shouted out to me, "I'm going to call your mom!"

I really wished that I had fallen for real. The ambulance raced off and I was on my way to the hospital. The female paramedic took my blood pressure and gave the statistics to the poker-faced man.

"What does that mean?" I asked, genuinely curious.

"It means your blood pressure is a little high because you're over-weight," he responded.

Tears flooded my face. The female paramedic tried to console me, telling me it was all right. I was glad there was someone with me who was being kind. I had no idea how I was going to sell my condition to my mother, especially since I had tried my illness techniques on her the two days leading up to my grand spectacle.

I was whisked out of the ambulance and into the hospital, where they took me immediately into the X-ray room. As I was being wheeled out, I saw my mother waiting for me. She did not look happy. She had been in an executive meeting when she was interrupted by the call from my school. I can imagine how shocking it would have been to get a call from the school informing her that there had been an accident and her son was being rushed to the hospital. What made it even worse is when she looked right at me, with her mother's eyes, and could see into my soul. She knew immediately that my injury was staged, yet she played along with the doctor's advice to have me keep off my leg until it "healed." The doctor told her there was nothing abnormal from the X-ray and that there didn't seem to be any swelling in my foot, which was a good sign for a speedy recovery. All I could think of was that my recovery was going to be very, very speedy. My mom thanked the doctor and wheeled me out to the car. I knew I was going to be in big trouble once we were in the privacy of her car.

The ride home was rather quiet, and the silence was ripping me up inside. I was prepared for something but was getting more nervous the longer nothing was said. I didn't know how long the silence was going to last, and since I was not tolerating it well, I made the first move.

"I'm sorry, Mom."

"Sorry for what?" she retorted.

I didn't know what to do or say in return.

She continued. "You must have had quite the fall. I'm glad your leg isn't broken."

She knew I had been faking my injury. It wasn't what she said, but it was her tone that made it clear. I decided it would be best for me to stop speaking about the incident altogether. I did my best limp into the house and kept up the charade for a while inside. At one point she asked me which leg had been injured. I indicated my right leg and she commented that I had been limping on the wrong foot. She was a cat, and I was her prey.

She didn't make much of a fuss about what had happened. It wasn't until a few weeks later when she received the bill for the ambulance that I finally received my dressing down.

"Forty-five dollars for your little ambulance ride!" she said as she threw the bill on the table in front of me one morning. "I hope your performance got you what you wanted at school."

I just sat in silence, taking it in. That was becoming my new method of coping. I would sit quietly and absorb the anger, letting it settle deep inside.

ᴈᕼ
I'M WITH THE BAND

My disappointment in your performance cannot be overstated.

— Supreme Leader Snoke,
The Last Jedi

By this point, my collection of Star Wars toys had grown. I cherished my toys and loved the boxes they came in. I made sure to return every toy to its original packaging after each time I played with it (which, at the time, was something unheard of). I was always so careful to take care of my precious Star Wars collection. R2-D2, however, remained at my side at all times.

At the height of my Star Wars toy collecting phase, I had amassed an impressive collection. As the franchise was quickly becoming a part of my young identity, I requested all sorts of the toys from the Kenner collection. I was especially lucky with my Star Wars bounty the Christmas after *The Empire Strikes Back* was in the theatres. I was proud of my AT-AT, Hoth Battle Set, X-wings, TIE fighters, and the Slave I—Boba Fett the Bounty Hunter's personal spaceship. I was equally proud of my assorted action figure menagerie. Every time I acquired a new toy, I carefully removed it from the packaging—much like a surgeon carefully makes their first incision.

Unlike previous toys, I treated my Star Wars collection as treasure. The packaging was stored away, complete with the instruction booklets and the ever-increasing catalogues that came with each boxed toy. My father added shelves along the walls of my bedroom upon which I proudly displayed my galactic treasures. I found that my display had a profound effect upon me. The presence of my creative dioramas brought me joy. By simply looking at them surrounding my room, I could easily transport myself into the Star Wars universe. They were as tantamount to my young self as religious artefacts are to a religious zealot. Hoth, Tatooine, Bespin, Endor, and Dagobah all provided me with a solace and tranquility—an inner peace for my meditative spirit to thrive. Star Wars was becoming my religion—my safe space. There were no adults telling me how I should interpret my feelings towards my toys and the films. My experience was personal, powerful, spiritual, and it was mine alone. No adult had imposed this spirituality upon me. My revelations regarding my soul and the Force were exactly what I needed to start the process of healing from the abuse I had survived at the hands of the Roman Catholic priests. When it came to Star Wars, I was a disciple of the Force.

Time passed.

I gravitated towards punk and new age music. Oingo Boingo, Black Flag, and The Clash were my favourites, followed closely by any number of Broadway show tunes and the Blues Brothers. My tastes, like me, were eclectic. My Walkman was my favourite companion. It allowed me to shut out the world as I walked to and from school, while helping me keep others from engaging me in conversations. I could choose when and if I would participate in discussions. Sometimes I just wore my headphones without listening to anything so I could eavesdrop on the conversations around me. I could hear what the latest school gossip was without people knowing I was listening to them.

I took to wearing camouflage. Partially, it was because I desired to emulate the Rebel soldiers on Endor in *Return of the Jedi*, but it was also due to the fact that there was still a part of me that wanted to go about my life unnoticed. At the Catholic school, it was important not to be singled out. Ironically, camouflage clothing was not in style in the early eighties, and so—despite my best efforts—I did stand out. A part of me craved attention and acceptance, yet I would try to avoid being noticed. I preferred to live in the shadows, where I could observe everyone from a safe and unnoticeable position.

I was in the high school band. I had chosen the trumpet specifically because of the music of Star Wars. The trumpets carried the opening theme, and I wanted to be able to play that melody just like it was in the movie. It was something I would never achieve, but I kept trying. I don't know what modern high school bands are like, but when I was growing up, the band kids were easily the most unpopular and weird group in the school. I could see from my surroundings that I could be the alpha of the band group. My primitive instinct to lead a pack tried to kick in.

My competition was a kid named Bill. Bill was even rounder than me, therefore I was better suited to be the head of the band gang. Bill compensated for his lack of physical prowess by commanding an advanced vocabulary. He used words I had rarely heard or didn't even know the meanings of. I saw my chance one morning as we waited outside the band room for Mr. Bakerfield, the band teacher, to arrive for practice. Bill was sitting in a chair, leaning back against the brick wall of the hallway so only the back legs were on the linoleum. He was rocking back and forth as he led a discussion on politics and the comic strip *Bloom County*. He had a much deeper knowledge of the strip than I did, and he wasted no time in humiliating me in front of the girls sitting on the floor listening to his theories. I picked my moment, walked up to him, and lightly kicked at the chair just as he was rocking backwards. The chair slid out from under him, and the back of his head rubbed over an exposed hinge on the custodian's closet behind him. Blood was streaked down the wall, and it looked like a murder scene.

Though I missed my chance of being an alpha, I suddenly became the bully. This was something I hated as soon as I saw how easy it was to hurt someone.

Bill was rushed to the nurse's station, and I was sent to detention. I couldn't explain myself. I was embarrassed for what I had done, but a very small part of me enjoyed the ease at which one could inflict sudden pain on someone else. The dark side was growing stronger inside me. It was a power that could protect me, but it could also do harm to others in the process. I apologized to Bill for what I had done, and after a few years, he finally warmed up to me.

My hostility towards other kids was fleeting. I saved and channelled my aggression into my martial arts training. I was still hiding my past, and I was now becoming a dark horse as a student—a dark chubby pony anyway.

35
SILENT BUT DEADLY

Choose what is right, not what is easy.

— *The Clone Wars*

My parents saw me withdraw further and further into my solitude. They thought I needed to occupy myself with a hobby. Although I had my martial arts training, I didn't see it as anything other than learning physical survival tactics. Maybe my mom saw this. She saw that I needed more than just physical survival tactics—I needed social ones.

Much to the anger of my Aunt Agatha and my grandparents, my mother surprised me with a computer. This was 1982. No one had computers in their homes—especially not fat, brooding, quiet kids who wore camouflage. Probably because she knew it would anger her family, my mom made no hesitation in purchasing me the Atari 400, with a pressure membrane keyboard and 4K of RAM. It was the pinnacle of home computing technology, and, even better, she bought me a game to go with it: Star Raiders! I was set. I thought of the game as a training simulator to prepare me for if I ever had to leave Earth to fly an X-wing in the Rebellion.

Not long after that, I was introduced to a phone receiver modem into which I could dial a number, place the handle of the phone into the casing, and log on to the internet. The internet was only in its infancy and was far from being the World Wide Web as we know it today. There was not much content available at that time. I did, however, figure out how I could hack into the Sears mainframe. If R2-D2 could do it, I thought, maybe I could too. I went to Sears and wrote down monitor information from the unattended staff computer tills, then returned home and attempted to access the system. One night I was even able to correctly guess the login password and was excited to see that I could order anything and mark it as paid. When I asked my parents what they wanted from Sears on me, I was immediately cut off from accessing servers through my computer for a while.

Though I was teaching myself computer basics (and some not-so-basics), I was still quite alone. I started to make home movies with my parents' Super 8 camera and my Star Wars action figures, but I hated having to wait for the film to be sent away for developing. This led to my mother purchasing me my first video camera. The camera was heavy and had to be connected to the recording deck, which was worn over the shoulder and weighed in at almost ten pounds. It came with a battery belt which added an additional five pounds to the set. It was incredible to record and review footage without having to develop film, but I didn't know anything about white balancing, exposure, or recording speeds. No one in my family did. Personal technology was new, so, to help me understand how to properly use my new gear, my mother (again guiding me) suggested I volunteer for the local cable station in Hopeless.

My Dad drove me to the CableVision station, and I went in for my first volunteering session. It was there I met the station manager, Owen. He was not much taller than I was, but I easily outweighed him by eighty pounds. He had a sarcastic wit and an easygoing nature about him.

"You must be in the army," he said as he looked at me dressed in my woodland camouflage.

"What? No," I countered.

"So, what brings you here? Why do you want to help out here?"

"I have a Minolta camera, tuner, and recorder that I want to be able to use better."

"What do you want to do with all that?"

"I don't know. Make movies?"

"Okay then, Cameraman. You want to be a cameraman. Best way to learn is by doing it."

Before I knew it, Owen had me in the studio, on a headset, and behind a professional studio Ikegami camera. He showed me how to zoom in and out and how to focus the camera. After an hour getting the feel for the camera, I was told that I would be operating the second camera on a studio shoot for the local gardening show. My job was to keep the host and her guest in frame as they discussed fungus and flora. I wore a headset, and Owen guided me through the shoot. During the monotonous discussion, he constantly made jokes and warned me not to fall asleep. He cracked the worst dad jokes I had ever heard.

"Hey guys, this is so exciting. Be sure to not wet your plants."

The other camera operator, Mike, joined in. "Is it thyme for this to be over?"

Owen countered. "This is unbeleafable."

As I listened to them banter back and forth, it was difficult to not laugh in the quiet studio. I also really wanted to fit in. I focused hard on my task. As the host ended her segment with a tip about wrapping roots, I became nervous as to what to say. My modus operandi with adults was to stay silent and hide away as best as I could, but I had already found myself standing out in the studio dressed from head to toe in army fatigues. Owen called cut from the control booth and the red recording light went off.

Owen's voice came through the headset. "Hey Nicker, was that as exciting as you hoped it to be?"

There was a pause.

Finally, I let go and went for it. It was time for my crack at a pun.

"Chive never been happier."

Silence.

Oh shit. This was it. I had obviously said the wrong thing. My heart pounded fast. The silence was broken when both Owen and Mike burst out laughing.

"Oh Nicker, that was terrible. You have a budding career here!"

At that we all laughed. Owen and Mike were accepting me for who I was. My size and sense of fashion were of no concern. Though I was young for a volunteer, Owen took a chance on me and let me carry on.

But, before I could be fully trusted, I would be tested.

I was soon introduced to late-night programming. CableVision was not an automated station, so content had to be broadcast manually, and I had been selected to do the late shift, from eight o'clock until midnight. Owen gave me the keys to lock up after finishing my shift. Mike, who had been the other camera operator on my first day, was getting ready to leave for the night. Before he left, he took me to one of the rooms behind the studio.

"Look at all these cable boxes. We just got dozens of them in."

"What are they for?" I asked.

"These are for people who subscribe to the premium cable channels. You attach your cable at home into one of these boxes and then you have full access to Super Channel, The Movie Channel, HBO, the Playboy Channel—all fourteen premium cable channels."

I was impressed.

Mike continued. "Yeah, if someone just took one of these, they would have free cable. There's no way for us to track them until we serialize them. If someone was to take one, there is no way we would be able to tell."

We exited the room, Mike wished me a good night, and I was left alone in the studio. It was just me and the programming that I had to keep queueing and switching for the next four hours. I had plenty of time to do homework, watch the premium cable feed on the other monitors, and think about the information Mike had given me before he left.

No one would know if I just took one.

I thought back to when I had travelled down that path before, swapping the Snowspeeder tags at The Bay. I thought about how easy it was but also about how bad I felt after. I reached into my jacket and pulled out my R2-D2.

"What do you think, buddy?" I asked my old friend.

I responded in my best R2-D2 chirps, and I twisted his silver dome to hear the clicking. He calmed me when I was anxious or scared.

"You're right, R2. What would Luke do?"

I did not have to contemplate long. I was not going to give into temptation this time. Sure, it would mean I could sneak access to the Playboy channel (and, as I was a fourteen-year-old boy, that was a major temptation), but I knew it was wrong. I had known that before even speaking with my droid.

The next morning, Owen called me to congratulate me.

"For what?" I asked.

"We like to see what volunteers do when they are alone without us there. You did a good job with the programming. You also gave up your opportunity."

"What opportunity?"

"Free cable."

It dawned on me. I was given a test of character. Mike deliberately led me to the room with the boxes to see if I would take their bait. I hadn't. From that point on, I was their number one volunteer and was given my own set of keys to the studio. Owen even let me drive the cable van short distances, even though it would be a few years before I had my driver's license.

Owen became my first real friend, and I became less withdrawn. Decades later, Owen and I are still in constant contact—and he's never stopped calling me Nicker.

∋ō
TO DATE OR NOT TO DATE

*I wish I could put my fist through
this whole lousy, beautiful town.*

— Rose Tico, *The Last Jedi*

When I was only eight years old, my grandfather had given me his car. It was a 1949 Dodge Club Coupe, and it had only 63,000 miles on it. Eight years later, it would be my first car. By this time, *Return of the Jedi* had come out, and I was driving. I was still round but starting to grow.

Daphne was in tenth grade. She had brown hair and looked like Princess Leia. She laughed at my jokes in class and seemed to take an interest in me. I really don't know why. I didn't know the first thing about dating, but I eventually got up the courage to ask her out. I was shocked when she actually agreed.

Socially awkward as I was, I suggested that I take her out for dinner. What? What tenth-grade nerd asks a girl to go out for dinner? Worse yet, why would a tenth-grade girl accept such a bizarre request from a short, round nerd? Why not a movie? Why not something more kid-like? Nope, it was going to be dinner, and I was going to pick her up at her house that Friday night. I have no idea where this bout of confidence came from.

The big question on my mind was what to wear. I had no idea how dates were supposed to work, aside from what I had seen on television and film. My half sister Melissa had been married a couple years prior, and I still had the suit purchased for me for the occasion. It was a three-piece, light brown, corduroy suit with a chocolate-brown shirt. I did not have a tie to wear with it, so the collar was left unbuttoned to show off my St. Christopher medal. (Though I was no longer a practising Catholic, the St. Christopher medal was the only jewelry I had, and I thought it made me look more mature.) Rounding off the look were my tan suede Hush Puppy loafers. I don't know what possessed me to decide this was how I was going to dress for my first date, but events were in motion, and yours truly was going to dress to impress.

Unlike modern cars made of lightweight alloys and plastics, my Dodge was built like a tank. The doors were almost a foot thick, and the vehicle was solid steel throughout. I had seen movies where the gentleman opened the door of the car for his date to enter. It was a classy thing to do, and so the afternoon of the date I spent time practising opening and closing the passenger door of my Dodge to make sure I could make it look effortless. I did not want any room for error on my big night.

Daphne lived on the outskirts of Hopeless, so I had time to focus on making a good impression as I made the drive over to her house. On the way, I listened to my inspirational Star Wars music, cranking the volume so the main theme blasted within the confines of the car. I was getting pumped, and John Williams music was helping me feel like a Jedi as I headed towards my date with destiny (well, Daphne, that is).

As I neared her house, I turned off the music and put the cassette in the glove box of the car. I loved *Star Wars*, but not everybody at my school did, especially the girls. I grabbed my cassette of *The Karate Kid* and pushed it into the deck. 'Cruel Summer' started to play. *Excellent mood music*, I thought, as I pulled into her driveway. The stage was set. In my mind I was a well-dressed guy in a classic car with excellent music and an all-brown ensemble. What could possibly go wrong?

I strode—or waddled, rather—confidently to her front door and rang the doorbell. She answered the door wearing a summer dress, her hair a magnificent tower of high, wide, and curly crimped perfection. If you are not familiar with hairstyles of the time, it's hard to really describe. The general rule of thumb for women's hair was *big*. Female high school students liked to add swoops in the front that went as tall as they could spray them to stay. Imagine the perfect wave for a surfer to ride. That was pretty much the way hair had to sit on top of the wearer's head. With television influences such as *Dallas* and *Knots Landing*, big wavy hair was the popular choice.

I spent a couple minutes nervously chatting with her parents as I stood in the doorway. I have this unpleasant condition known medically as palmar hyperhidrosis, otherwise known as plain old sweaty palms. Whenever I get nervous, my body reacts by alerting my hands that it's time to sweat. Meeting someone's parents for the first time is an excellent trigger for the reaction. I had hoped Daphne's father wouldn't shake my hand, but he walked towards me, hand extended. For some reason, only my right hand was sweaty, clammy, and cold. My left hand was totally fine. Room temperature. I knew that a clammy handshake was going to send a poor message of confidence to Daphne's dad, so for some inexplicable reason, as he stood there, right hand extended, I reached out with my left hand and twisted it into a very unnatural position—thumb facing down—in order to grab his hand. He looked rather shocked, and I pretended that my technique was very normal. It wasn't. I could feel Daphne's doubts about the success of this date. This very well might have been strike one for the night. I let them know I was taking Daphne to the local Greek restaurant for dinner, and that I'd be bringing her home shortly after that. I exited the house and walked down the stairs in front of Daphne. I was going to gentleman-the-shit out of this night.

The next step was to open the door for her. I moved to my position and opened the door. Daphne moved past me and entered the vehicle. I learned something very, very important in the next few seconds that night. People who wear dresses don't just sit in a car. They tend to lean out as they gather any fabric that may get caught in the door. I had not factored for this when I was preparing my gentlemanly actions for that night. I had rehearsed my moves rather robotically. Open door. Girl gets in car. Close door. There was no factoring the possibility of waiting for girl to tilt away from the car with her head as she adjusted her sitting position. So, as Daphne entered, I closed the door. Not a gentle action either, but a really firm shutting of the door since the car was so old. As the handle left my hand, I saw what was about to unfold. This was strike two. Daphne's head was on a collision course with the steel frame of the window. Everything was in motion and the course was irreversible. I watched in horror as the door connected to the right side of her head. She momentarily popped up in a perfect sitting position before gaining more speed as she continued to double over, the left side of her head now on a collision course with the giant Bakelite steering wheel. She nailed it and slumped over, now unconscious. I rushed over to the driver's side and propped her back up to a sitting position. Her parents looked on from the living room window. I thought I had killed her. She was breathing, but her hairstyle had changed. There were two noticeable lumps on her head, the result of the two blows. Her permed and crimped hairstyle with the long swoosh in the front now had two smaller hills on each side, giving her head the look as if she was sporting a new mountain-range style. Soon enough, her pupils rolled back into position as she gained consciousness. She screamed in pain, but I was just happy that I had not killed her.

Her first words were, "You fat fuck!"

I cannot remember much more than that as she stormed out of the car, stumbling back to the house in a daze and leaving me sitting alone in her driveway. Her mom came out and helped her up the stairs and her father looked at me disapprovingly.

Strike three. I started the car and began my drive of shame back home while 'Cruel Summer' played on:

> *It's a cruel, cruel summer*
> *Leaving me here on my own*
> *It's a cruel, cruel summer*
> *Now you're gone*
> *You're not the only one*

"Fat fuck" rang in my head. I drove down the road back home, defeated. I started to cry. I failed. I was a fat fuck in a brown suit. I looked in the rear-view mirror as I drove and thought how my suit made me look like a fat piece of shit. The anger and the humiliation were flooding in again. I didn't deserve anything or anyone. It would be best if I just killed myself. That's what I would have to do. It was the only way to save my parents from God's wrath and save me from any further humiliation.

There was a truss bridge that I had to drive over on the way home. The river flowed about eighty feet below. If I swerved off the bridge, the car would plummet into the quick-flowing river. My car did not have seat belts, so I would likely break my neck as I slammed against the roof of the car, and if that didn't kill me, I would at least be unconscious as I drowned. Good riddance. I could hear a voice inside goading me on. It sounded like Emperor Palpatine.

Yes ... yes ... feel your hate swelling inside you.

I stepped on the gas pedal, making sure to get enough speed to break through the barrier at the centre of the bridge. I was sweating all over now.

Almost there ...

I was getting to a good speed.

Almost there ...

I was on the bridge.

Almost there ...

I was approaching mid span.

This is it ...

I cranked the wheel hard to the right and the car responded; the right wheels were on the pedestrian walkway. I was going to do this and not fail. For once I would do something and do it right. But then as my car continued to veer right, I felt a sudden hit of adrenaline and fear.

I swerved back onto the road. I couldn't do it. I was scared. I was scared to die. I was scared to live. I was scared, terrified, and alone. I couldn't even muster up the courage to kill myself. I was an utter failure in life.

My heart pounding, I pulled over once I crossed the bridge. I held myself and cried for what seemed like hours. More and more I was slipping down the path to the dark side.

I saw Daphne in the halls at school the following week. She did not speak to me. The lumps on her head were thinly disguised with a hairband. Thankfully, I was not a murderer. I found out a few weeks later that she had lost a bet, and her penalty was to lead me on and have me take her on a date. It made sense—after all, who in their right mind would want to go on a date with me? She was popular, and I was not. I was awkward—a good target for those who loved to make fun of others. She was a member of the mean group. I should have seen that, but in my eagerness to fit in with others, I refused to see that at the time.

I couldn't wait to leave Hopeless.

17

OF KENDO AND JEDI

Hokey religions and ancient weapons are no match for a good blaster at your side.

— Han Solo, *A New Hope*

The balance between light and dark is something that I continue to grapple with to this day. There are times I feel a strong temptation to succumb to the darkness that stirs deep inside. Perhaps that is why *The Empire Strikes Back* remains my favourite film of all the series. It was dark, and the lessons I took from the film helped fill the space in my soul that organized religion had left gaping. I wanted to believe in something, and the movies provided that for me.

I believed that I could never enter a relationship with anyone after what had been done to me as a child. I was damaged goods. What teenage girl would be able to deal with the baggage I was carrying around with me? I wanted to be loved so deeply, yet I believed that I was unlovable. I was in puberty and had a difficult time coping with my sexual desires and urges, and I was feeling more than just teenage guilt. I felt constantly dirty, and every time I was aroused, I punished myself. Sex, to me at that time, was something horrific and one-sided. I had been a toy for pedophiles in my childhood. I was manipulated, beaten, sodomized, and humiliated by the men who were trusted with the responsibility to educate me and nurture my soul. Instead, it felt as though they had methodically murdered me from the inside.

Sometimes my frustration and anger pushed me further down the path to the dark side. My mood and the focus of my karate training shifted class to class. Each time I trained, I imagined it was in preparation for taking the path of the Jedi. I had seen all of the original movies in the theatre sequentially. I owned the VHS versions of them to watch over and over when I was bored, or studying, or just to have on for comfort in the background. I knew all of the lines by heart.

I felt that there was a connection between the philosophies of the Jedi and that of the Bushido code, which I was learning of through karate. Martial arts rely heavily on the training of the mind and body in harmony. The code of the Samurai warrior includes justice, courage, compassion, courtesy, truthfulness, honour, and loyalty. Good martial artists do not let emotion get in the way of their training. Countless hours are spent on meditation and self-reflection.

Japanese traditional training can be described in three stages: Shu, Ha, and Ri. The first stage, Shu, is represented as an egg. In this stage, the student is taught to protect the form of their martial art. It is a very difficult stage of learning that involves protecting the form much like a bird would protect eggs in a nest. The next stage, Ha, is the breaking form. To continue with the analogy of a bird, the chick breaks through the hard shell of the egg. The shell breaks in many pieces, and this represents that the fundamentals of the martial art are developed and applied to all situations. The final form is Ri. This is the releasing form, representing the bird leaving the nest. This is where the student must forget all that has been learned and focus instead on the formless technique, thereby letting old ideas and conventions go and allowing the student to be free within the form.

In *The Empire Strikes Back,* Yoda explains to Luke:

> *A Jedi's strength flows from the Force. But beware of the dark side. Anger ... Fear ... Aggression. The dark side of the Force are they. Easily they flow, quick to join you in a fight. If once you start down the dark path, forever will it dominate your destiny, consume you it will, as*

it did Obi-Wan's apprentice ... For my ally is the Force.
And a powerful ally it is. Life creates it, makes it grow.
Its energy surrounds us and binds us. Luminous beings
are we ... not this crude matter. You must feel the Force
around you. Here, between you ... me ... the tree ... the
rock ... everywhere.

I was intrigued by Yoda's lessons. Yoda is the perfect ideal of a spiritual leader. He is unassuming and small, yet he contains a powerful spirituality within him. Never does he train Luke to wield a lightsaber. Instead, he focuses on his mind and his Zen conditioning. He teaches Luke that the power of the mind is far greater than the physical ability of the body. I liked this lesson. While my body had been violated, the priests could not touch, or physically fuck, my mind. It was the only untouched place I could escape to. My mind could still conceive a form of purity and resilience far beyond anything that had been physically done to me. I knew I could use my mind to overcome.

I practised everywhere I went. If I found myself getting scared, I would tell myself it was a Jedi test. I was beginning to be able to turn my fear around. Instead of being afraid of roller coasters, I convinced myself I was training to fly X-wing starfighters, and I turned that fear into excitement. I was learning to work with my fear instead of letting it rule me. I was learning to be with myself, and I was often surprised how simply focusing on my breathing helped me relax.

Perhaps the most exciting thing about this new spirituality, and my own path to becoming a self-professed Jedi Knight, was that there was no concept of the Force as God. I could relate to the Force. It was all around me: in the flowers and other animals. It surrounded me. God, however, was this entity that allowed his ministers to abuse me. I feared and hated the concept of "God" as taught by the Catholics, but I embraced the idea of the Force. I have come to understand the Force as a powerful energy. Energy can neither be created nor destroyed; it simply changes from one form to another. I have also come to understand that there are equal amounts of light and dark energies in the Force. Bringing a balance into the Force is bringing both light and dark into harmony. At times one may dominate the other, but to be in harmony is to balance the light and dark in the universe.

As a growing boy with anger that absolutely could have taken me to the dark side, I was fortunate to be learning about control through martial arts and the Star Wars trilogy. As Yoda says to Luke, "Control, control, you must learn control." It was a lack of control, and the dark side turned outward, that led Ignatious and Vitus to abuse me and who knows how many other innocent children.

I often wonder what would have happened to me if I had not accidentally stumbled into that theatre in 1977. I easily could have followed the path of my half sister, turning to drugs and alcohol to cope with the aftermath of abuse. But instead, I turned to martial arts.

It was the climactic duel in *The Empire Strikes Back* that made me first want to be a Jedi Knight. I had no idea what kind of swordplay I was watching, but I knew I had to learn whatever it was.

The beauty and efficiency with which the lightsaber ignites immediately aroused my desires to use one when I first saw it on the screen. I wished I had one with me the night that I was stabbed and left for dead in the snow. At the time I would have not hesitated to ignite the blade and cut off Alex's hand when he came towards me. I dreamt of ways that I could possibly build a lightsaber of my own. I never succeeded, but I did want to learn the art of the lightsaber fight. Bob Anderson was the fight coordinator on the original Star Wars films, and I learned that kendo was the basis for the fights he designed. Even as a dedicated karate student, I knew that one day I was going to find a kendo club of my own. It was my destiny.

38
UNIVERSITY

*It's a chance for you to
make a fresh start.*

— Mon Mothma, *Rogue One*

As I progressed through my final grade of high school, my parents hoped I would find a career path that would be both lucrative and exciting. My mother had turned down a career opportunity in New Zealand because her parents did not want her to move too far from her family. She told me that although she was glad that she didn't follow her dream to travel, she wanted to make sure I took advantage of any opportunity to see the world. My dad had travelled, for work and for war, and also felt that travelling was important. They encouraged me to find a job that would allow me these opportunities. I started to think that perhaps a consular job in government would be an exciting and rewarding career path. I think it was more likely that, much like Luke, I was anxious to see where the stars could take me.

Following the desire for a life of politics, I attended a youth leadership conference at the Terry Fox Centre in Ottawa, became a young parliamentarian, and went to the Soviet Union on a two-week school trip. I was excited to see what was unfolding behind the Iron Curtain. International calls were becoming stronger for reuniting East and West Germany, and as relations with the Western world opened, there were more opportunities for tourists to see how the Soviets really lived. Our high school planned a two-week trip that took us to many amazing historical sites. It was an exhilarating educational tour, but the fatigue of travelling such a distance took a toll upon my health. Soon after returning, I became severely ill and spent two months in bed drifting in and out of consciousness—and in and out of dreams and nightmares.

I dreamt I was in the alley the night I was stabbed. A cold blade thrust into me, and the snow was sketched with blood. I could not feel the pain but instead suddenly found myself surrounded by sharp triangles. I was in a boat circling a black hole and feeling a strong temptation to drift into it. It was calling me to let go and give in. I drifted hauntingly towards the edge, feeling my muscles melting away. A voice echoed in the dark.

Run, Luke!

Listening to these words, I suddenly found a paddle in my hands and paddled away from the increasing strength of the current pulling me into the hole. Then I felt hands around my waist and a painful thrusting sensation. I could feel myself being thrown into a wall, falling down the stairs, and my head smashing onto the floor. When I picked myself up, I was wearing a cassock and was standing in front of a large congregation in a church. I was covered in blood, and they pointed at me, laughing.

You're not going anywhere!

Admiral Ackbar, from *Return of the Jedi*, suddenly appeared.

It's a trap!

Father Vitus appeared, pointing at me accusingly.

If you tell anyone, God will kill you!

Worthless.

Death was calling me. Darkness surrounded me. And yet, a light. My mom and dad were standing over me.

Fight!

Brother Ignatious appeared, grabbing my hand and pulling out a strap.

It will be over in the morning. Blame yourself. Kill yourself.

More light, and then nothing. It was as though my dream was taking a long caesura before recommencing.

Then, the voice of Obi-Wan Kenobi echoed all around me.

Run, Luke. Run!

Suddenly, I was awake in my room. My parents were standing over me. I was alive.

I was told I was likely not going to pass my final year of school. The teachers had warned my parents that I would have to repeat twelfth grade.

Run, Luke. Run!

There was no way I could spend any more time in that town. Somehow, I was going to graduate, get out of Hopeless, go to university, and become a diplomat. That was what I was going to do. It was my destiny. I planned to do an undergraduate degree in politics and pre-Soviet history before going into international politics. I was very excited to start my life outside of Hopeless, leaving the past behind me once and for all.

My faith in the Force and my tireless studying paid off. I not only passed but made the final honour roll and had been accepted into the University of Victoria. I was finally going to leave Hopeless. I was finally getting out.

In late August of that summer, I made the inevitable and difficult decision that it was time to take my prized Star Wars possessions and put them away as carefully as I could. They had been on many adventures with me, and I wanted to make sure they were preserved for the day I imagined passing them on to my own children and watching them create their own Star Wars adventures.

I took great pains in repackaging them in their boxes. The carefully preserved instruction booklets were replaced, and the toys were put back in their inserts—exactly as they had been when I first opened them. Even the old toy catalogues were put back in their original homes. I was careful to use clear magic tape to keep the lids shut. Storing them away was ritualistic and extremely emotional for me. I was ending a chapter of my life. Storing my toys provided a passage from my childhood into the unknown challenges that adulthood would present. I stored them in a safe spot in my dad's garage—high above the miscellany that accumulates in such places.

The next morning, I got into my car, placed my R2-D2 action figure in the cup holder, and started my journey south. I pulled out of the driveway and waved to my parents who watched me as I left.

"Well, R2, I guess this is it," I said, feeling the excitement of leaving Hopeless and the fear of beginning a new chapter in life. "Plot a course for Victoria, R2." And we set out on the long drive to university. I played the soundtracks to all of the Star Wars films during the drive to my new home and imagined university as my inevitable Jedi training.

I was very excited to discover there was an actual kendo club at my university. I signed up immediately. My first sensei was Ted Davis. He was an unassuming man—slight and not too tall. He wore the traditional clothing of the kendoka—a dark blue hakama and keikogi. He stood majestically in his robes. Though he was only five-and-a-half feet tall, he seemed much taller when he was gliding across the floor demonstrating the martial art to the new group of students observing his class. My eyes were wide open. I had finally found my ultimate martial art. The uniform resembled that of a Jedi, and the shinai, the bamboo practice swords, were facsimiles of lightsabers. I could not wait to begin training. It had been six years since I first learned karate, and now I would become a dedicated student of kendo.

For the first several weeks, I did not have the privilege of wearing the robes I so desperately wanted to wear. I was a beginner and needed to learn the basics. Dutifully, three times a week, I would go to the university rec centre and repeat the footwork necessary to the art. My feet bled over the hardwood floor as I developed calluses. My fingers blistered from holding my shinai too tight. I often left the dojo dripping with sweat and limping from the pain of the open wounds on the bottom of my feet. It was difficult. I was determined. I kept going back.

Eventually I was allowed to wear the uniform and then the armour of the serious kendoka. I learned how to fold my uniform properly to keep it pressed and to keep the pleats of my uniform pants straight. I was not only being disciplined in the techniques of kendo, but I was also learning the respect for the techniques and the history of the art I was devoting myself to. We all took care of our uniforms. After class, no matter how tired we were, we would kneel and fold our uniforms properly, with respect for our learning. We did not speak during this. We folded our uniforms in silence, allowing ourselves to reflect on the lessons we had learned during the practice.

I have seen students of other martial arts show little respect for their attire. They practise in wrinkled, unwashed uniforms. I strongly believe this is not the student's fault. It is the instructor who must take responsibility for the actions and inactions of their students. Much like a parent, the sensei models the behaviour and habits that the students will ultimately adopt. Ted was a fantastic instructor.

My first year at the university went by far too quickly. I had loved my classes, but in April, I found myself heading back to Hopeless. I planned to work as a server in a restaurant while I plotted my next course on my journey to becoming a diplomat. I thought this was a perfect career path: the Jedi were guardians of peace and justice in the Star Wars universe, so a diplomat was really a Jedi without the ability to attain mind control (though how perfect would that be in foreign politics?).

Quite by accident that summer, I fell into performing at the local theatre with a number of high school acquaintances who were involved with a summer stage program. I started hanging out with them during the day, and then started writing sketches and mono- logues, and, quite by accident, I began performing with them. I had not been officially cast with them, but, somehow, I was performing comedy, and I was loving it. My mother saw what was happening and tried to keep me focused on my career as a future diplomat. I assured her that was my plan; but I felt as though I belonged on the stage, and I felt such a thrill when my sketches made people laugh.

The following year at university, I became more intrigued with the possibility of being an entertainer *and* a diplomat. Obviously, as I had been told by my banker mother, there was no career to be made in the arts, but perhaps I could join the USO and travel from base to base. I started taking acting workshops while studying that year and was even so cocky as to audition for a position with Disney. It seemed that my cockiness paid off, as that summer my jobs included not only managing an acting company but working as a cast member in Disneyland as well. I was starting to feel that the path I had originally chosen to study was not for me. For many years I had not wanted to be visible to others, but all of a sudden I was craving the attention to be watched as I performed. I loved the feeling of acting. I felt so free. I was coming out of my shell as a performer and could be myself around my new coworkers and friends.

The people I worked with at Disneyland did not know who I was or what my history was. They found me fun and engaging, unaware of the years of sadness I had experienced, and I was eager to spend as much time as possible away from where I grew up so that I could truly discover who I was. Disney became my constant fun-place and my escape. I loved the feeling of creating magic. I loved interacting with guests and making new friends who just saw me as a fun-loving, "goofy" kind of guy.

I learned so much in my time working for Disney, but the part that hooked me was the children. I saw the magic that a performer could make for a child in need—a child like I had been—and I knew this was what I wanted to do.

I worked with a young woman named Beth who was "good friends" with Princess Aurora (you may know her as Sleeping Beauty). I have always had respect for the princess characters as, unlike the masked characters, they do not have the ability to have their faces hidden. One morning she had been assigned to a character breakfast where she moved from table to table, visiting the guests and engaging them in pleasant conversation. She approached a family of three having their breakfast, who were eagerly awaiting visits from the various characters. Princess Aurora greeted them with a smile and spoke with the parents as the girl in the wheelchair looked at her with a huge smile, unable to speak due to being plugged into an oxygen tank and other medical equipment. They told Princess Aurora that she was their daughter's favourite princess. Happy to be interacting with a genuine fan, Princess Aurora asked them what they were celebrating. The parents told her that their daughter only had a short time left to live, and it was her wish to come and see the park before she died. (Many groups come to the parks with children who are facing challenges, and that's why making magic for them is so important. Sadly, it is not unusual to find out that a child has come to the park as their last wish. I honestly don't know how the princesses, with no mask to hide behind, can carry on when they hear these things.) Princess Aurora spent a few more moments with them and the family took a picture with her—the young girl awestruck to meet her favourite princess.

Although there was nothing more Princess Aurora could do for this young girl, Beth felt the need to keep the magic alive. She left to change after her shift and before long was at the Emporium to buy an Aurora doll for the young girl. Beth was able to find the family exiting from their breakfast, and she approached them and told them she was "good friends" with Princess Aurora. Beth said that the princess had asked her to give the young girl the Aurora doll as a special gift. The family was excited. Beth had created magic on her own.

Weeks later, Beth was called into a meeting. The family had written the park and shared how incredible Princess Aurora and her friend had been to them. They wanted to share that their daughter loved the special present given to her and wanted to thank Princess Aurora for what she did. The young girl loved the doll so much that the parents had her buried with it.

A little magic can go a long way.

I was developing an empathy for people who were suffering. The Force was showing me that perhaps good *could* triumph over evil. I had the power to make a choice. I could sit in the sorrow of my past, letting my pain overshadow my potential, or I could use the pain and suffering of my past to help others—others like that young girl. Light over dark. I realized that *I* had the power to create real magic for others—for children. I decided to make it a point to create magic wherever and whenever I could.

My Disney training helped me secure another acting job—this time on a tour with Anne Mortifee in a show called *The Bluebird of*

Happiness. My character skills were useful as I played Heathcliff the Seagull. The tour was an initiative to bring a story of hope to schoolchildren and orphans. It was my second trip to the Soviet Union and my first as a semi-professional artist. At the end of performances, we were often invited to speak with the children and adults we entertained. Though there were often language barriers, my physical comedy and the songs we sang resonated without need for interpretation. I could see the power that play gave to people. Storytelling had value. We performed for Raisa Gorbachev as well as orphans from Chernobyl.

I felt so energized when I witnessed how performance could bring happiness to all types of people. For brief moments of time, suffering and social and cultural barriers were suspended, and messages of joy and hope could be sent and received instantaneously. How could I ever return to normal university studies after working as a performer? I believed I had found my calling. It was during this trip to the dying Soviet Union that I realized I was already working as a diplomat. We had been called Cultural Ambassadors of Peace, and I finally saw the value of storytelling across cultures. My Russian studies had not been wasted, and I had impressed our hosts with my historical knowledge of the places we visited on our tour. In between shows I entertained my fellow performers with improvised comedy based on our group experiences. I could not stop performing.

After we returned, I knew my education needed to focus on developing my skills as a performer. George Lucas had filmed much of the Star Wars trilogy in England, and I knew that many aspiring actors travelled there to train in the profession. If I could try out acting in a summer course there, I would be able to truly know if acting was for me.

So, the next summer, I travelled to England to take a four-week course in acting. While I was there, the dean had noted my enthusiasm and approached me to ask if I would be interested in taking a spot in the full-time acting program that fall, which was only two weeks away. Although I knew my mom would not want me to make a career of acting, I had made my decision that performing was what I wanted to do, and I was determined to remain in England to pursue it.

I called home from London. I remember speaking to my mom from far away. It was much easier to tell her my plans that way.

"Hey, Mom."

"Hey, honey. How is summer school?"

"I love it. I really love it."

"When are you coming home?"

"I'm not."

There was a very long pause on the line.

"Mom, I was accepted into the full-time acting program. It's a big deal. I can't come back. This is what I really want to do."

"How are you going to earn a living? You can't be an actor. There is no money in it."

"I can feel it. I know I have to do this. I am sorry, Mom."

"Your dad and I cannot support this. You're going to be on your own. You can't make money as an actor."

"I have been working as an actor, Mom. I get paid to entertain. I know I can do this."

"What about the university? How can you drop your courses this close to the start of term?"

"I never enrolled for this fall."

My mom hung up the phone.

I felt scared. Here I was, in England, not knowing what I was going to do to live, yet I knew I had to stay.

The next day my mom called back.

"Honey, your dad and I were talking. If this means that much to you—"

"It does, it really does—"

"We'll find a way. Nic, your grandmother stopped me from going to New Zealand when I was young. I had a job lined up, and she guilted me into staying in Canada. I can't do that to you. Your dad and I love you."

"I love you too, Mom. And Mom ... Thank you so much."

"Please let us know what we will need to send over."

"Definitely my kendo equipment. There are lots of clubs over here."

"You were pretty cheeky not enrolling at the university. What if you didn't get a position over there?"

"The Force is with me. This is my destiny."

"Cheeky monkey."

That fall I started my official acting training. When I was not in class or rehearsing, I was practising kendo. Kendo was a great exercise for me to purge my ever-present frustrations. I was starting over, and while I became close with many of my fellow students, they initially were relentless teasing me about my Canadian accent and my unfortunate terminology for things.

As people know, the British have different terms for common items. For example, a sweater is a jumper, an undershirt is a vest, a truck is a lorry, and so on. On the second day of class, Kate, a lovely woman from Kent, came into one of the rooms as I was gathering my belongings.

"Nic, we're going to the pub. Did you want to come along?"

"Sure, just a sec. I'll just grab my fanny pack."

There was a jarring pause. She stared at me.

"Your what?"

"My fanny pack."

She darted out of the room. I could hear laughter in the hall, though I didn't know what was so funny. As I finished collecting my things and approaching my pack to tuck them away, Kate returned with another student, Peter. She nudged Peter and he spoke.

"So Nic, what's that you have there?" he asked as he pointed towards my pack.

"It's my fanny pack," I said a little self-consciously.

There was an outburst of laughter in the hall behind them from several other first-year students who had been listening. I felt my face getting flushed. Kate approached me once more.

"Nic, in England a fanny is a woman's vagina."

I was completely embarrassed now.

"But what do you call these then?" I asked as I picked up the pack.

"Bum-bag" she said.

I wasn't in Hopeless anymore. I made a mental note—bum-bag. I clipped it around my waist and joined my new mates on the way to the pub.

I trained at the same dojo where the British National Kendo Team trained near the University of London. Training in kendo balanced me, and I was excited that I was training with Britain's best kendo athletes. It was a privilege and an honour for me.

Many of the team members were soldiers, and they were being gradually deployed to the Middle East as Operation Desert Storm was escalating. Initially I was asked to be a tournament alternate in case they needed someone to fill a position should too many of their members be unable to attend. Not long after that, I was offered a spot representing Britain in tournaments in Europe. I was officially a part of the team.

Kendo was providing me with many amazing opportunities, and since kendo was the art of the Jedi, I readily took advantage of them and of my abilities. It was in Zurich that I competed and ranked internationally. I treated my teammates and opponents with respect. I allowed myself to breathe and to focus on my spirit within and through the shinai. Star Wars was always on my mind.

Our senior instructor was an amazing kendoka. His name was Colin. He was fierce in tournament. He had four distinct scars—the result of an opponent's blade breaking during a strike to the head, sending four sharp sections of bamboo into Colin's face. It was sheer luck that Colin did not get any shards thrust into his eyes, yet there remained the four memories of that event. Colin liked to make his younger teammates fearful of him. We all dreaded having to fight him during practice. It was impossible, or so we thought, to hit him at all. One night, as Colin and I were in the middle of our free-practice, we locked into taiatari, which is a technique where two people come in body-to-body contact with each other. I could look straight into his eyes through our masks. His eyes were focused and gazing through me. I could feel his energy pushing through.

I looked straight back at him and said in my best Darth Vader voice, "I am your father, Luke."

Colin burst out laughing and looked down—I took full advantage of this moment and delivered a decisive hit to the top of his head. I had done it. I had landed an incontestable point upon the unbeatable Colin. My victory was short-lived, however, as Colin almost immediately returned a flurry of hits and worked me hard until I was exhausted, battered, and bruised.

Colin was assigned as my roommate while we competed in a tournament in Zurich. While he was physically intimidating, he and I soon bonded through our love of Star Wars and a mutual warped sense of humour. We spent the whole weekend laughing. He became a good friend of mine after that weekend, and though I have not spoken to him since I returned to Canada, I will always remember his incredible prowess at my beloved martial art.

It is hard to describe how kendo made me feel. The uniform, consisting of Japanese keikogi and hakama, reminded me of the Jedi robes worn by Obi-Wan Kenobi. Though his were in earth tones and mine were indigo, when I put them on, I could feel a transformation within. Whatever I was dealing with outside the dojo went away when I put on my uniform. When I would look in the mirror, I imagined myself as a Jedi apprentice. The gym where we trained became a Jedi temple. We would line up and kneel as we donned our armour. It felt as though I was preparing for battle. In my mind I was arming myself for an inevitable battle against evil.

In practice, when I was feeling too tired to go on, I would imagine Ignatious or Vitus in front of me and I would tap into my inner anger to see me through. Yet, drenched in sweat after each practice, I could not bring myself to shower in front of the other men. As hard as I tried to be one of the team, I could not stand in front of others naked. I would carefully fold up my uniform, pack it away, and take the hour-long tube ride to my flat, wet with perspiration.

My training was bringing up many emotions. Anger was a great motivator, though it was a sign that the dark side was growing within me—and it was. I was entering the age of the warrior. In my early twenties now, I was in prime shape and ready to take on the world, or in my case, the Church. I was starting to feel a sense of betrayal from my former educators. My anger against them came out in my martial arts practice.

Yoda warns Luke, "... beware of the dark side. Anger ... Fear ... Aggression—the dark side of the Force are they."

I started to question why the dark side was so bad. Anger gave me strength. It gave me power when I was feeling too tired to attack. Anger gave me the strength to move on. The fantasy of destroying my enemies brought me sycophantic joy. If I tapped into my anger, I could ensure that I would not be put at risk again. Yoda's further warning, that once someone had started their journey down the dark path, it would dominate their future, also weighed upon me.

One of the most difficult things I found when training new kendo students was letting them practise targeting upon me. The senior students would wear their kendo armour and allow the beginners to strike. Beginners do not have the control that more advanced students have, and, as a result, they tend to hit heavy and even miss the armoured parts of the body. Whenever my exposed body was hit with the shinai, I was immediately brought back to the years of beatings at the Catholic school. Sometimes I would start crying beneath my mask. No one knew what I was going through during practice. I hated working with the inexperienced students and made a point of initiating them when they were finally allowed the honour of wearing armour. Since they were then wearing protection, I could return the strikes upon them. I knew who had been hard-hitting, and I would hit them back harder. We were supposed to pull back our strikes, but I enjoyed the feeling of power when I struck them hard. It was a dark time for me. I wanted to hurt others, and much like the abusers of my childhood, I was doing it in plain sight of others under the guise of training.

In *The Empire Strikes Back*, Luke finds himself targeted by both the light and dark factions of the Force. He meets Yoda and trusts him to educate him in the ways of the Force, yet he doubts that which Yoda teaches. This opens him up to the dark side. Through his meditations he senses bad things happening to his friends and leaves his training to go help them. On Cloud City, Luke meets Vader who manipulates Luke's emotions and attempts to seduce Luke to the dark side of the Force. Luke resists, but it seemed to me that there was a chance that Luke could follow in Vader's wake.

I felt that I had a darkness in me that I could exploit. I could use my anger to hurt others as I was hurt. It felt good when I could overpower my opponents. It was a very dangerous time for me. I had spent so much of my youth being hurt and oppressed, and now there was an opportunity for me to make it my turn to *Do unto others,* as had been done unto me.

Could I ever find peace within, or was peace a lie?

⪥ ⪦
IT'S ALL ILLUSION

Your eyes can deceive you.
Don't trust them.

— Obi-Wan Kenobi,
A New Hope

I ultimately enjoyed my time in England, and I especially enjoyed the stage combat component of my theatre education. My fight instructor was Angela Goodall. She inspired me to excel in my pursuit of becoming a fight director. I was able to take lessons from William Hobbes, the fight director I admired from watching his work on classic films such as *The Three Musketeers, The Four Musketeers,* and *The Duellists*— to name only a few. His approach to stage fighting was to relate the style to the period the drama was set in. Rather than the fights being merely modified fencing, Hobbes, and other fight directors such as Bob Anderson, looked to the styles and weapons of the period. Their work and dedication to staging entertaining and exciting fight scenes inspired me to make stage combat my main focus for a career.

I wanted to be a fighting actor. I wanted to perform fight scenes, and, even more importantly, I wanted to act out scenes where I was the victor. I found performing fights exhilarating. In my head, I was beating my abusers and always succeeding. I found that, due to the abuse I had suffered, I was able to tolerate the pain that comes with performing stunts. I could easily handle it. Physical exertion was not something I shied away from either. I was a keen student of all things pugilistic. I was thirsty to fight and to win. William Hobbes introduced me to Alan Meek, the sword maker for many great films, including *The Princess Bride* and Kenneth Branagh's *Henry V*, and I even became the proud owner of a few of Meek's swords.

I was eager to begin my acting and stunt career in Vancouver. I was able to find an agent without too much searching and spent the first few months of my acting profession waiting tables at a popular restaurant. There was a series shooting in Vancouver that was a pop culture hit. Based on the hit film, *Highlander* was an action-based series that required actors with sword skills. The fight director on the show was Bob Anderson.

Bob Anderson was a man whom I admired greatly. He was a British national fencing champion and more importantly, he had been the sword master on the original Star Wars films. Though Bob was a fencer, he designed the fights for *Star Wars* drawing heavily upon Japanese culture—mainly from kendo. He was the reason I became a student of kendo, and he was a person I desperately wanted to meet.

I knew that most of the cast and crew for the series were put up at the Sutton Place Hotel. My ignorance of all things film-related resulted in my audacity to call the hotel and ask directly for Mr. Anderson. I could feel my heart pounding in my head when I dialled the number and reached the hotel operator.

"Sutton Place Hotel. How may I direct your call?"

"Um, Bob Anderson please."

"One moment."

There was a click and the sound of silence. I thought for a moment that I had been hung up on. After all, it couldn't be that easy, could it? Then there was ringing, and an English voice answered.

"Hullo?"

"Yes, um, is this Bob Anderson?"

"Speaking."

"You are the fight director, Bob Anderson?"

"Yes. Has my call-time been changed?"

He thought I was an office PA. I had him. *Him!* The actual Bob Anderson on the phone. The man who put me on the path to kendo. The man who created the Jedi way of fighting. He was now on the phone ... with me! Unfortunately, I hadn't planned what to do if I actually was to get him on the phone.

"Mr. Anderson, I am not with the production."

"I'm sorry, I don't quite follow."

"I'm sorry. My name is Nicholas Harrison. I wanted to call you and let you know that I thought your fights were incredible in *Star Wars*. I loved your fights for *The Princess Bride*. I was a student of Angela and Roy Goodall in England ..."

"Oh, yes, I know them. Lovely people."

"Yes. They were, uh, are. Listen, Mr. Anderson, I just wanted to call you to say you have been a huge inspiration and I really want to work with you one day. In fact, I know I will work with you one day. Your fights are the best. Did I say I really loved your work on *Star Wars*?"

"Well, yes you did. Listen, I must go now. It was nice chatting with you. All the best to you. Goodbye."

"Bye."

There was a click and that was the end of my contact with Bob Anderson. I couldn't believe that he had actually spoken with me and that it had been so easy to get in touch with him. I felt several emotions come over me: I was exhilarated that I had spoken with him; I was embarrassed that, although I actually spoke with him, I didn't have too much to say; I was sad that I had possibly missed my chance to meet him. I told everyone I could that I had spoken with him, even though not many people knew who I was even talking about. I thought about meeting him for weeks after that.

A few months later, I had an audition for *Highlander*. The episode was 'Epitaph for Tommy.' I auditioned for the part of a character named Ned, and, best of all, he had a fight scene with Duncan, the main character. If I was to book that part, I would be working with Bob Anderson. The first audition went well. I received a call-back, and the second audition went well. Then, it happened. I booked the part. I was more excited that I was going to work with Bob Anderson than I was about working with Adrian Paul, the star of the show.

Bob and I spent a few days together working out the choreography for my fight scene with Adrian Paul. I told him that I was the one who had called him months before, and we shared a laugh over my brazen call. We spoke about *Star Wars,* and he claimed that he really knew nothing about kendo until he was asked to stage the lightsaber fights for the film. He knew, once he spoke with George Lucas, that fencing wasn't going to be right. George had asked him to make it more "solid, graceful, and full of suspense." Much of kendo is the contemplation of the moment, so it seemed like a perfect fit. In *A New Hope*, the fight between Vader and Kenobi has those moments which create incredible on-screen suspense. Watching that fight as a child set me on the path of the Jedi, and Bob Anderson was the master.

My love of *Star Wars* introduced me to kendo as well as all forms of swordplay. *The Princess Bride*, another one of Bob Anderson's films, inspired me to pursue the art of rapier fighting. Though historically inaccurate, the beautiful fight between Inigo and Wesley is one of the most memorable sword fights in modern cinematic history. Bob loved telling me about his time on that film, which he said was his favourite that he had worked on. He told me that the script for the big sword fight was written as "and then commenced the most epic sword fight of all time." He was impressed with the dedication the actors had in working on the fight scene; they spent every available moment rehearsing it. Bob was proud that they did not need to use the stunt doubles for much of the fight. He knew he was going to be remembered for that fight, and it had the fun and elegance of a fight from the golden film age.

Bob Anderson has been, by far, the greatest fight director I have ever worked with. I ended up working on my episode of *Highlander* for two weeks and was excited to have been choreographed by my fight directing hero.

40

THE MASTER'S DEGREE

*I cannot teach him, the
boy has no patience.*

— Yoda,
The Empire Strikes Back

After a few years of working as an actor and fight director, I applied to study for a master's degree in directing. I attended the University of Victoria, my alma mater, and spent time as a sempai in my old kendo club. Ted Davis was not instructing much at that point, as his health was failing, but I enjoyed my sessions as a senior member of the club. Training gave me an outlet for the anger I was still fostering within.

Returning to university after being away for a long time made me feel as though I was an outsider. I was becoming an expert in period fighting styles and weaponry, but the challenge of communicating my experience in an academic box was stressful, and I felt as though I did not belong. The history instructor, Dr. Hughes, led the graduate students in approaches to historical methodology. It was, as he put it, a casual class where we would discuss methodology and theatre history. Our first assignment was to read a book from his reading list and present it in class. Foolishly, I volunteered to present first.

The book I chose to report on was *The Face of Battle*, by Westpoint historian John Keegan. It was a fascinating book. Keegan looked at three key historic battles that all occurred on the same area of land:

the battles of Agincourt (1415), Waterloo (1815), and the Somme (1916). I will not go into details of the book other than to write that it is well worth the read. Our assignment was to report on the book. That is all we were asked to do.

I enjoyed my reading and felt confident that my report was going to be compelling. I was one of five graduate students in the class. Our weekly meeting space was the small department library. It was cozy, and we were getting to know each other. Dr. Hughes asked me to share my report. I began by giving a brief synopsis of the book and who John Keegan was. I had only been speaking for a couple minutes when Dr. Hughes interrupted my report.

"So, what is the book about?"

"It's about these three key battles ..."

"Yes, but what is it about?"

"It's about Agincourt, Waterloo—"

"Yes. But *what* is it *about*?"

Dr. Hughes was getting physically agitated. His face turned red. His tone became condescending.

"What is the *methodology*?"

"... Well, there are these three key battles—"

He snapped.

"What is the fucking methodology? Can you tell me what the fucking methodology is? Why the fuck are you here? If you don't know what the fucking methodology is, then you should not fucking be in a grad class!"

He slammed his writing pad on the table and stormed out of the room. Our two-hour seminar class had lasted less than ten minutes. I started to cry in front of my peers. They all looked equally shocked.

Inside, the tempest of emotion was underway. Dr. Hughes had stirred up memories from my past. The memories I had been suppressing—of my teachers humiliating me, abusing me, raping me—came flooding back. Nightmares returned. My sense of self-worth plummeted. I began dreaming about the black ball chasing me in the maze again—a dream I had not had for years. I started to get flashes of images from my childhood. I sank into a deep depression. Dr.

Hughes's actions had triggered me, opening a portal to the pain of my past. A portal I had hoped was sealed shut. Shame, guilt, and rage surfaced once more. I started to hate myself and came close to dropping out of grad school, feeling, as Dr. Hughes had said, as though I didn't belong there.

My fellow grad students and I discussed what had happened when we were back in our shared office. While they were shocked with the way our instructor had led the class, they were all quite relieved they were not the first one up that day. Each one of them had prepared their reports the same way I had. Dr. Hughes had set a trap for us. His way to drive home the point that we were at a different stage of our education than he was, was to make an example of the first student so that everyone worked harder to avoid that type of humiliation. From that point onwards, I fell back on the survival behaviour I had learned as a child. I kept my head down and focused on studying, doing everything I could not to be seen or heard for fear I would be made an example of again. I silently hated Dr. Hughes for what he did to me in that class.

As the term went on, I found myself becoming more and more introspective. Memories from my elementary school came back. I finally started to see that what happened to me was wrong. I was also extremely afraid. I did not want anyone to know that I was the victim of rape and abuse. By now I knew God was not going to kill me if I was to tell, but I still felt ashamed. At that time there had not been media attention given to victims of clerical abuse, and priests were still seen as infallible.

I decided I needed to speak to someone about my thoughts and about what happened. I didn't want to share it with those who knew me, so I decided to see a therapist. I took advantage of free counselling the university offered and started to see a student therapist. I was asked a lot of questions and never felt free to discuss how I felt. I was given information on the mind and was told to meditate. This initial experience with therapy was terrible. I gave up after only four sessions, vowing to deal with my issues on my own.

My disastrous date with Daphne affected my relationships moving forward. As a teenager in puberty, I longed for contact, yet I could not stand anyone getting close to me. As I grew up, I found myself distrusting of anyone who wanted to enter a physical relationship with me. I looked to Star Wars and observed that the Jedi did not engage in physical relationships. This made me feel somewhat better with myself. As I grew and slimmed down, I desperately wanted to have the normal teenage experiences I saw on film, but I wouldn't engage in anything sexual until I was in university.

I was unable to sustain and maintain relationships for any length of time because I did not trust my girlfriends. I was afraid to make the first move in any relationship, yet I wanted desperately to be the one in control. This is a problem with being a sexual abuse survivor. Sex, to me, was a form of power. While it was supposed to be pleasurable, for me it was a constant battle of desire and shame. I had been groomed to be an object and a tool for old men to maintain power over me. To this day I cannot be naked in a locker room. I still change alone. I have a difficult time in change rooms because I think back to being alone in the room with Father Vitus. I cannot stand being in a room unless I have a clear exit in the event that I have a panic attack. I never thought I was going to enter a long-term relationship.

And then I met Rebecca.

We started dating within a year of my return from England. I was directing a play and she auditioned for me. I was smitten. I tried to encourage my friend to ask her out because I didn't feel that she would like someone like me. My friend assured me that I should ask her out myself, which I eventually did, and we began dating. There was something familiar about being with her. I could feel something that connected us. I wasn't sure what it was.

"Nic, I need to talk to you."

This is never a good thing to hear when you are on a walk with a new girlfriend or boyfriend. This was the dreaded, I-love-you-but-I'm-not-*in*-love-with-you talk.

She continued. "I've been thinking. You are really nice, but ..."

"But what? You're not into me, right?"

"No, no. It's not you, it's me."

Right … Of course. She wanted to break up with me.

"I don't think we can be together."

She broke into tears. For twenty minutes, I just held her as she cried. Finally, she calmed down enough to carry on her conversation.

"You are not going to want to be with me when I tell you this."

"Well, why don't you try telling me?" I tried to joke.

"I've never told anyone this before. Not even my parents."

I could sense something. I felt a sense of familiarity with what she was about to say. She looked at me, embarrassed.

"I was abused when I was eight years old. Sexually abused. You don't want me. You don't need this. I have a lot of things I need to work out."

What the fuck? I held her close to me as she sobbed. I was dumbstruck. Here was another abuse victim confiding in me.

"No. I am going to be here with you. I will do whatever I have to do to support you through this."

She found this hard to believe. Why would I? I, of course, did not dare say that I was a victim too. I told her that it was not her fault, that I would never hold that against her. She stayed with me, and I watched her process and untangle the bonds that were holding her back. I watched her go to therapy, I listened to her, and all that time I kept thinking that I could never share my secret with her. I knew that must have been what brought us together, that common bond. I owe her a lot for being brave in front of me. She showed me what strength is, and she dealt with her abuse with grace and dignity. She unknowingly helped prepare me for the time that I would eventually come out about my own abuse.

41
SNOW FALLING ON CEDARS

We're gonna do this.

— Poe Dameron,
The Force Awakens

As I was finishing my degree, I received a phone call out of the blue from an old friend, Shayne, who was working with The Kennedy/ Marshall Company in Los Angeles. I had first met Shayne while working on the series *Sliders*, where he and I bonded over our mutual love for warped comedy and all things film.

Shayne asked me if I knew of anyone who could teach or choreograph kendo techniques. I thought he was joking as he knew kendo had been my main martial art for years.

"Uhhhhh ... me!" I replied.

"What? Well, that makes my job much easier then," he teased.

He had been tasked to find a kendo choreographer for the feature film *Snow Falling on Cedars*, to be directed by Scott Hicks. I sent him as much information as I could on kendo, as well as some video clips of me teaching kendo at the university. He then sent me a script and I looked at the scenes. I sent them my interpretation of how I would stage the physical action and what traditional kenjitsu technique would be important to support the script. I was also asked to send them a video of a traditional tea ceremony, which I did. Scott Hicks flew up to meet me, and we had a long conversation about tradition and kendo. A few months later, I was asked to create the kendo scenes for the film. I spent months working alongside Kathleen Kennedy, Frank Marshall, and Scott Hicks. I loved it. There I was working with film celebrities on their passion project. It was on that film that I earned my first film nickname—Kendoboy. I had no idea that my love of Star Wars, and as a result kendo, would put me in such an amazing position and incredible learning experience.

I had first seen Kathleen Kennedy's name on *Raiders of the Lost Ark*, another favourite of mine. Her and Frank Marshall have produced most of my favourite films, and I felt like a fanboy working with this powerful husband and wife team.

Bob Richardson was the Director of Photography and I worked closely with him, letting him know how the sequences were going to play on our set. Perhaps the most magical moment was the day we were shooting a memory sequence where the audience sees a wide shot of a field. Kazuo and his father are practising kendo. His father trains him roughly, preparing him for the way of the sword, knocking the young boy to the ground and yelling at him to get up and keep going. I helped Scott set up the shot, and then, when it came time to shoot the sequence, Scott handed control over the set to me. To *me*! My heart pounded as the cameras rolled. Sound was speeding, the slate was struck, and then it was my turn to call "Action!" We shot the scene three times. During one of the shots, a flock of geese flew into frame, and Bob Richardson thought they looked incredible. When we were watching the 2000 Academy Awards—*Snow Falling on Cedars* had been nominated for Best Cinematography—I was excited to see they used the shot I had called as part of the film clip for the ceremony.

My love of Star Wars and kendo made that experience possible, and it solidified for me that I was on the right path. My love of staging fights would help me focus the anger I had inside for what had happened in my past.

What I really enjoyed was that I had proven myself as a legitimate fight director. I had trained Rick Yune and Cary-Hiroyuki Tagawa to perform their fight scenes, choreographing and coaching them along the way. The female lead, Youki Kudoh, and the rest of the Japanese cast began calling me Sensei, while the rest of the cast and crew all knew me as Kendoboy. I had earned the respect of my film peers, and it felt great. I was a part of the production, and I was contributing my skills to the film-makers I had looked up to as a child. I was excited to be a part of the on-set huddles with Scott Hicks, Kathleen Kennedy, and Frank Marshall. For the first time in my life, I really felt accepted and respected as a professional.

As I write this, Kathleen Kennedy is currently the head of Lucasfilm Ltd.—home of Star Wars. I was excited to see the fights in the latest films still had the essence of kendo. The prequels lacked the form that *The Force Awakens*, *The Last Jedi*, and *The Rise of Skywalker* have recaptured. Whenever I see someone holding a lightsaber with their hands in the wrong position, I cringe. I am a kendoka, and I understand the importance in the posture, technique, and the ways of the sword. I love the speed, grace, and strength that kendo offers. I do miss competing. I really miss choreographing it. Perhaps one day I will be able to be in a filmed lightsaber fight. I would have never dreamt that kendo would lead to me being a top fight director.

It was during filming of *Snow Falling on Cedars* that I began seeing a new therapist. Her name was Carol, and her specialty was dealing with victims of physical and sexual abuse. I found her name in the back of a community newspaper. After a hiatus following my first terrible experience with therapy, I knew it was time to find another therapist. My attempts at working things out on my own were not helping at all. I needed someone to help me with the work I knew I needed to do.

Carol was an older woman, well into her sixties. She was unassuming and had a large German Shepard that waited with her clients in her reception area. I filled out several forms while I waited for my appointment. When I did see her, we sat and chatted. She went over her policies with me, and I agreed to her requirements. Initial sessions consisted of me telling her about my childhood, my family, my education. She asked why I had come to see her, and I shared that my experience with my university professor had stirred up memories of my time in Catholic school. I was frank about the physical abuse, but I had decided that I would not share anything more than that. I was secretly hoping that those feelings of shame would subside by focusing on the physical abuse by the priests and the dominance of my mother.

I stayed clear of discussing anything remotely connected to the sexual abuse with Carol—or at least I thought I did. She sat back and listened, at times prompting me for more information. She never interrupted, nor did she draw conclusions with what I was saying. She let me sit and talk, talk and cry. It felt good to see her in between my times on set with the film. I thought I was doing a great job at covering up the truth and hiding what was really going on inside me. My secret was tormenting me, but it felt like I was going to get away with focusing on the physical and hiding the deeper secrets.

Then it started to unravel. The film was starting to wrap up, and, perhaps due to the long hours combined with the lack of sleep, I was becoming more exhausted. I was in the middle of a session with Carol. She had given me some written work to do from a previous session. We were discussing my responses when I stopped and became quiet. Several moments passed in silence as I stared blankly at the paper.

"Nicholas, what are you feeling?" she asked.

I did not respond but sat staring at the white paper on the table in front of me.

"Nicholas?"

I tried to speak. My mouth opened. I was trying to keep the doors to my deepest secrets shut, but I was losing my strength. Visions of candy, beatings, and rape began to come to me—slowly at first. Perhaps I was going to be able to hold them back. It was similar to the feeling a person has when they know they are about to throw up but believe that by being still they will be able to prevent vomiting. The visions flashed with increasing speed in my mind. Now it was as if the vomit was in my mouth. If I opened it, there was going to be a mess that no one would want to see or clean up. I tried to swallow my feelings back. It wasn't working. The door to the secrets of my past was being obliterated. Still, I was silent. Carol again spoke.

"Nicholas?"

"I ... I ... It's all my fault." I couldn't believe I had spoken. If I could just shut up. Maybe she didn't hear me.

"What is your fault, exactly?" Carol asked.

She had heard me. Too late. Could I turn back now?

"It's all my fault ..." Memories now were rushing back. I wanted to stop, run out of her office, and never come back. I started to cry as I confessed what had happened to me as a child. I told her everything, sobbing as I recounted the horrors I faced so long ago. The memories were coming back as fresh as if the events had only recently unfolded. I felt a combination of terror, fear, and relief as I shared my deepest secrets with her. She let me share my story. She didn't judge. She thanked me for sharing.

My path to healing had begun. She was the first person I had shared my story with. Even Rebecca, whom I was now engaged to, and who had confided in me about her own abuse, did not know these horrible secrets. We were to be married the following month, and I knew I had to speak with her.

We walked along a wooded path near our apartment. It was a warm day, and the sun was bright. I knew I had to tell her my secret. My heart pounded, and though I knew Rebecca intimately, I was afraid of what I was about to reveal. I had been raped and beaten as a child. I was worried that Rebecca might see me as less of a man because of it. I was trying to find the words as we walked along the path. She could see that I was struggling.

"You ok, hon?"

"Yeah, great," I quipped sarcastically. "Hey, I need to talk to you."

"Okay, so talk."

I could not find the words.

She stopped and looked at me. "Hey, you're starting to worry me."

I took a breath and tears started to roll down my face. I ignored them as I fought for words. "Remember years ago when you told me about being abused?"

"Yes ..." I could hear the apprehension in her voice.

"Well, I ... I ... was abused at my private school."

"What?" She looked shocked. "Abused? Beaten?"

"Yes ... and ... well ..."

"Honey, you can tell me anything. I am not going anywhere."

"I was raped and sexually abused too ... It's disgusting, so I understand if you—"

"I'm not going anywhere. I love you."

"Even though I was raped?"

"I am so sorry that happened to you. You can tell me anything and everything. I am here for you, hon. I am right beside you."

Rebecca became my confidant, and Carol became my Yoda. My sessions with Carol were my trips to Dagobah. I sat before this tiny older woman and began to start the much-needed healing I had yearned for all my life. I was hopeful that I could keep this between me and her. My mom and dad would never need to know. I could still protect them from the deep pain of my childhood. I was going to spare them from that.

Or so I thought.

42
CAN I LET YOU IN
ON A SECRET?

Help me Obi-Wan Kenobi,
you're my only hope.

— Princess Leia, *A New Hope*

My last days of shooting *Snow Falling on Cedars* were on Whidbey Island in Washington State. I arrived home on a Saturday afternoon after finally wrapping the film and enjoying the three-hour drive. I opened the door of my apartment, bent over to untie my shoes, and collapsed to the floor—my lower back going out. Really going out. I couldn't get up. The pain was excruciating. I dragged myself across the apartment to my phone and dialled Rebecca. She was working but was able to get me the phone number for a nearby chiropractor. I called in a panic and spoke to the receptionist. She could tell I was in pain and put the chiropractor on the phone. He agreed to come by the apartment and told me to get on a bed or couch so he could attempt an adjustment. It was going to be an hour before he was there. For that entire time, I tried to get myself up on the couch, the pain making each movement almost unbearable. When he finally arrived, I was still crawling up on the couch. He waited patiently for me to ascend the summit of my personal Everest. When I finally made it, he attempted to do an adjustment but was unable. He told me I would have to wait until Monday morning when he was back in his office.

The next day and a half passed very slowly. I could not even kneel. I realized how much I had taken mobility for granted. Until that time, I never fully understood how debilitating back pain could be.

I had a small footrest in the living room. It was black leather with a circular metal frame. When Monday arrived, I knew I could not walk all the way to the car in order to get to the chiropractor, so I had Rebecca put a set of my stunt knee pads on me and I crawled up onto the footrest, allowing my chest to rest against the top. With the pads on my knees, I was able to crawl down the hallway to the elevator and then down to the parking garage. I was not able to sit in Rebecca's car, so, like an old Golden Lab, I awkwardly climbed up into the back seat, coming to a rest on all fours, with the footrest still supporting my upper body. I made my grand entrance to the chiropractor crawling along the sidewalk and into his office. He was able to get me on his table and was able to get a bit of an adjustment. I could hear my back popping as he pushed my knees up to my chest and used his body weight to torque my hips in line. I felt an intense combination of pain and relief. I was finally able to stand, and, with the aid of a cane, I ambled out of his office and sat in the front seat of the car for the drive back home. I was able to tolerate small amounts of time standing but was told to rest while my back settled down over the next few weeks.

I was forced to lay back and heal. During that time, I had much on my mind but was unable to see Carol. One evening I was watching a special on the CBC about abuse in Newfoundland at a Catholic school named St. Vincent. Beatings, mental anguish, and rape—I knew all about those things and could relate to the victims out there. The phone rang. It was time for my nightly check-in with my parents. I picked up the remote and silenced the television.

"Hello." Even with the advanced technology of call display, I did not answer in the familiar.

"Hi, honey. It's Mom and Dad."

My mom was (and at the time of writing this, still is) the biggest worrier. Finding me covered with bruises all those years ago had made her overly protective of her little boy. She was always worried that any injury was worse than I told her. She hated the fact that I was a stunt performer and a fight director. Try as she might, she could not hide her nervousness over the phone.

"How are you feeling, honey?"

I had so many emotions swelling deep inside me. My body was finally breaking down after trying to carry the secrets of abuse with me throughout the years. If my body was a dam, then the flood of emotions butting against the edifice was going to finally break it down. The problem was compounded with the simple fact that I could not move. I could not stand up and run off, distract myself, or deflect. As I lay there, the documentary of abuse played on in silence. My mom's worried voice added to the force cracking the walls that surrounded my emotion and my secrets. I needed to answer my mom, but what could I possibly say? How could I masterfully avoid revealing how I was feeling? After all, the darkness inside me reminded me that I would destroy my family if I ever revealed what had happened to me as a child. It was my fault. I deserved to be abused. I answered my mother's question dismissively.

"Fine."

Perfect. It was simple. I was hoping we would move on from there. Those of you who are mothers know that this just opened further inquiry.

"You don't sound fine."

"No really, I'm fine."

"What are you doing?"

"Oh, you know, just watching TV."

"Oh. What are you watching?"

What the hell was this? Was this twenty questions? I was getting agitated. The storm brewing inside was growing.

"Just this show about abuse in Newfoundland."

"Oh."

There was a long pause. Phew, I made it. Time to move on to a new subject.

"Are you okay?" my mother asked.

"Yeah, I'm fine. Really."

"Okay."

"Yeah, it's just this show. It's pretty sad. It's about these kids who were at a private Catholic school, and they were abused and stuff."

Why did I have to say that? I tried to shut up my unconscious mind, but it wasn't working.

"You don't sound fine. What's wrong?"

What is it with mothers and their uncanny ability to sense when things are wrong with their children? The dam was starting to break.

"Nothing! I am fine, okay?" I shouted into the phone.

Oops. There was an even longer pause.

"Look. You can tell your father and me anything."

"I know. Mom ... Dad ..."

They both answered. "Yes?"

"There is something ..."

"You can tell us anything. Anything."

The tears started to flow down my cheeks. "I don't know how to tell you this. Please don't hate me."

"There is nothing you could tell us that would make us hate you, Son," my dad chimed in.

My mother went right for the meat of the conversation.

"Are you gay?"

"What? No? What?" Now that was a curveball. I was living with Rebecca. I suppose my parents really wanted to be with the times—there was so much television at the time where the biggest thing a child could reveal to their parents was that they were gay.

But now there was no turning back.

"Please don't hate me."

"What is it? Please let us in."

"I ... I ... was abused at school."

My mother was a little shocked at this answer. After all, this was old news to her.

"We know, honey. That's why we took you out."

"No."

A longer pause. I was now crying. The hot tears were running down my face and soaking into the couch. I was finally able to get some breath back into my body, and I eventually continued.

"There is so much more. Mom, Dad, I am so sorry."

I apologized to them. What the fuck was that? It wasn't my fault, and I was now apologizing to them for being abused. My mom interrupted.

"No, don't be sorry. There is nothing to be sorry about. I am sorry. Please, you must tell us what happened. What do you mean?"

Yoda's lessons from *The Empire Strikes Back* came back to teach me in that moment. Yoda tells Luke, "You must unlearn what you have learned ... Feel the Force."

There was no thunderclap. No lightning strike. God was not about to strike me dead. The path of the Jedi was opening to me. I could be quiet and enter the dark side, or I could use the Force as my ally and reveal the truth. Unless you have been in such a situation, you have no idea how hard that choice is to make. If I stayed silent, how would the secrets of my torture and rape manifest?

It was time to heal, to stop ripping off the bandages before wounds could turn to scars. It was time to become a Jedi.

I told them everything.

Ч∃
OUT IN THE OPEN

*The more you tighten your grip,
Tarkin, the more star systems
will slip through your fingers.*

— Princess Leia, *A New Hope*

Telling my parents what happened to me was one of the most difficult things I have done. It has also been one of the most cathartic things I have done. Years of hiding the secrets of my abuse were at an end. I was worried that they might try to justify what had happened. I was worried that they would ask me if I was sure that what I was telling them had occurred. They did not. They listened on the phone as I finally told them everything that I had hidden from them. They cried with me and let me tell them without interruption. I held nothing back. After an hour or so of telling them the truth of what had happened to me, I finally stopped talking. My throat was sore. The phone line was quiet. I wasn't sure if they were still on the phone. I was too exhausted to speak, so I just continued to hold the handset to my ear, wondering if I had lost them.

Finally, my mom spoke.

"We love you. What are we going to do?"

I wasn't expecting to hear my mom ask what *we* should do. This was my burden. It was mine to bear. Now, at long last, my parents were ready to stand behind me. I didn't know what to say.

"Press charges?"

"You're damn right we are going to press charges. Those bastards are going to pay for what they did to you. I—We are so sorry we allowed this to happen to you."

"*No*. Please don't say that, Mom. You did everything you could to protect me."

I was worried that my parents would take on the guilt for what had happened. I knew that they would have removed me the moment there was the tiniest hint of abuse. There wasn't. In hindsight, of course, I can see the signs of crying out. It was in the early artwork I drew. It was in the writing. But unless you were looking for signs of abuse, the clues have little meaning.

When I was able to walk again, I resumed my therapy with Carol. I told her what had happened and how my parents reacted. My revelation about the sexual abuse only brought more tears and more self-blame, but it meant the work of healing could finally begin because I was no longer attempting to wall it up deep inside. I had unleashed decades of pain and suffering. The real hard work of therapy had begun. I was ready and I was not going to run from it.

Carol reminded me often that fear was something easy to fall into. I was afraid, but I was willing to do the work to get back on the path to navigating balance in my life. For the first time, I was learning how to put myself first. It was difficult and emotionally exhausting, but it was necessary for my healing.

After a few more months of coming to terms with the fact that I was not to blame for the abuse, it was time for me to take the next important step along my path of healing. I wanted to hold my abusers accountable. I warned my parents that I was going to file criminal charges against Father Vitus, Brother Ignatious, and the Blessed Virgin of the Bleeding Heart Elementary for what had happened to me while in their care. My parents supported my resolve and intent. They embraced me.

I met Carol at her home office, and we drove to the local police station to report the crimes committed against me as a child. In Canada, there is no statute of limitations for cases involving sexual abuse of a minor. My heart was pounding hard in my chest as we parked outside the detachment. I looked at Carol, my Yoda.

"Nicholas, you must do what you feel is right. I will be right beside you." She touched my shoulder.

We exited my car and headed up the stairs to the main entrance.

The officer on duty at the front desk was a young female constable. She was occupied with papers in front of her. I was nervous, my heart feeling as if it had jumped into the back of my throat in an attempt to run away from this situation, yet I continued to move towards the constable. I was going to do this. Justice needed to be served.

I looked at Carol. She looked up at me. As I moved closer to the desk, I thought of the moment Obi-Wan tells Luke that he was taking his first step into a much larger world. I was bringing my fragile courage. I was going to make a stand. I was going to fight for the small child within me. It was a huge moment in my life. I could feel my heart throbbing in the back of my head. The constable glanced up at me, momentarily taking her attention off of her papers.

"Can I help you?"

"I ... I want to report a crime."

She put her papers down and gave me her full attention. She looked right into my eyes.

"Yes, of course. What kind of crime are you reporting?"

My eyes began to tear up. I swallowed hard. This was it. I could visualize Red Leader in *A New Hope* barreling down the Death Star trench, focused on the destruction of the Empire.

Stay on target ...

"I was raped."

The young constable's expression changed. Her face became flushed. This was obviously uncomfortable for her. Here was a six-foot-plus man starting to cry and telling her he was raped. Men didn't act like that, did they? She started reshuffling her papers, looking around her station for a means of escape from this situation. I started to cry. I wasn't trying to. It was a combination of embarrassment, shame, fortitude, and resolve. I looked back at Carol, she nodded at me with a *You've got this* look. I carried on before the increasingly fidgety police constable.

"I was raped when I was a child ... at Catholic school ..."

Stay on target ...

She held up her hand, silencing me as she picked up her phone and turned away. She stopped looking at me as she clutched the receiver to her ear, looking everywhere but at the sobbing man-child standing before her. She hung up the phone and, without looking at me, pointed to a chair and dismissively told me to have a seat.

Carol came and put her hand on my back. The human touch made me cry more.

Carol whispered, "You're doing fine. I am proud of you."

Proud? Really? I felt anything but. Still, I could hear Red Leader

Stay on target ...

After what felt like an eternity, a sergeant approached me. I stood up to meet him. He was an older man, in his late fifties most likely.

"Where and when did this happen?" was how he began his conversation with me.

I was a little thrown off by his comment—*this*. I had been beaten, raped, humiliated. It was more than *this*. Still, I wiped the steady flow of tears and responded that it had occurred on multiple occasions in a private Catholic school in the small town of Hopeless. He looked relieved.

"You need to report this kind of crime to the local detachment. You cannot report it here."

"What?" I could feel my heart sinking. My cheeks flushed with embarrassment.

"You can't report this kind of a crime here. You have to go back to the town that it happened in. You can call them or do it in person." He turned and disappeared back into the recess of the lobby, dodging his duty of dealing with a male survivor, leaving me in tears and frustration.

Red Leader was still commenting in my head.

Stay on target ...

Carol and I regrouped at her home office. We decided to try again from her phone. I called the detachment in Hopeless and was told that

I could not report such a crime over the phone. I would have to do it in person in Hopeless.

Stay on target ...

A few weeks later I was in Hopeless, outside the police detachment by myself. I walked in and attempted to report the abuse to the officer on duty, but he refused to start a file and suggested that I pursue my quest for justice through a civil court. I didn't know what else to do.

I could see Red Leader's X-wing destroyed. My hopes of bringing my abusers and the powerful Catholic Church to justice were crushed. I could feel the dark side calling to me. I wanted to burn the church in that town. I thought about it. I fantasized about dousing the cathedral with gasoline and lighting a match, sitting back, and watching it go up in flames. Of course, I wouldn't do such a thing, but it sure made me feel better to imagine it.

How easy it would be to let the dark side dominate my destiny.

44
INCOMING RADIO TRANSMISSION

I am fluent in six million forms of communication.

— C3P0, *The Empire Strikes Back*

Shattered by the prospect of never having my case picked up by law enforcement, Carol and I decided that perhaps civil court was a good alternative. She had a few contacts who specialized in pedophile cases, and before too long, I had retained a lawyer. This lawyer appeared to be sympathetic to my cause and cautioned me that it would be a tough case as I did not have credible corroborating witnesses to back up my claims. At this time, cases of abuse against the Catholic cult were few, and those that did make the headlines were often unsuccessful. In Canada, at the time, cases that succeeded against the Church focused on the systemic and horrific suffering of generations of Indigenous children forced into the residential school system as a form of religious "cleansing." These cases were presented together and were undeniably damning. Stand-alone cases taking on the Church were, as I was to learn, not taken seriously or with any real attempt at justice. It is important to keep in mind that many of the same priests who committed abuses at residential schools were also abusing children at Catholic schools across Canada.

At the same time that I was engaging in my civil attempt at justice, I was employed at a major market radio station. It was the number-one station in Vancouver, and I had found myself as the morning show stunt guy. A result of my Star Wars obsession.

I had built myself a Star Wars stormtrooper costume from a kit I found on a now-defunct site called *Wookiee Cantina*. It was a PVC vacuum-formed suit of armour that I had to trim and put together. I was excited to become a life-sized action figure. I spent a few days putting it together, with dozens of pieces littering the living room floor of my one-bedroom apartment. When it was completed, I wore it wherever I could find a costume event. At that time, the second Star Wars trilogy was in production, and the opening of *The Phantom Menace* was weeks away. My favourite morning radio show hosts were Darren and Janice. I knew Janice from the Vancouver TheatreSports League where I was a professional improviser and Janice was an alumnus. I called her at the radio station and left a message telling her I had a real Star Wars stormtrooper suit and that I was willing to do something on their morning show in exchange for tickets to the movie premiere in Vancouver. The station often hosted movie premieres, and I was not going to risk missing out on a chance to see the movie ahead of the general public.

Within a couple hours, the phone rang.

I was excited to hear back from her so soon.

"So, you have a real stormtrooper costume? That's incredible. Darren and I would love to do something with you on the air."

I had never thought I would be a radio guy—but this was it. My chance to see a new Star Wars film ahead of the general public was going to happen.

"But I hate to tell you that we don't have any passes for the new movie. They are being pretty strict about it. But doing something with you as a stormtrooper sounds like it would be hilarious. If you are into it, we can definitely hook you up with some swag to make it worth your while."

Swag is the term radio jocks use to refer to free stuff they give out on air. She assured me they had a lot of swag to throw at me. Hey, I was going to get to be a stormtrooper on live radio. That was pretty cool to me.

We decided that the bit I was going to do would be "What can a Star Wars stormtrooper get for free." Their street guy, Freeway Frank, picked me up at my apartment at five in the morning and drove me downtown. We arrived, and he helped me dress in my costume (no small feat). I was given a wired two-way microphone that plugged into my mobile phone with enough cable to extend away from my face. This was to catch the responses from the people I engaged with. The earpiece helped me listen to Janice and Darren as I set about the tasks given to me. It was exciting. Darren made sure everything was working.

"Hey, Nic. Just so you know ... there's no pressure, but we can only record you doing two short segments. You are going to have to be descriptive without being boring, and you have to really paint the picture for our listeners. You have about three or four minutes, and we'll coach you if we have any ideas to jump on. Other than that, have fun and make it funny."

No pressure there. I had to be descriptive and provide colour commentary without being boring.

Part of the training I received years earlier as a Disney cast member was about the importance of being in character at all costs once the costume was on. I don't think Janice and Darren were prepared to deal with me once I put the helmet on, because once I started, I was not Nic, but TK 426, an edgy stormtrooper. Darren and Janice laughed when they addressed me as Nic, and I corrected them that I was an Imperial stormtrooper hanging out on Earth.

And so it began. My very first on-air bit was to walk into the very prestigious Hotel Vancouver and approach the desk clerk. I only had a couple minutes to get things going, so I had to make it snappy. Luckily, there was no line at the check-in desk that early in the morning. The clerk looked up from his computer screen.

"Welcome to the Hotel Vancouver. How can I assist you today?" they asked as if there was nothing odd addressing a soldier of the Empire.

"I believe the Empire has a reservation for a D. Vader?" I asked as my amplified voice was heard clearly through my chest speaker, making me sound just like a stormtrooper in the movies. It was obvious that I was starting to annoy the clerk. I could hear Janice and Darren laughing. This gave me confidence to carry on.

"I am here under the direction of Lord Vader to book his room."

"How do you spell the name?"

"V. A. D. E. R."

"We don't have anyone booked under that name."

"Can you check under TK 426?"

"Security!"

I heard Darren and Janice in my earpiece. "Run! Get out of there."

I shuffled away in my plastic armour, and they could hear how difficult it was to move. They broke out laughing. When I exited the hotel, Janice and Darren asked if I could try again somewhere else. I was happy to oblige. The next target that morning was a local Starbucks. Again, I entered in full-on Imperial character.

"I am requiring a free beverage for the Empire."

This time the employee was a little more playful.

"So, what do stormtroopers like to drink?"

"Chocolate chip Frappuccinos. With extra sprinkles, please."

Again, Janice and Darren erupted in laughter. The morning was a success. As I removed and repacked my costume, Frank was on the phone with Darren and Janice. He looked over at me and asked if I had time to drop by the station with him to meet the hosts and to pick up some free stuff. Later that morning, I met with the Morning Crew, and they offered me a job as their stunt guy. They wanted to give me a radio name, and Janice kept repeating they wanted me to be the kind of guy that people would find friendly and fun. By the time I left that morning, I was the newest employee of the radio station and had my new name: Nick the Guy. Morning radio was never going to be the same, and the only reason I was able to have a sixteen-year career as a comedy radio personality (and eventual morning show producer) was because I had a Star Wars costume and picked up my phone to tell someone because I wanted free tickets.

I spent three years with the station, and I quickly became a favourite with their listening demographic. I was zany, quirky, and was able to be a colour commentator. As an improviser, my skills at setting up a comedy bit, enhancing an environment, and making myself the fall-guy of my own jokes resonated. I had fan mail and free trips around the world, and it was amazing. Darren thought it would be better morning radio if people didn't think of me as a married guy with responsibilities—so Nick the Guy was a single, crazy, lovable loser.

Within a few months of starting, Janice left the morning show, and I learned how quickly the radio world works. She was replaced with Floyd. Floyd was intense and was not keen on having jokes played on him. He loved my work as Nick the Guy, but there was friction between us as I was becoming increasingly more popular with the listeners than he was. The program manager, Eric, a great guy and huge fan of my comedy, left to take a promotion in Ontario. He was replaced with an alpha male named Chip. Chip was shocked to learn that I was not really the character I portrayed on the radio, and he was even more shocked to discover that I was married and expecting my first child. He really thought it was important to ensure that information didn't get out. He wanted to continue the idea that I was a big loser-type that always got into trouble. As a result, my morning radio spots were becoming less fun and more jackass in presentation. I was not excited about that change. The promotions department did not like his approach to things either, as he helped himself to gift cards and items that were supposed to be used as gifts for the listeners. Chip loved what I was doing. I loved doing my morning comedy. But it was all about to fall apart.

By this time, my civil case against the Catholic Church was underway, and a local television station wanted to do a story on me. They sent out a camera crew to follow me as I did a morning radio stunt. They were gathering footage to add to their story about me as a comedian to contrast my sad story of abuse. They were set to interview me later that week, and I told them I was going to clear everything with my new boss, Chip. The morning I went to see Chip, he told me how funny I was and how great an asset I was to the Morning Crew. Some of my on-air bits were so funny that other sister stations across the country were playing them. I was an ace in his pocket as far as he was concerned. He asked me why I wanted to see him so urgently, offering me a beer from his bar fridge. I declined. It was nine-thirty in the morning.

"So, what can I do you for?" he asked, laughing at his own version of a joke.

It was hard to tell this guy what had happened. I managed to get through it, telling him the length and degree of the abuse, the civil case, and the upcoming television interview. He became visibly upset.

"This is not good. This is not good for ratings. Have you had the interview yet?" he asked. His tone became unusually serious. I told him it would be later that week.

"Okay. Well, I have a meeting to get to. Thanks for telling me."

Our meeting became instantly cold, and suddenly the man who had just offered me a morning beer had a sudden appointment to go to. He did not shake my hand as I left.

I called the television station to find out when the interview was scheduled for. They told me that it would be in a day or so and that they would call back to schedule a time for me to come in.

Later that night I received a call from Chip, asking me to come to the radio station as soon as I could. I suggested the next morning, but he wanted it to be later on in the day—long after the Morning Crew team would be gone. He was serious on the phone. I asked him if it was because of the court case. He told me it was not. I asked him if he was calling me in to fire me. There was a long pause. Again, he responded by asking me to come in the following afternoon.

The next afternoon I arrived at the station and stopped at the receptionist's desk.

"Hello. How are you doing?" I asked.

There was no response and I noticed she answered the phone that wasn't ringing. It suddenly felt very awkward. As I rounded the corner, past the broadcast booths, I noticed a security guard standing outside of Chip's office.

"Can I help you?" he asked.

"I am here to see Chip. I have an appointment."

"Stay there." He went inside the office.

I looked around. The normally busy hall was disturbingly quiet. After a few moments Chip came to the door, and the security guard resumed his post outside. Chip tried to come across as friendly.

"Oh hey, Nic. Come in."

I moved past the guard and into the office. Chip sat down and started to play with a paperclip. I looked at him as he focused on his paperclip-bending technique. I could feel a disturbance in the Force.

"So, I wanted you to know we are shaking things up around here. Nothing personal. Just, you know, changing things around."

"Okay," I responded.

He trudged on. "So, I am going to have to let you go."

Silence.

Chip cleared his throat. "I mean you're doing a great job. It's just time for change."

He finally looked at me and I sat, calmly looking back at him.

"On what grounds are you firing me?"

"Just, you know, shaking things up."

"You know I am your number-one rated radio personality at the moment?" It was true. The ratings had come in a week before and, to everyone's surprise, I was the top-rated personality on air.

Chip stood up to usher me out.

"Hang on," I said, "can I have a day or two to clear out my email? I have some stuff in there I would like to make sure I get."

Chip dropped his paperclip on the desk and adjusted his tie. "Yeah, okay. Sure." He motioned to the door behind me. The security guard came into the room to escort me out of the building.

"I'd like to say goodbye to the promotions people," I said.

"Can't do that. Policy," was Chip's reply.

I walked over to their office anyway. I didn't freak out or cause a scene, but I stepped inside the promotions office to say goodbye. They had no idea I was being let go. The guard grabbed my arm, and we did the walk of shame out of the office. At the entrance, I was asked for my keys and security card. I handed them to the guard as he held the door open for me to leave. As soon as I exited, he locked the door from the inside just in case I tried to regain entry. It was a bit dramatic.

When I returned home and tried to access my email, it had been disconnected despite Chip assuring me I would have a day or two to clear things out. The television reporter who had been wanting to do the story on my abuse also suddenly stopped responding to my calls. I learned that Chip had called him after our initial meeting. Suddenly, my interview was dropped. Chip was more concerned over his ratings than about justice.

Thinking my radio career of three years was over, I went to bed feeling sad and angry. The next morning, however, I received a phone call.

"Hello. Is this Nick the Guy?"

"Yes."

"Hi, it's Clay and Karen, the hosts of the local country radio station. We heard you were fired last night. Do you want to come work with us?"

I met the following day with the program manager, Gord. I was worried that my court case against the Catholic Church was going to make them change their minds.

Gord was a pleasant man and had much the demeanour of my original program manager, Eric. He had been listening to me for some time and was very excited to welcome me as an addition to the morning show team. I knew I had to tell him that my case against the Catholic Church might bring unwelcome publicity to the station.

"Bring it on," he replied.

He was happy to hear that I was standing up so bravely against the Catholic machine. I was so relieved. A few days later I began my fourteen-year run with Clay and Karen of the Waking Crew. Chip was upset that I was able to keep my radio name as I transferred over. The first radio bit I did with Clay and Karen involved me "auditioning" for the job as the stunt guy for them. All morning they boasted how they were happy to take me on after I had been wrongfully fired from the other station. I am sure Chip was fuming. I was even successful in filing a wrongful dismissal claim. I won. And I heard that Chip did not last too long in his managerial position. When my son, Benjamin, was born, my new Waking Crew team sent over the biggest baby welcome basket that I have ever seen. It was a huge difference from the treatment I had been getting at my former station.

I maintained a fun and easy-going relationship with Clay and Karen over the years I worked with them. When I was finally let go in 2016, it was on amicable grounds. My ongoing comedy had run its course. Though it was sad to say goodbye, I knew it was time to retire Nick the Guy. I created a lot of fans, did a lot of crazy things, and loved my time bringing joy to those who listened to my antics.

45
DISCOVERY

Do. Or do not. There is no try.

— Yoda,
The Empire Strikes Back

Newly settled into my role as the Waking Crew stunt guy, I found myself having to take a few days off to go back to Hopeless. My lawyer was able to track down Brother Ignatious, who was living in a retirement home for oblates in Florida. The Diocese of Hopeless was bringing him in and had lawyered-up to fight the allegations against him. My lawyer wanted me to go up to Hopeless to face him in discovery for two days at his lawyer's office.

I was terrified to go up to Hopeless and see him. As a child, Ignatious was towering, oppressive, and all-powerful. He was an angry man who had beaten me, raped me, made me bleed, and threw me down the stairs in an attempt to kill me. He was still alive and relaxing in the warmth of Florida. The last time I had been alone with him was when he raped me against the pommel horse in the gym of the school. I was now going to face him as an adult.

I told my parents that I was coming up for the discovery. I flew in the night before and all my mom could talk about was how much of a bastard Ignatious was. I met with my lawyer for dinner, and she prepared me for what I might be facing the next day. That night I was unable to sleep. In the morning, my dad drove me to the law offices. It was a quiet drive. I could feel my heart beating hard in my throat. I met my lawyer outside the office, and we went in together.

It was shocking to see how small Ignatious was. He was at most five-foot-eight, perhaps even smaller. In my child's mind, Ignatious was huge and towering. Looking upon him as an adult, he seemed so much smaller, weaker. But his eyes. His eyes were exactly the same. Piercing grey cold dead eyes. His eyes said everything his body did not. He was an evil man who had chosen to hide behind his collar all his life. I tried to look him in the eyes, but throughout the discovery, he avoided eye contact. The only time that he did make eye contact with me was when he was asked by my lawyer if he ever abused a child when he worked at the diocese.

He looked straight at me and said, "No."

The oddest thing that he did confess was how he took pleasure in giving kids a "little kick" if they were too slow to get inside. My lawyer looked at me as if to say, *What a winner*.

The next day, when my dad drove me back for the second round of discovery, we started the drive in silence. My dad was not a man of too many words.

"Son, this is a good thing you are doing. I know it must be hard for you. It's hard for your mom and me. I just want to let you know how proud we are of you for standing up to him. I just wish that you had the ability to tell me what was happening to you all those years ago. I wish you had. If I knew how much you were suffering, I would have gone to that school and shot that son-of-a-bitch right in his office. I would have been out of jail by now."

His voice was shaky as he spoke. I believed him. He was a para-trooper in the Second World War. He was trained to kill, and he was an excellent marksman. He was also the kindest man I have ever known. As a father now myself, I really can understand what he was saying. I know I would do all I could to protect my children—he would have done that for me. My dad was my Han Solo. He was rough around the edges but was more of a gentleman than anyone. He was quiet. He had been beaten by his father as a child. He never wanted me to go through what he had gone through. He wanted to make it right. He loved me so much, and he was proud of what I was doing. Though it felt like I was alone, I had my small band of Rebels alongside me.

After the discovery, I was tasked with finding other survivors of Ignatious's abuse who would speak up. I decided to approach some former students who I knew had been abused. I was able to track down one who was working as a used car salesman. I blindsided him at his dealership. Looking back, it was probably not the best way to approach the subject. I asked him if I could speak with him. We went into his office. He had no idea what I was going to say or ask of him. The conversation started friendly enough, but as soon as I brought up the school and abuse, he immediately became agitated. He started yelling at me to leave and told me he was "never abused, just hit." In his heightened emotional state, he did not connect that being hit was a form of abuse. He told me to get off the property or he would call the police. Again, in retrospect, it was not the best way to handle the subject of abuse.

My lawyer had contacted a survivor in a small town just north of Hopeless. He agreed to a meeting, though he was scared to step forward. My mom confided in her close friend, Henny, about my lawyer's contact with another survivor who might help support my case. The next day, my lawyer received a call from the survivor who suddenly refused the meeting and denied the occurrence of any abuse at the school. Henny had notified the diocese, and the survivor had been visited by a priest the day before his meeting with my lawyer. It seemed Henny's allegiance to the Church was more important than her friendship with my mom.

Without more witnesses, I was facing the fact that my story would not be heard in court. My lawyer informed me that that I did not make a good client for her as I was not impoverished and because I came across as a person who had their shit together. I was "functioning." The people in Hopeless rallied around the Church despite the fact that the bishop of the diocese was involved in his own pedophile scandal. I played a waiting game with my lawyer, hoping that someone would come forward. I was very upset that my half sister did not stand with me. She was too scared. I continued to wait.

It is said that timing is everything. The discovery I had in Hopeless happened a couple years before the Boston scandal broke by the newspaper Spotlight. My lawyer continued to sway me away from continuing to fight the Church. She thought I was just wasting valuable time, and because I did not have success lining up corroborating witnesses, my story would have no weight against the Catholic lawyers defending the institution of the Church.

Years passed.

In total I waited eight years from having the courage to speak out to being told I had to give up. I didn't want to give up. I wanted to have my time in court. I wanted to look in the eyes of the judge and share my story, a story similar to many others who have continued to be silenced by men in power. But, unfortunately, without witnesses to stand with me, I was told I would not have a chance. I wanted desperately to share my story, yet my lawyer did not want to lose. My case was ultimately dismissed, and I felt deep down that I had failed.

46
GOODBYE

The Force will be with you ... always.

— Obi-Wan Kenobi,
A New Hope

What happens after a Jedi fails? As Yoda said to Luke, "Do. Or do not. There is no try." Well, I did what I needed to do. I spoke out and attempted to take on the Catholic Church alone. At that time, the Church was too powerful and the fanatics that follow them were quick to jump to the word of a pedophile priest over that of a man who dared to speak out against the horrific abuses he endured as a small child.

I will admit that it was hard for me to return to Hopeless to visit my parents after my failed attempt at justice. My parents' neighbours joked with their friends about me being abused. I was sent images of disgusting Halloween costumes of pedophile priests—the comedy of the costume being a small child mannequin, on its knees, attached to the front of a priest costume, waist height, face buried into the groin area of the cassock. A quick google search will still show that costume for those who are curious to see what it looks like.

Disgusting.

I did not tell my parents that the case had been dropped. My father had fallen ill in March of 2006 with what he thought was an impacted tooth. My parents came to visit us—Rebecca was now pregnant with our second child. When he arrived at our house, I couldn't help but notice the side of his face. The left side of his jaw was bulging out in the shape of a golf ball.

I drove my dad to see a doctor. We waited briefly in the clinic before being let into the doctor's office. My dad was quiet.

"You're going to be okay, Dad."

"I'm not worried, Son. My doctor told me it was just a swollen gland. It's going to be okay. Don't you worry."

My dad was not worried about himself. He was worried about me being scared.

The doctor had little in the way of bedside manner. He had my dad open his mouth, took a brief look inside, and was direct with us.

"It's cancer."

"What?" I couldn't believe what I had just heard.

"It's aggressive," he continued. "You have to get this dealt with right away."

My head was spinning. My dad just sat there and wrapped his lower jaw with a scarf he was using to prevent people from staring at his face. He did not seem emotional or phased by the sudden diagnosis. It was as though he was an old Jedi Master, in control of his emotions, while I, his Padawan, grasped to control my own.

What followed were a few months of radiation therapies in Vancouver. In between treatments he sat in a chair in our living room and looked outside. He spent hours sitting, looking outside. Rebecca and I would sit with him and talk with him as long as we could. I knew that I would miss my dad if I was to lose him. I didn't want him to go. I told him there was still so much to do and to see. He nodded and looked at me.

"I'll do what I can, Nic, but life is funny like that." Then he looked straight at me. "How's the lawsuit going?"

His eyes, his light blue eyes, looked right at me.

He continued. "You know your mom and I are proud of you. We are behind you. You know that, right?"

"I do, Dad, I do." There was no way I was going to tell him it had all been lost—that I had failed. I didn't want to give him bad news. Not while he was in this condition.

He continued to look at me while he spoke. "Your mom and I are so proud of you. We want you to know we support you going back to school."

I had just been accepted into the PhD program at the University of British Columbia. I had found out about my acceptance at the same time my dad got his cancer diagnosis.

"Thank you, Dad."

"You're going to do alright, Son. I know it."

"How do you know, Dad?"

"I see it in your eyes, Son. You're a fighter. I am so damn proud of you. Your mom and I both are."

"Dad, there's something I want to tell you."

"Yes, Son?"

"I ..." I wanted to tell him I failed in my lawsuit. I tried. What came out was, "I love you, Dad."

"I love you too, Son."

The tumour, which grew to the size of a grapefruit at one point, was responding to the treatments and we were all excited that maybe, just maybe, it was going to work out.

I was so relieved when we heard the news that the salivary gland cancer had been beaten. My daughter was due in September, and it was now July. My mom and dad were able to celebrate Ben's fourth birthday with us before they headed back to Hopeless, and I was excited to think my dad would be able to meet his other grandchild.

In early August, my dad went in for a routine examination. The cancer that had been in his salivary gland was gone—but it had spread into his lungs. He was dying. How long? Days. Weeks, maybe.

I flew up to see him. They were keeping him in the hospital in Hopeless. He was happy to see me. I brought him coffee. I had to give it to him by placing a straw in the coffee cup, placing my finger over one end of the straw, and then putting the straw in his mouth and lifting my finger so the coffee in the straw could drip into his mouth.

All I could think about was Luke Skywalker coming back to see Yoda in *Return of the Jedi*. Yoda sees Luke and asks him, "That face you make. Look I so old to young eyes?"

I knew my dad saw how sad I looked. He looked at me, his eyes looking deep into my own.

"It's okay, Son. I love you."

"I love you, Dad."

Through the night, it became difficult for him to speak. His words slurred, and he drifted in and out of consciousness. I spent two nights in the hospital with him, dripping coffee into his mouth, and he seemed to enjoy it. He completely stopped being able to speak the second night.

Yoda tells Luke at one point that he needs rest. My dad could squeeze my hand. He tried to speak. I sat beside him, holding his hand. I looked into his eyes—those blue eyes I wish I had. They were beautiful.

"Dad, I had to drop the court case."

I didn't expect a response. He looked at me. His eyes watered.

"Oh ... Son ..." he forced out. "I'm ... sorry. You'd better not tell Mom." He tried to force a smile, though I know he meant it. She would have been devastated.

"Dad, I'm sorry. I failed. I am a failure, Dad."

I started to cry. He squeezed my hand.

"No ... Son ... it's just a case. You ... have a voice ... you're going ... to be a doctor." He was speaking as best he could. He continued. "I am proud of you. Your mom and I ... we ... love you."

"I love you too, Dad."

He turned over and started to choke. I pushed the button for the nurse. She came in and took a small vacuum hose, stuck it in my dad's throat, and I could see what looked like raspberry jam getting sucked into the hose.

"What's that?" I asked the nurse.

"Blood clots. It's okay. It happens."

The rest of the night I sat with my dad, and each time he started to choke I pushed the button, and the nurse came in to suck up the clots. In between, I would sit with my dad and talk to him. He couldn't really speak to me anymore. I told him I was afraid. I told him I didn't know what to do without him. I imagined that I would sit with him, like in a movie, and we would have one last meal together.

Then, early in the morning, my dad, who had been fighting to speak earlier, sat up in the hospital bed and reached up to the ceiling and cried out.

"Fly to the baby!"

The first time this happened it scared me like a horror film. I know my dad had hoped he would meet his new grandchild. He was holding on, and for some reason I could feel it. I looked at him and held his hand.

"Dad. I love you. The Force is with you. If you have to let go, it's okay. I am here. I love you. I will always love you."

"Fly to the baby!" he cried out again.

I sat, holding his hand, crying. And though I wish I could write that that is how we spent the night, it wasn't. More hours passed, and I became angry. Not at my dad, but at the way life must end. I suddenly despised everyone. I hated everyone. I could feel my hate swelling. And so, I left that morning to return to Vancouver and to start fight rehearsals and my PhD at the University of British Columbia. I had only just arrived at the theatre when it happened.

Just like the moment Ben Kenobi pauses and has to sit down on the Millennium Falcon after he feels Alderaan blow up, it happened to me. Sword in hand, I had started to demonstrate a fight combination.

"I want you to parry to this side and then bind his sword over—"

I stopped, with my sword in mid-air. I could sense it. There was a disturbance. I held my arm up as if I was frozen.

"There is a disturbance in the Force," I said jokingly though I seriously felt it. I took a breath. "Okay, let's try this again." I started to execute the move but froze again. This time, the instructor, Stephen, approached me.

"Hey Nic, what's happening? You don't look so good."

"Stephen, I think my dad just died."

As soon as I said those words, my phone started to vibrate. I looked at the call display. It was my mom.

"Excuse me, I need to take this." I stepped outside the theatre doors. I wasn't even able to speak when I answered the call.

"He's dead," my sobbing mother yelled.

"I know, Mom. I can feel it." I could, I really could.

I walked back into the theatre. Stephen and the two students were sitting on the stage. I just looked at them.

"It appears that my dad has died. I think I better go now."

There was a tremble in the Force, and that day I felt it.

I never really told my mom the case was dismissed. It was something best left unsaid. I think she secretly hoped it would come back and I would be able to get my day in court.

So, much like the disbanded Jedi after Order 66 was followed, I went into a sort of hiding. I was able to hide myself away in my PhD program, keeping quiet about the court case and focusing instead on my studies.

During my years of being quiet about my failed case, news broke about the Boston sex abuse cases in the United States. In Canada, the Truth and Reconciliation Commission reached out to the Indigenous communities, and truths about residential schools were collected and shared. Many voices were being heard, yet mine was not one of them. As much as I wanted and wished for someone to come find me and ask to hear my story, I knew that it would be up to me to speak out and continue to share my voice if I was to be heard.

I ended up speaking out through my studies. I asked my advisor, Jerry, if I could write a paper about abuse and how popular culture can be used as a therapeutic tool for recovery. Jerry allowed me to write it, and within a couple months I had written a paper titled *How Star Wars Saved my Life; Reclaiming a Stolen Childhood Through the Power of the Force.*

Jerry called me into his office after I submitted it. I was worried I was going to be yelled at. I had used myself as the case study. Jerry stood up when I entered his office. I was expecting him to lose his temper with me as Dr. Hughes had done years before when I was working on my master's degree.

"Hey, so I read your paper. Pretty interesting stuff."

"Thank you."

"Nic, I know you want to write your dissertation on origins of stage combat, but ..."

But? This was it. He was going to kick me out of the program.

"... but this is pretty powerful stuff. It's not too late if you want to make this the focus of your dissertation."

"Really?"

"Of course. Nic, it's powerful stuff. So let me know what you want to do. I really got to hand it to you in writing this. It's raw and it's powerful."

Jerry was becoming my Qui-Gon Jinn. It was my second time at grad school, and this time I was being heard. I could feel the presence of my dad around me, and, in that moment, I started to feel like I was finally starting to belong. The Force was growing stronger within me.

ㄐㄱ
BREAK A LEG

Into the garbage chute, fly boy.

— Princess Leia, *A New Hope*

There is a term that stunt people use when a stunt or gag presents very limited risk. Those days on set are called gravy days—and they make up for the days that result in injuries. In the stunt community, it is commonly accepted that any day you get to walk home is a good day.

On his deathbed, my dad told me to "fly to the baby." A month later, right as I began my PhD studies at UBC, Olivia was born. I suddenly had two young children and needed to earn more money to properly support them. Luckily, my reputation as a stunt fighter allowed me to easily find more work in the film industry.

Because of my skills as a swordsman, I was able to perform in some of the fights I choreographed. Most notable was my performance as the larger-than-life Dark Knight in *Scooby-Doo 2: Monsters Unleashed*. It was an exhilarating few years, but I found it difficult to balance my education, work, and family life.

Two years flew by and suddenly it was 2008. Olivia was getting close to her second birthday, but because I was so often away, the two of us had never really bonded. She wouldn't come to me when I arrived home, and she didn't allow me to pick her up. It broke my heart. I wanted to be home more with her and her brother.

And then it happened.

I was starting work on a fantasy television series, stunt doubling the lead actor. My wardrobe consisted of long Fabio hair, leather pants, and pirate boots. It was day one of filming, and there were two stunts on the schedule: a fairly easy leap to the ground (as the heroine and my character evaded attacks from a flying dragon) and a simple six-foot drop onto a ten-inch pad (to create the illusion that my character was being dropped from the clutches of a dragon high above). Later in the series, I was going to be doing more fighting.

When I arrived on set, I noticed that they were setting up two stories of scaffolding in the marsh. We were shooting at an estuary, and the marshlands provided a good representation of a feudal land-scape. I watched as the scaffolding fell over in the distance. No doubt it was going to be used for lighting later on. I paid little attention to the chaotic construction behind me.

The first stunt went off without a hitch. I asked the stunt coordinator where the next stunt, the six-foot drop, would be happening later in the day. He did not answer me. A few moments later, the first assistant director approached me.

"Did you want to go check out the scaffolding over there? We'll be getting to you soon."

I was confused.

"You're dropping from it in a bit." The AD turned and walked away, and I looked over at the stunt coordinator.

"Don't worry. You're just going to sit on the first level and jump into some boxes and the pad. It's only an extra four feet or so." He tried to sound reassuring.

I heard Han's voice in my head.

I have a very bad feeling about this.

I walked through the marsh towards the leaning tower of scaffolding. My stomach was churning. When I arrived, the rigging crew was doing everything they could to secure the construction for my stunt. Dwight, an experienced rigger I had worked with many times before, greeted me.

"Welcome to the shitshow," he said.

I tried to smile. I tried to speak. All I could do was manage a weak smile and nod. Dwight led me to the side of the structure.

"You can climb up this way. It's been a bitch putting this up on this soft ground, but it should hold. Climb up and have a look."

I climbed up to the first level. It didn't look too bad. There were some boxes taped together under a crash mat, so it wouldn't be too jarring of a landing. My heart rate slowed.

"This isn't too bad," I called to Dwight, below.

"You have to go to the top platform," Dwight called back.

I was trying to look cool and calm.

"Oh, yeah. Okay."

Fuck.

I have a very bad feeling about this, I thought to myself as I climbed another level.

I was now sixteen feet above the ground. If they brought in a porta-pit or two, this could just work. I was curious to see what the stunt coordinator had brought for me. I looked below and saw him approaching. In the distance the camera crew was starting to set up for the shot.

"Do you need help bringing the pit over?" I called down.

"No. We don't have one. They changed all of this last minute."

"What about boxes?"

"No, I don't have any."

Cardboard boxes, when assembled, can make a good makeshift crash area when you're in a pinch. It's very old school, but it works. Sometimes two levels of boxes can even provide good cushioning for high falls. But it seemed there were none to be had.

"What are we going to use?" My voice was getting shaky.

"I have the ten-inch pad. We can fold it over to make it twenty inches."

The ten-inch pad was eight feet by eight feet and made of ten inches of high-density foam. It was a perfect pad for a six-foot drop. Not sixteen. I looked down from my perch. Being over six feet tall, my eyes were approximately twenty-two feet from the ground. It was a long way down.

Now I could hear Lando Calrissian in my head.

This deal is getting worse all the time.

The ten-inch pad was being folded on the ground below me. Far below me. I remembered watching an episode of Bugs Bunny, when Yosemite Sam was running a circus act and Bugs Bunny was supposed to do a high dive from the top of the tent into a small bucket of water. The point of view from the diving board to the bucket was exactly what I was now seeing. I took a step back from the edge of the top platform. The scaffolding rocked. This was not going to be a gravy day. Today I was going to earn every penny.

I closed my eyes and took a breath. I could do this.

No.

I tried to put the negative feelings out of my head. I needed to clear myself of doubt.

Breathe. Use the Force.

No. Don't do it.

I looked over at the camera crew. They were watching me.

"Let's roll on the test," I heard the AD call out on the megaphone in the distance. When they record a test jump, it usually means danger is high and the stunt may not be repeated.

I walked over to the ledge of the scaffolding and started to sit.

"What is he doing? We can see his legs."

I looked over to the stunt coordinator. He just looked at me and shrugged.

Shit.

"Rolling!"

I stood and looked down. Below me was the pad. One of the stunt riggers was hidden underneath the scaffolding. He was holding on to one of the handles of the pad to prevent it from moving when I landed. It was then that I realized the pad was on a decline that led to the edge of a sudden six-foot drop-off, at the bottom of which was mud. Lots of mud. I looked back at the pad. It looked so small.

"We're still rolling."

I thought about one of the first things I tell my students when I teach stage combat. "You can always say no if you don't trust the gag." I was not trusting the gag. I could walk away. I had a choice. As every

Jedi knows, their path before them is not set in stone. I could choose and choose wisely.

"Tell him if he doesn't jump, we'll get a real stunt person out here."

Ego got in the way.

I looked down, saw my mark, and leapt. I hit hard. I dropped to the pad feet first and rolled out of it. It hurt, but I was okay.

"Cut! We can't use it. We can't have the feet land first."

The stunt coordinator responded over his walkie-talkie and then looked over at me. "You have to do a sider."

A sider, or cowboy fall, is when the stunt performer drops and lands on their back or side. I could do it, but it was going to hurt. I climbed back up to the second level. I didn't move as quickly, nor was I smiling. I got to the top and moved to the ledge. I heard the call for action over the megaphone. I looked down at the pad and back to the camera crew. It reminded me of Luke Skywalker on the skiff in front of Jabba's sail barge waiting to leap into the Sarlacc. I would much rather be there than on this marsh.

I dropped.

I hit the pad, but my left knee hit something off the pad—the remnants of an old beaver dam. My knee was throbbing.

"One more!"

The coordinator looked at me. "Can you do one more?"

Foolishly, I nodded.

"Resetting!"

As I climbed to the top of the wobbly scaffolding for the third time, now with my left knee aching, I thought about how I'd be hobbling home that night. Still ultimately a good day.

"Rolling!"

I tried to jump. My feet were stuck to the scaffolding. My body had had enough. The Force was telling me to stop. I tried again. Nothing. I had to motivate myself. I hummed the opening bars of the *Star Wars* theme and thought about how the Jedi could use the Force to soften their landings. I was going to use the Force that day. I had to. I just wanted the day to be over.

I jumped.

I hit the pad. But the pad had angled slightly, so I hit it like a slide and kept going. I went over the ledge and dropped another six feet, and landed feet first in the mud. Shin deep.

My momentum was still moving forward, and I heard snapping. Blood curdling snapping. I hit the mud with the rest of my body. The pain was excruciating. I cried out and tried to get up. That's when I saw Dwight leaping from the ledge of the bank on top of me. He landed a knee across me and pinned me to the ground.

"Don't fucking move, Nic!" the rest of his rigging crew jumped down to surround me.

"Can we get one more?" the AD called out on the megaphone.

"He's done. He's broken his leg. Call a fucking ambulance!"

One of his crewmembers cut off a piece of their leather belt and Dwight put it in my mouth. "Bite down on this."

There should have been an ambulance on standby once they changed the drop from six feet to sixteen feet. One of Dwight's crewmembers, a former firefighter, carefully dug my foot out of the mud and got me on a pack board. He wrapped his shirt around my foot, which was now all but detached from the rest of my leg. It was all very surreal. I was starting to imagine the pain Luke experienced as he hung from the bottom of Cloud City with his right hand severed from his body.

"That's lunch!" the AD called out on the megaphone.

The ambulance had now been called, but the nearest hospital was over thirty minutes away. They decided to drive me as far as they could themselves, meeting the ambulance part way. Dwight and his crew walked me carefully out of the marsh and past the lunch line. It must have been awkward for the crew to be lined up for lunch while a stunt man dressed as Fabio was paraded past them with his detached foot being cradled like a football. They put me in a transport van and drove me, very slowly, down the dirt road to meet the ambulance, which took me to the local hospital for immediate surgery on my foot.

It was not a gravy day.

I almost lost my foot. Even after the surgery, my doctor had to monitor me for signs of infection that would result in amputation.

Several of my tendons could not be reattached, so I was going to have to strengthen others to compensate if I was going to learn to walk again. It was going to be a long process.

On the bright side, my toddler daughter suddenly had a new playmate. It must have been two or three days after I was home, lying in bed, when I heard her tiny footsteps approaching. A small pillow was thrown on the bed, and Olivia pulled herself up and onto the bed beside me.

"Hey there. You want to watch Dora?"

Through the soother I heard her response. "Mm-hmm!"

I picked up the remote and turned on the television. As we watched Dora and Boots on their adventure, Olivia snuggled closer and closer to me, eventually resting her head on my shoulder. I put my arm around her. This became our routine for the next several months.

I was able to bond with my children so much while I slowly healed at home. Olivia was well into her toddler phase, and Ben was five. He was still so small and fragile, yet he was the same age I was when I had started receiving the strap. How delicate my children suddenly seemed.

My own childhood had been ripped away from me, so it warmed my heart to now be part of their playtime. They included me in their games and brought me books for us to read. It felt as though my children were teaching me how to be a child.

Watching Ben and Olivia, seeing their excitement and innocence, I wondered how it could be possible for any adult to inflict such harm upon a child. It was clear to me that we really do owe the deepest respect to our children.

There is no doubt about it, the stunt that day was horrific. That day also taught me how easy it was to succumb to pressure to do something I knew was dangerous. But in spite of all that, those months of healing I had at home turned out to be profound bonding moments for me and my children.

Those were my real gravy days.

48
A NEW HOPE

Let's keep a little optimism here.

— Han Solo, *Return of the Jedi*

Instead of being a victim of abuse, I choose to be a survivor. I continued to find lessons within the Star Wars films. The Rebellion against the Empire began as fragmented elements working in isolation. It was only over time, and as their many voices were heard, that the Rebels began to join together in their fight against the Galactic Empire. The Empire itself presented an image of strength as a way to prevent groups from rising up against it. If you can take hope away from the oppressed, then you can control them. If you rule with fear, you can keep potential challengers to your power from speaking up. Though fragmented, the voices are becoming stronger and stronger against the Church. I have a duty as a survivor to speak out so that what happened to me does not happen to future generations of children.

So, I do. Whenever I can, I do.

Seeing the elegant and powerful use of lightsabers when I was a child is the reason that I wanted to learn how to use them. It was one of the main reasons I wanted to be a Jedi. I loved the idea that the lightsaber or sword could create a safe space around the person who held it.

In combat, the safe space is the area around you in which you are protected from attacks. Usually this means you are out of striking distance. Through kendo I learned how powerful a safe space was in order to defend myself. Sometimes avoidance of an attack is all that is necessary. Not every attack requires a counterattack. And in maintaining a safe space, a kendoka is aware of the *go no sen*—the ability to counterstrike from a safe space after avoiding an attack. Essentially, it is best to take the high ground in a fight, physically and morally. I think of it as: to be prepared to fight so I don't have to fight.

As an abuse survivor, I am always aware of my personal space and do my best to maintain a safe distance from everyone I interact with. When I am in restaurants, I sit with my back to the wall in order to avoid people getting too close to me from behind. When I was a teenager, my friends thought it was fun to sneak up on me because I could flip them over me. It was always terrifying to me because my impulse to defend myself was not a game but was coming from a place of self-defence.

I have now taught stage combat to hundreds of acting students and stunt performers—I feel as though I have a natural edge when it comes to doing this. Afterall, I have spent most of my life fighting. Fighting in different ways.

As a child, I was fighting to live. No matter what happened, something guided me to carry on. I believe it was the Force. Martial arts gave me the strength and conditioning I needed to gain the confidence to physically stand up for myself. Having been stabbed and beaten, raped and abused, I have now turned these experiences into lessons for students of combat. I know what it is like to be stabbed. I can explain to an actor what happens to the body when a blade is thrust inside. I know the physical change in a person before they attack. I can teach the unspoken language that is exchanged between people when words fail and before physical aggression begins. I can share with actors the feeling in the body when you make that decision to give up rather than to fight—the excruciating pain from someone forcibly entering you against your will. I know what it is like to have someone force their fingers into your mouth and force your head towards them for oral satisfaction. And I can do this without falling back into the void of my time as a victim.

Time.

Time does not necessarily heal old wounds, but it does leave scars. It places waypoints that remain for the traveller to come back to when they need to. I have used, through years of therapy and martial arts training, my experiences to help me grow as an artist. When I was stabbed, I vowed it was the last time. I have spent the rest of my life continuing to develop my skills as a fighter so I will never be the victim again. I have also been able to share my knowledge of my time as a victim to help actors and students understand the physical and psychological changes in the body and the mind when someone is hurt, raped, or beaten. My power in this, and my ability to teach it safely, comes from my personal knowledge and experience in this area.

The portrayal of the violence is cathartic. I know my work is successful when the actors and stunt people can execute a fight I have developed with the care and attention that helps further the plot, excites and moves the audience, and can be performed with precision every night. I let actors know when I don't believe their reactions. I have a unique ability to blend my in-depth knowledge of stage combat and martial arts with a first-hand experience of violence. I am proud that in my many years of choreographing violence, I have not caused hurt to anyone. Acting is being, and I can now use my past experiences as teaching methodologies for the benefit of the performing arts.

I also wanted to do more to help the less fortunate. But how would I be able to combine my love of Star Wars and my desire to do good? This is where the 501st came in. Vader's Fist.

40

BAD GUYS DOING GOOD

Save the dream!

— Saw Gerrara, *Rogue One*

If you know what the 501st is, you may be asking the question, *Aren't they the bad guys?* The short answer is yes. In the Star Wars universe, the 501st Legion is part of the Empire, and the Empire are the bad guys. On Earth, however, the 501st Legion, is a worldwide club that brings together adults who love Star Wars and costuming. There are also sister clubs, of course: the Rebel Legion, Droid Builders, Mandalorian Mercenaries, and the Saber Guild. I belong to three of these clubs. If I had more time, I would undoubtedly belong to all of them as I am proud of my nerdiness when it comes to all things Star Wars.

It was the 501st that started it all. The founders of the club are Albin Johnson and Tom Crews who created it in 1997. As of me writing this book, there are over thirteen thousand members worldwide. Members must have a screen-accurate villain costume from the Star Wars franchise to be admitted. The guidelines are pretty strict. In addition to uniting Star Wars fans with a passion for replicating screen-accurate costumes, the mandate of the 501st is to contribute to communities through fundraising and charity work. Their motto is *Bad Guys Doing Good*. It is awe-inspiring to see Darth Vader flanked by ten or twenty Imperial Stormtroopers walk past you while 'The Imperial

March' plays. Impressive does not begin to describe the sight or the fan reaction.

As a result of the abuse that I endured as a child, I developed post-traumatic stress disorder (PTSD) and obsessive-compulsive disorder (OCD). My OCD started shortly after I left the Catholic school. It began with obsessively washing my hands, my buttocks, my groin, and making sure anything I drank out of was clear of specks. It became worse over time. To this day I cannot drink out of a glass without inspecting it closely. My OCD also manifests in not being able to leave unfinished jigsaw puzzles alone. I have missed entire evenings because I cannot pull away from an unfinished jigsaw puzzle, and it is for that reason I do not have any in my house. I cannot stop myself. If I spend more than a few minutes in a room with an unfinished puzzle, I will stay to finish it—I therefore cannot have them around me. I know it must sound funny, but there is something about leaving things unfinished that gives me anxiety. This has also manifested in creating historically accurate costuming. If I am unable to faithfully recreate a costume or prop from a particular period of time, I obsess on how to correct it until I am satisfied that it is presentable as a faithful repro-duction. This is both a curse and a blessing. Because of this, my Darth Vader costume took me over two years to complete. I obsessed over every detail of the costume to make it as close to screen-accurate as possible. I was not happy with just *creating* the costume, however.

My former Disney training has also compounded my obsession with screen accuracy. In creating magic, it is important to create not just the image but the entire atmosphere surrounding the character being represented. I like to call it the *actmosphere.*

Creating the proper actmosphere is important to me. If there's one thing that has carried over from my training, it is that the magic created must be believable. There is something powerful in watching your favourite character engage with you in real life. The illusion is powerful. And that is why I find it so unfortunate when people break character in public—they are breaking the illusion. I have seen profes-sional characters stop in a crowd and remove their character's head to say hello to friends, or just to show that they are the ones inside the costume. It disturbs me when I see that behaviour from a masked character in public.

To be representing any iconic character requires study in that character's movement, voice, and attitude. Prior to building my own Vader costume, I observed that other Vader cosplayers were often shorter than I was. Having a Vader shorter than a stormtrooper greatly diminishes the overall reaction from fans—as I am only one inch shorter than David Prowse, the actor who plays Vader in the movies, Vader was the most logical costume for me to build. You may be wondering why I chose to portray a character that is so frightening. It's true that in my childhood Vader terrified me and reminded me of the priests in the school where I was abused. Screen Vader *is* terrifying. Yet, as an adult, I understand that the balance between the dark and the light is important, and that Vader has his role in the balance of the Force.

I decided that I would create a perfect *actmosphere* for my representation of Vader. My Vader would speak. However, much like the Evil Queen in Disneyland, My Vader would have fun with his ominous presence. I added a soundboard that allowed my voice to replicate Vader. I used phrases from the movies such as "This will be a day long remembered" and "Join me, and together we shall rule the galaxy as ..." as well as improvising my own reactions to my engagements with the public. It is important to me to keep the image menacingly fun while also respecting the intellectual property of Disney and Lucasfilm Ltd.

In addition to helping fans create screen-accurate costuming, the 501st raises millions of dollars annually for charitable causes. Some of the local garrisons of the 501st go far beyond the basic levels of charitable fundraising to create lasting magical memories. Bad Guys Doing Good.

I started noticing a young fan and her family at some of the events my Vader attended. We often had events in the largest toy store in British Columbia, Toy Traders. The lineups to take pictures with Darth Vader weaved throughout the store and wait times were always in excess of two hours. Gemma was not hard to miss. She used a specially made wheelchair and was on a constant oxygen supply. I noticed that the owner, Matthew, would make sure Gemma and her family were brought to the front of the line when they arrived. I learned that this was important for her because of her limited portable oxygen supply. Matthew always made exceptions for fans in need.

I soon learned that Gemma's favourite character was Darth Vader. She always arrived dressed in her Vader costume when she came to see the 501st.

"Do you remember me?" she would often ask.

"Of course, I do, Gemma. The Force is strong with you," I would typically respond.

I was asked by my garrison commanding officer if I would do a private appearance for Gemma. She was turning eight years old, and her parents requested a special visit from Lord Vader. Normally we do not attend birthday parties, but I had no problem in saying yes to Gemma's family. I was accompanied by two stormtroopers and, honestly, it was one of the most memorable times I have had. Gemma made a present for Vader, and she kept taking my hand to show me around. Before we left, she made us dance with her to 'Uptown Funk.' Twice.

When we were leaving, one of the children asked me, "Are you going back to the movie now?"

"Yes," I replied. "We are going back to the movie."

The following year I was asked by Gemma's mom if I could help her. Gemma was going to be nine years old, and though she still loved Vader, she wanted to meet Kylo Ren. I was able to line up a stormtrooper, Kylo Ren, and a Tusken Raider. Because Vader was not making an appearance, I was able to attend as a handler since Gemma wouldn't recognize me out of costume. When we arrived, Gemma greeted the Star Wars characters by name, but then looked at me and asked who I was. She wanted my name and wanted to know why I had shown up at her door. I told her I was the Star Wars representative on Earth who helped the characters when they visited this planet. She looked at me for a moment before letting me come in. This time it was not Darth Vader who had to endure the dance party. The stormtrooper,

Kylo, and the Tusken Raider had to dance while I watched. It was wonderful watching my fellow garrison members developing a magical actmosphere for Gemma and her birthday guests. Gemma held Kylo's hand as she moved her wheelchair in time to the music, dancing with her favourite Star Wars guests who were there to celebrate her special day. Even as just a witness to this event, I couldn't help laughing and smiling. The exuberance was infectious.

Bringing the magic to Gemma in her home was incredible. I learned that Gemma was born with a rare, undiagnosed neuromuscular condition. Though she was confined to her wheelchair, the Force was strong with her. I also felt that if I was going to help create magic when I was accompanying costumed characters to events such as Gemma's party, I was going to have to fit in more.

That's when I decided to create an Imperial officer costume. While Imperial officers are portrayed as stern and unsmiling, I decided to take it further but with more flair. I created the character Major Poppins. He is Mary Poppins's brother, and is practically perfect in every way. I also created a Hero of the Galactic Empire medal to present to people like Gemma.

Just like I had promised years earlier in Disneyland, I was still committed to creating magic whenever I could.

In 2018 we inducted Gemma into our local 501st garrison with a big fundraiser and medal ceremony at Toy Traders. We offered special challenge coins and patches to be sold and were able to raise over four thousand dollars for muscular dystrophy research. When I presented Gemma with her medal, she told me that I was her hero. I was not hidden behind a mask, only in my officer costume, and I was taken off guard by her comment. I started to cry but was able to pull myself together and told her she was my hero too.

My love of Star Wars costuming as a professional cosplayer has led me to build other characters within the 501st and our sister club, the Rebel Legion. At the time of writing this, I have two characters in addition to Darth Vader and Major Poppins that I love to cosplay when raising money for well-deserving charities.

I love my Chewbacca costume. It is amazing to see the love that Wookiee gets. People cannot seem to get enough of the walking carpet, and I love engaging people when I am in that incredible costume.

Montgomery Starstalker is my other costume. He is a Rebel pilot from Blue Squad. Monty wears a larger-than-life moustache and saunters around with the wit and banter of a World War II Royal Air Force pilot. He is boisterous and fun—and that is really what this level of cosplaying is all about. I love the excitement these characters bring out in everyone when they appear. It's as close as I can get to living within the Star Wars universe. Every time I am in costume, I truly feel the Force is with me.

So again, I ask, what does a Jedi do when they fail?

Yoda's response is "Do. Or do not." However, I feel that at times there is *Try*. I tried to follow the path to justice. I secured a lawyer. I spoke out and stood up. No one stood up with me aside from my mom and dad. My parents' long-time neighbours made fun of my court case with their friends. I received death threats from zealous Catholics. People were too scared or ashamed to stand with me. My own lawyer talked me out of continuing with the lawsuit.

But I did not give up.

So, is it really failure? When I am drawn into my dark moods, I do think of my pursuit of justice as a failure. It echoes in my head. It consumes me. I look at my life and think of the years I wasted pursuing justice, and I can feel the hate within. But I am not ashamed, for I did stand up. The justice system failed *me*. I do not accept the failure. I continue on. I have learned that there is strength in continuing to speak out and in being a voice for others.

I have spoken at events about my story. Often, I am approached afterwards by people who thank me for what I share. I have had people tell me they are too afraid to do what I do. They tell me that they were abused, but it was "not as bad" as what I had endured. To this I always tell them that it is. It is as bad. Once is too many times. Verbal, physical, mental, sexual abuse is all as bad. Yes, I spent years being tortured—my soul being murdered over and over. My story is very traumatizing for some to hear. But it is not about comparison. I will sit and listen to those who tell me of their stories, and the pain I sense from them is just as powerful as the pain I endure retelling my own story. It is all bad. No one should walk away from any survivor's story comparing degrees of suffering. What we need to do is thank survivors for sharing. Giving voice to our suffering empowers all victims of abuse. I get angry and sad when I hear of others' suffering. Therefore, I am not a pure Jedi. I live in the grey—the overlapping borders between the light and the dark. I would like to think I gravitate to the light, but I am not pure. I was set on a path to the dark side when I was a child. It was my abusers' intentions to make sure I did not find the path to the light—for if I was to dwell in the dark, I would not be a threat. It is hard work striving for the path to the light side of the Force. In the moments where I could turn to the darkness, I feel guided to the light. I've given myself to the Force and it continues to show me the path.

My half sister Melissa stumbled deeper into the darkness. A life of drugs and alcohol abuse has been her way of coping with the horrors of her past. I am fortunate that, for whatever reason, I did not choose that path. Yes, I have been familiar with self-harm and depriving myself of happiness because, at times, I listen to the voices that tell me I am not worthy. Yet, I know I am. I know we are all worthy of love and acceptance. We are all surrounded by the Force, and it will guide us if we trust in it.

The 501st has continued to bring me much happiness. During the COVID-19 pandemic, I began going on ten-kilometre walks in a Star Wars costume every Friday during the lockdown. The first time I did so, I was worried people driving by were going to have accidents as they stopped to photograph Chewbacca. Residents of my neighbourhood posted their pictures of the "Star Wars Guy" walking around their neighbourhood. One TikTok member has received over two million views posting his encounter with me while on that walk.

Rebecca found it infuriating to be out with me on long costumed walks like this, because it meant that she had to buy into the actmosphere—engaging not with Nic but with Chewbacca. When Chewbacca is walking down the road and people stop to ask for pictures, does Chewie speak? Of course, he does, but it's in Shyriiwook. Imagine if a child was to hear Chewbacca suddenly complain in English that the mask was too hot, or if he suddenly swore. The magic would die. It must not die. You never know who is watching or how impactful the magic can be. That is what I love about the power of the Force and the magic of representing Star Wars characters in public.

After the first week, people wondered if the "Star Wars Guy" would be out again. And I was. It became a thing. The local paper reported it, and as I walked people would stop and thank me for what I was doing. People enjoyed the hope that I was providing. Hope. A new hope in troubling times. People started driving around the route at the time I normally would be out. They wanted to see me. Here I was, a grown man in a Star Wars costume walking around—and people wanted to see it. It made them smile. It also made *me* happy to see that the message of hope within *Star Wars* is still as powerful today as it was in 1977.

As a Rebel Legion and 501st member, I have seen firsthand the effect we have when a group of us show up in a hospital ward for a special visit. There is an energy that happens that is contagious and magical. Patients young and old love the interaction they have with us, and you can see—momentarily—their pain and suffering disappear as they spend a moment with us. For some, this is their last magical memory as they end their time on this earth. Magic is so important.

50
JEDI SCHOOL DROPOUT

*Oh, no, my young Jedi. You will find
that it is you who are mistaken ...
about a great many things.*

— Emperor Palpatine,
Return of the Jedi

Years of having been beaten, raped, and bullied could have led me toward following a path to the dark side. To be able to inflict pain and misery on another both fascinates and terrifies me. Why do some people strive to keep others down? There must be some benefit that perpetuates such abuse to continue. I eventually learned that neither the light side nor dark side are free of challenge. Knowing when to strike and when to walk away from a fight can make the difference between death and survival.

If you were to meet me, you might initially feel intimidated by my stature. I am tall and strong. I tower over most people. Yet, inside this shell of a man lives the child who was not allowed to play freely and experience childhood the way it is depicted in stories. I have had to look over my shoulder most of my life to avoid danger. After completing my PhD and working as a university professor, you might conclude that things turned out great and all is well. However, for the Jedi, vigilance is key to survival.

In 2011 I became a member of the regular faculty at a local university. The faculty appeared to be pleasant, and the students were fantastic. I was hired to teach improvisation, acting, and stage combat; but my PhD also qualified me to teach theatre history. Things were looking good. The senior administrator of the theatre department, Sam, would assign the workload each year. Although there might be the occasional question as to whether I would prefer one class over another, he was in control of what, and how much, I was to teach. Sam had applied for the same position I had been hired for, but his lack of teaching qualifications precluded him from being able to competently instruct in those areas.

Sam had been a behemoth in the film industry. He was feared by many, as it was believed he could make or break their careers. He was used to getting his way. Unfortunately for me, he had decided I was his rival and spent the years following my hiring calculating how he could step over me. Sam had underestimated me.

My failure in seeking justice had made me stronger. My emotions were more in my control. I discovered that Sam was strategically plotting a way to remove me from the university in order to benefit his advancement, and so I challenged him and his leadership.

"If you don't like it, why don't you run against me?" he scoffed.

His position as senior administrator and department coordinator were both up for re-election, but no one dared run against him.

"I think I will, Sam," I retorted.

"Nic, I am going to request you be underloaded next term," he sneered as he threw a printout of the faculty workload on my desk. He continued, "I am going to be surpassing you in seniority, and there aren't enough courses to go around." He was gleeful.

"What if I were to beat you in the election?" I asked.

"I have been the coordinator for years. That's never going to happen."

He confidently strode out of my office, and I could swear I heard him snickering. By now I had two children, and I was not going to let another bully have his way with me. I could feel the anger and fear within me. I sat back in my chair and closed my eyes.

Breathe.

I thought of Yoda training Luke.

Control, control. You must learn control.

The warrior within me wanted to lash out. I knew I could not. I needed to strategize. Sam was convinced that he had his coordinator and chair positions solidly entrenched. I reached out to the voting faculty and ran on a platform of change and hope.

Sam was shocked when I beat him in both elections. The votes were not even close. Sam—who had intimidated, bullied, and coerced faculty to achieve his goals—had lost to me. Unable to deal with his defeat, Sam left the university. He also left a mess for me to clean up.

I was soon asked to track funds he had loaned to two other faculty members to make a research trip outside the country. It was my duty to ask for those funds to be returned to the department. Cordially, I emailed the two parties asking for more information on the funds and the terms of the repayment to the department. I was barely two months into my new position when I would be challenged once more.

The entire faculty knew of my history of being an abuse survivor. I made it a policy to keep my office door open at all times—both for the comfort of my students as well as for my own. The offices in that area were quite small and claustrophobic. My office was narrow with the door at one end and a window at the other, while the width of the room itself was only eight feet wide and barely twelve feet long. As an abuse survivor, I felt much more comfortable not being confined in a small space—and as a teacher now myself, I always wanted my students to feel safe.

I arrived at the office early in the morning to prepare for more cleaning up of the mess Sam had left for me. I opened the door, turned on the light, and put down my tea. Less than five minutes had lapsed when there was a gentle knock on the door. It was Donny—one of the faculty members I had emailed about the missing funds.

"Can I speak with you for a minute?" he whispered.

"Sure, come on in," I said looking up from my desk towards him.

I felt uneasy when Donny slipped in, closing the door behind himself.

"You're harassing me," he said as he took a step towards me in the small office.

"What?" I pushed myself back from my desk.

"You're harassing me," he calmly said again, taking another step closer.

I stood up, the warrior in me assessing the threat. Donny was well aware of what I had endured as a child and up until now had respected my boundaries and open-door policies. The way he had entered my office, shut the door, and then blocked my potential escape was clearly a tactic to pressure me into action. It worked. My breathing became shallow as I saw myself trapped. He, too, was a larger man, standing almost as tall as me. I could not get past him without having to shove him aside. I could not climb out the closed window behind me. I felt like Han, Luke, Leia, and Chewbacca must have when trapped inside the Death Star's trash compactor. I had a bad feeling about this.

"Back off, Donny," I said, taking a step away from him.

"You're harassing me, and I am going to report you to the dean," he threatened as he took yet another step towards me, now getting within my personal space.

"Stop it! Back off. I mean it!" I shouted.

"Or what? What are you going to do? What are you going to do, huh?" He was now only a foot away from me, backing me against the window of my office. I could hear Emperor Palpatine's voice in my head.

Use your aggressive feelings, boy. Let the hate flow through you.

"Get out!" I shouted at him.

He smiled at me. Once again, I could hear Palpatine's voice.

Strike me down.

I wanted to hit him. I could have. I was close enough. Yet I heard Yoda once more.

Control, control. You must learn control.

Donny poked his index finger hard into my chest in an attempt to provoke me.

I stepped to the side and behind the chair, putting it in between Donny and me.

"Get the fuck out of my office! Now!" I started to cry.

He looked shocked and puzzled. This was not the reaction he was hoping for. He backed up to the door and left. I slammed the door shut and locked it from the inside, collapsing from the rush of adrenalin and emotion. My instinct was to hit him, and I am sure that's what he was hoping for. If I had struck him, I would have been immediately fired. I am sure he must have calculated that as a stunt performer and fight director my instinct would be to hit him. My sudden emotional outburst was likely not what he was expecting.

I was trembling and did not feel safe. I had to get out. Memories immediately flooded back to me—being trapped in the office with Ignatious, being raped by Vitus. I was the victim then, but I was a survivor now. I grabbed my jacket and closed the door, writing *I QUIT* on the whiteboard as I ran out of the building to the safety of my car. I didn't know where I was going, but I had to leave. Reaching into my glovebox, I pulled out my R2-D2 action figure—the one my mother had bought me. His silver dome, pitted with years of companionship, gave me some calm. I had only been in my car for a minute when human resources called me.

"I quit," I cried into the phone.

"No, Nic, you aren't quitting. You are just going on leave," they reasoned with me. "Are you going to be okay?"

"I don't know," I cried—a combination of embarrassment and anger.

I didn't know where to go. I drove to my doctor's office and asked the receptionist if I could see him. She took one look at me and though he was booked solid, I was in his office within minutes. I explained, through tears, what happened. He commended me on my strength and control.

Donny lodged a complaint of assault against me. I also filed a complaint of harassment against him. He had been close allies with Sam, who I had overcome in the recent election, and I felt Donny was purposefully provoking me in my office to cause me to lash out and hit him. That would have immediately removed me as a threat to him and the unpaid funds he had. When I was asked for a statement from the arbitrator, she warned me that if I was found guilty, I would be fired. I told her that I had no problem with that as I was not the attacker, so I knew I could not be found guilty. The Force was going to be on my side. I told the arbitrator that I would not return to work until I was emotionally ready, and that I would not step foot on that campus until Donny was gone. The arbitrator was to meet with Donny to hear his version of events; however, Donny refused to meet with her. When Donny was informed that if he was found guilty, he would be fired, he instead chose to retire immediately.

I stood up for myself and insisted on not returning until I was emotionally ready. Instead of retreating into my fear and anger, I stood my ground and took care of myself. My doctor told me this was a sign of great strength. He knew all about my past, and he often told me that I was a Jedi. He told me that I had demonstrated a Jedi's wisdom in how I had handled the attack in my office.

It took me almost two years to return to work. When I did, the entire atmosphere had changed. The caustic atmosphere Sam and Donny had created amongst both faculty and students had been cleared. I learned that one of the other instructors also had several grievances against Donny, and she thanked me for "throwing myself on the grenade" to save the department.

My strong stance was important for me and for the department. I believe that is when I finally crossed the threshold from being a Padawan of the Force to a Jedi Warrior. I stood up for myself, protected my allies and my family, and did what was right for the child inside me. I proved to myself that I could stand up and fight when I needed to. It was one of the hardest things I have done in my adult life, and one of the most rewarding.

51
REMNANTS

Luminous beings are we,
not this crude matter.

— Yoda,
The Empire Strikes Back

Back in 2002, Rebecca and I were blessed by the birth of our son, Benjamin. I had done many years of healing and thought I would be ready for fatherhood. Then, one day, I bought a house. How does that happen? Children. Houses. Life. With the acquisition of property came the inevitable visit from my parents to see the new home, and with them came the remnants of my childhood life. Boxes of my childhood treasures—the comics, the toys, and my Star Wars artefacts were brought down to my new home. I had a special place where I decided to store my Star Wars toys. I glimpsed at the boxes and put them away quickly, as my toddler son was very curious about new boxes. Boxes could be easily destroyed if there were prizes within. Like many Star Wars fathers, I regarded my childhood toys with perhaps a little too much reverence.

Safely out of reach from young hands they remained.

Until that one day ...

I decided to clean up some of the clutter that had accumulated in my office. As I was picking up some old scripts off a shelf, one of the Star Wars boxes caught my eye. It was the box containing my AT-AT from *The Empire Strikes Back*. Something was different about it. I had not paid attention to the condition of the boxes when they arrived, and I especially had not noticed the way in which the boxes—all of them—had been sealed. Instead of the clear magic tape I had carefully and meticulously used to seal each and every box after making sure the toys were properly stored, I noticed they had all been re-sealed with a brown two-inch carpet tape. This was an alteration I had not made. I stopped what I was doing and took down my AT-AT. Perhaps nosy people had peered in to see what the boxes contained.

Perhaps.

I found a box cutter and carefully cut the crinkled carpet tape to open the box with a surgeon's care. The brown carpet tape had been hastily applied to the box and I could see that it had been removed and reapplied causing damage to the pictures on the boxes that I had so carefully packed away years before. This was not my doing.

I have a bad feeling about this, I thought to myself as I finished my incision. I cautiously opened the flap, pulled out the plastic insert and peered inside. My face became hot and for a moment it felt as if I had forgotten how to breathe. My precious toy had been replaced with a number of wooden cut-ends—the useless pieces of wood that accumulate on the floor of a shop and usually get swept away with the sawdust. I felt sick to my stomach. Box after box showed the brown tape, and box after box contained not one toy—instead being stuffed with the bits of wood. My toys were gone. It slowly dawned on me that my childhood place of worship had been sacked.

I called my parents and told them what I had found. I was upset and angry that my personal property had been stolen. They were all gone forever. Ripped away from me. My personal church was robbed of the icons that had made it so important and special to me.

It turns out that Melissa, her boyfriend, and her son had gone into my parents' garage when they had been away on business. They had taken it upon themselves to not only steal my toys, but to avoid suspicion by making sure the boxes remained. They even went so far as to replace the contents with the scraps of wood to make the boxes feel as though they were untouched. It was the brown tape that gave it all away. I was angry with them and felt betrayed. My property was gone. The only remnant I had of my childhood toys was my R2-D2, which I had kept with me (and is in my coat pocket as I write this now).

Deep inside I like to think that perhaps the toys she stole and the money she took for those things helped her in some way. After all, though I attached so much meaning to them, they were only pieces of shaped plastic. Maybe, even if only for a minute, she was able to get a breath of peace before returning to her nightmare. I hope that maybe one day there will be a realization within her—an awakening. Her adopted lifestyle, as a way of coping from the abuse, has now become a generational spiral through her children and, in turn, through theirs. At times I light candles for them—hoping in some way the light of the flame will glimmer within them all. It's a faint hope, but hope, nevertheless.

I pray that the Force be with them. One day, perhaps, they will see the light side or the balance between the light and the dark. As I learned watching *Return of the Jedi*, it is never too late to want to change. Vader redeemed himself at the end of his life and turned to the light. As I continue to see the beauty of the light within my family and the light within my mother, I hope that one day, so too will Melissa and her family see that light within themselves.

As a survivor of abuse, I was terrified that I would fail my son. Ben has grown up in a home where he has witnessed my ups and downs, my triumphs and my failings. At the time of writing this, he is a teenager. He is an incredibly intelligent young man, finally finding the balance between the light and the dark as he continues to grow. But it seems to me that he may have inherited some of the demons that continue to haunt me. He experienced bouts of darkness in his early teenage years, during which he spoke of suicide and self-harm. Now, on the precipice of his adult life, he has finally started to flourish in his ambitions and his personal life. In the years that he was unable to find a path to loving himself, I blamed myself—and, to a larger extent, I continue to blame the Church. During my children's formative years, they witnessed my struggles with justice and the depression resulting from my failed attempts. My self-guilt and self-loathing affected me as "Dad," and though I tried to be the role model for them as my dad was for me, I know I have been flawed.

As much as I admire Luke Skywalker, I cannot live up to the heroism he embodies. Luke chose a path to the light. I continue to find myself in the grey. A grey Jedi is a Jedi who lives on the line between the light and the dark side of the Force. I find myself at times turning to the dark side, and at other times turning to the light. I am a continual work in progress. The Force is strong in my family. I believe in it whole-heartedly. Yet, day to day I find myself waking up not knowing which path I will start upon. I want to be good. I try to be. Each morning I shave across the scar I was given when Ignatious tried to kill me. It brings me back. My son's anger brings me back to the teenage years I endured when I was lost and searching for meaning. *Star Wars* was my saviour. What will be his? I am not devoid of anger, fear, and aggression. I try to maintain control of these emotions when they come up. It would be so easy to give in to the hate that surrounds me. I sometimes worry that it is a losing battle, that eventually the light will turn to eternal darkness. But I have hope. Hope is what allows me to carry on. I see the good in my son. I see it in my family. I see it and sense it in me.

When I watched *The Force Awakens,* I cried watching Han Solo confront his son, Ben. Han, despite the evil his son embodied, saw the light and the love within his son. I see that too. Han sacrificed himself to help save his child. I, and any loving parent, would do the same. I have watched that scene over and over, and I know I would do it in a heartbeat.

Melissa has had children, yet she did not raise them. She tried, yet two were taken away and two were raised by one of her partners. I truly believe the dysfunction and inability to provide for her children are a direct result of the abuse she has not been able to heal from. She and I have dealt with the aftereffects of abuse in vastly different ways. Though she is related to me, I cannot relate to her. I can only wish her well and forgive her for what she has done to hurt me in the past. I know it is not entirely her doing but largely the result of years of abuse.

Life has granted me many opportunities. I have accepted some and shied away from others. I live in a continual state of past and present. My daily experiences are linked to the tumultuous events of my youth. I try not to think about what happened back then; however, I cannot forget either—for the events of the past have shaped me. The lens through which I view the world has been skewed. I struggle with trust. I struggle with opening up to others for fear of being hurt. These are the scars of the past that continue to weigh upon my mind on an almost daily basis.

My goal is to live in the present only and to not dwell on the past. I am working towards creating peace within. My past is my past. It is the map of who I am. It shows where I have been and where I currently exist. The path I have taken, dangerous as it has been, is one that has made me who I am. I am a child of the Force. The Force is what guides my every move. It is an energy field binding me and all living entities together. My experiences may not have been the fondest, and the lessons I carry are heavy. My story is not one that is easy to share, but what I have to share is important. Change begins with one soul, one voice. The faintest cry is heard if it is sustained. While there are those who would wish me to stop telling my story, my belief in what is right and what is just prevents my silence.

We, as a society, have a duty to listen to our elders and our children. Children come into this world vulnerable and dependent upon adults to protect and guide them. We owe children the respect and dignity to be listened to. We need to hear them—truly hear them. Every person has a voice, and every person has a right to be heard. All too often throughout history, voices have been silenced. I have heard people say to me "but you are only one person," and indeed I am. Over time I have started to hear more voices speaking out against the horrendous abuse by the Catholic Church. Every day new voices are daring to speak up and out. I hope this continues. I hope that one day the multitude of voices will be strong enough to blast through the walls of injustice. The abuse of one child is too much. The time has come for people to stand beside survivors and let them know they are not alone any longer. One day justice will come. Truth will win. Balance will return to the Force. As humans, it is our destiny.

May the Force be with us, everyone.

EPILOGUE

Confronting fear is the destiny of a Jedi. Your destiny.

— Luke Skywalker,
The Rise of Skywalker

I deal with the aftereffects of abuse on a daily basis. As a sexual abuse survivor, I have difficulty being naked in front of other people. This makes it very awkward in changing rooms and at the doctor's office. I cannot open my mouth for long periods without gagging, and this is very difficult in dentist chairs. I obsess about washing my hands, keeping my breath fresh, and washing my clothes. I cannot sit with my back to others in restaurants. I have difficulty with navigating personal space in social situations and always end up stepping away from people rather than getting close to them. This really does make saying goodbye to people very awkward. As a result, new acquaintances and colleagues often think of me as snobbish. I am rarely found at cast parties or other events. It has made my networking very difficult. In short, it sucks.

Having lived in both the light and the dark side of the Force has allowed me to create a unique balance within. There are many positives to come out of what has happened in my past. It has forced me to learn how to defend myself. It has given me the opportunity to be able to look people in the eyes and to not back down. My martial arts training has provided me with much more confidence than I would have had without it. The Star Wars films have provided me with spiritual guidance. I believe in the Force. I believe in all living things. I believe in balance and that we come together to learn from each other. I also believe that the Force has helped me navigate difficult obstacles in my life. The Force is my ally. When I stop and breathe and see the life around me, I see that there is so much more than me. I see the joy in the young and in the old. I feel we are all connected, and that balance is key to us finding our way. I believe it was the balance in the Force and the lessons of Yoda and Obi-Wan that helped me stay on the path between the light and the dark, and I believe the Force has made me stronger as a survivor. *Star Wars* has given me the strength to speak out against the evils of abuse. For these things I am thankful. The Force continues to be my ally, and a powerful ally it is. As long as I have the Force as my guide, I know I will continue to appreciate life and the delicate balance between the light and the dark inside each of us.

Did I overcome my abuse? No. I don't believe anyone can. Like a physical scar, it will always be a part of me—like the gold bonds of the Japanese practice of kintsugi. We survivors of abuse are all connected by our common horrible experience. When we have the strength to grow from victim to survivor, we are linked by a shared experience that strengthens our resolve. I hope that the relative number of people who have suffered abuse is small compared to the world's population, because I would hate to know of such momentous suffering. I speak out on behalf of those who cannot. I want all survivors to know that I am their ally. I continue to heal and grow—not only for me, but for them. I am never shy to share and show my scars of abuse. I often think of the final message Obi-Wan sends out to the surviving Jedi in the animated series *Rebels*:

> *This is Master Obi-Wan Kenobi. I regret to report that both our Jedi Order and the Republic have fallen, with a dark shadow of the Empire rising to take their place. This message is a warning and a reminder for any surviving Jedi: Trust in the Force. Do not return to the Temple. That time has passed, and our future is uncertain. We will each be challenged. Our trust. Our*

faith. Our friendships. But we must persevere. And in time, a new hope will emerge. May the Force be with you. Always.

I spent most of the COVID-19 pandemic finishing the book you have just read. Collette, my editor, has been most generous with her time throughout this experience. By September 2020, we were wrapping up the loose ends and preparing the book to be printed. It was done. It was time to move on and to finally let go of my attempts for legal justice.

Then it happened. As Obi-Wan's holocron message predicted, "... a new hope will emerge."

It did.

I received a message from a friend of mine who told me about a lawyer who may be interested in taking over my case. She was aware of my increasing frustration of not being heard.

My lawyer had done her best to represent me and my case, but taking on the Catholic Church seemed much like trying to find the weakness hidden in the Death Star plans. From time to time I had asked if there was more we could do, but although she had worked hard to find me justice, there seemed to be no options available to us. Eventually, I stopped asking for help.

I lost hope.

My case sat dormant for fourteen years.

But times were changing. More people were coming forward and sharing their stories about abuse. And then, after having accepted defeat for so long, I met with this new lawyer. And she agreed to renew my fight against the Church.

A new hope.

Much has changed since I first attempted to hold the Church accountable. In *A New Hope,* Leia warns Moff Tarkin that the more the Empire tried to suppress insurrection and rebellion, the more civilizations would rise up against the tyranny. In the past fourteen years, so much has come out about how the Church has tried to crush, demean, discredit, and silence survivors who dared to speak out. The more they have tried to silence survivors like me, the more voices have spoken out, shattering the silence with a force that demands to be heard. I may have started my fight years ago, but it is far from over. I am so thankful that an ally has joined me in my rebellion against the Catholic Empire. I am discovering a new balance of the Force within me. I have heeded Obi-Wan's message, "... we must persevere."

I don't know what the outcome of my case will be. I know I am doing the right thing for myself—for the child who still lives inside me. I am continuing my rebellion for the many children who are suffering within the shells of the adults they have become. It is time for us to be heard and to let the healing continue. We are survivors. We are Jedi. It is our duty to persevere for the greater good of the universe. As Jynn Erso says to her fellow Rogue One warriors, "We have hope. Rebellions are built on hope."

Hope.

It is my hope that you who have picked up this book will find the inspiration to speak out against abuse. If you are a victim of abuse, I want you to become a survivor. If you are a survivor, I encourage you to become a Jedi. "Trust in the Force" and know that while our faith and friendships are constantly challenged, as long as we believe in the Force we will persevere. This is my Safe Space. The Force is with me. May it help you find your balance as it has helped me find mine.

Safe Space

ACKNOWLEDGEMENTS

This book has been years in the making. I have had countless conversations with people about my fears and excitement in putting my story to paper. If you were one of those people, I thank you. Those conversations challenged me and inspired me, frightened me and reassured me. Each conversation brought me a step closer to finishing this book that is now in your hands. And for that, I can never thank you enough.

I want to thank Rebecca Harrison, who has seen the best in me when I could not. Her belief in me has helped steer me through the most difficult times in my adulthood.

My children, Ben and Olivia, mean the world to me. Family is important, and I truly feel the Force is strong with my family. I thank them for giving me the space to work from home and for their understanding in the importance of this work to me.

To my mom and dad, whom I love dearly. They supported me in my ongoing attempts to speak out against abuse, even as it affected them in their work and social standings within the small town where I was abused.

This book's origin began when I wrote a paper for my PhD advisor, Jerry Wasserman. His enthusiasm gave me the courage to initially tell my story. Ken Hollands read my paper and encouraged me to create a play on this subject: *How Star Wars Saved My Life*. He also put me in touch with Valerie Methot who became the dramaturg and director. Elyse Maloway helped me keep my sanity in rehearsals, and I want to thank them and the entire creative team for making this story come to life in Vancouver in December of 2017.

I would also like to thank my therapist, Carol Spencer, to whom I first came out about the abuse I endured. Mental health and therapy are so important to survivors of abuse. To that end, I wish to also thank my current therapist, Noa Rabin, and my doctor, Johannes van Eeden, for their ongoing support through the years in helping me navigate this world as a survivor.

Thank you to my fellow Star Wars cosplay enthusiasts within the 501st and the Rebel Legion for helping me express my love of Star Wars in positive ways that benefit the many great charities we help raise money for.

No work like this happens on its own. The tireless efforts of a great editing team must not be forgotten. Collette Berg has taken on a huge task in the editing of this book. Thank you, Collette, for making this book even stronger through your careful eye and attention to detail. I am thankful you did not fall asleep during our coffee meetings as the book took shape.

To Ian Boothby and Pia Guerra, thank you. Ian, you gave me the great title for the book: *Safe Space*. Pia, your talents as an artist are incredible. Thank you for designing the book cover. I am so humbled by your generosity.

I am thankful for the many organizations out there that help survivors who have experienced abuse and, specifically in my case, abuse by priests. The Survivors Network of those Abused by Priests (SNAP) has been an invaluable resource to me. Leona Huggins, my local representative for SNAP, deserves thanks for her tireless efforts to assist those of us who dare to stand up for justice. In 2020, Leona introduced me to Sandra Kovacs, a lawyer. I want to thank Sandra for meeting with me and for providing the child within me a new hope that I may one day see justice for the horrors I endured from kindergarten through grade four and the ongoing effects of surviving such trauma since my escape from that school. I am thankful for the chance to dream of justice once more.

George Lucas, thank you for creating the amazing universe for this boy to play in when he believed all hope was lost. *Star Wars* means the world to me. I shudder to think how different my life would have been without the story of Skywalker and his comrades to help me through the darkest of times.

Finally, I would like to thank you, the reader, for picking up this book and giving it a chance. Victims of abuse need to share their stories. We can all learn from those who have suffered. I believe that sharing stories of abuse and survival, shedding light on the effects such events have on the life of a child, can help bring an end to such atrocities and make the world a better place. I will always speak out about abuse. May the Force be with you as it is with me.

I have spoken.

STAR WARS REFERENCES

Throughout this book, I have made countless references to Star Wars films and the universe George Lucas created. Although this book is not affiliated with George Lucas, Lucasfilm Ltd., or The Walt Disney Company, I am forever grateful for the existence of their films, and I acknowledge that the intellectual property of these films and the entire Star Wars universe belongs to them.

Star Wars: Episode IV A New Hope. 1977. [film]
Directed by G. Lucas. United States: 20th Century Fox.

Star Wars: Episode V The Empire Strikes Back. 1980. [film]
Directed by I. Kershner. United States: 20th Century Fox.

Star Wars: Episode VI Return of the Jedi. 1983. [film]
Directed by R. Marquand. United States: 20th Century Fox.

Star Wars: Episode I The Phantom Menace. 1999. [film]
Directed by G. Lucas. United States: 20th Century Fox.

Star Wars: Episode II Attack of the Clones. 2002. [film]
Directed by G. Lucas. United States: 20th Century Fox.

Star Wars: Episode III Revenge of the Sith. 2005. [film]
Directed by G. Lucas. United States: 20th Century Fox.

*Star Wars: Episode VII The Force Awakens. 2015. [film]
Directed by J. J. Abrams. United States: Walt Disney Studios
Motion Pictures.*

*Star Wars: Episode VIII The Last Jedi. 2017. [film]
Directed by R. Johnson. United States: Walt Disney Studios
Motion Pictures.*

*Star Wars: Episode IX The Rise of Skywalker. 2019. [film]
Directed by J. J. Abrams. United States: Walt Disney Studios
Motion Pictures.*

*Rogue One. 2016. [film]
Directed by G. Edwards. United States: Walt Disney Studios
Motion Pictures.*

*Solo: A Star Wars Story. 2018. [film]
Directed by R. Howard. United States: Walt Disney Studios
Motion Pictures.*

*Volpe, Giancarlo, dir. "The Zillo Beast." Clone Wars, season 2, episode
18, Cartoon Network, 2010.*

*Lee, Steward, and Steven G. Lee, dirs. "Spark of Rebellion."
Star Wars Rebels, season 1, episode 1 and 2, Lucasfilm
Animation, 2014.*

NOTES

INTRODUCTION

Bloch, Ernst (1923, 2000). *The Spirit of Utopia*. Stanford: Stanford University Press.

Bourdieu, Pierre (1984). *Distinction: A Social Critique of the Judgment of Taste*. Cambridge (Mass.): Harvard University Press.

Jenkins, Henry (1992). *Textual Poachers: Television Fans and Participatory Culture*. New York: Routledge.

Mathijs, Ernest (2008). *The Cinema of David Cronenberg: From Baron of Blood to Cultural Hero*. London-New York: Wallflower Press/Columbia University Press.

Phinney, Alison (2018). "Self, Lost and Found," in Philippe Tortell, Mark Turin and Margot Young (eds.), *Memory*. Vancouver: UBC Press, 243-251.

Spigel, Lynn and Henry Jenkins (1991). "Same Bat Channel, Different Bat Times," in Roberta Pearson and William Uricchio (eds), *Many Lives of Batman: Critical Approaches to a Superhero and His Media*. New York: Routledge, 117-148.

Staiger, Janet (2000). *Media Reception Studies*. New York: NYU Press.

PROLOGUE

"A long time ago in a galaxy far, far away ...": *Star Wars: Episode IV A New Hope*. 1977. [film] Directed by G. Lucas. United States: 20th Century Fox.

CHAPTER 1: BEGINNINGS

"If there's a bright centre to the universe, you're on the planet that it's farthest from.": *Star Wars: Episode IV A New Hope*. 1977. [film] Directed by G. Lucas. United States: 20th Century Fox.

CHAPTER 2: FAMILY

"Luke's just not a farmer, Owen. He has too much of his father in him ...": *Star Wars: Episode IV A New Hope.* 1977. [film] Directed by G. Lucas. United States: 20th Century Fox.

"It is an energy field created by all living things. It surrounds us and penetrates us. It binds the galaxy together": *Star Wars: Episode IV A New Hope.* 1977. [film] Directed by G. Lucas. United States: 20th Century Fox.

CHAPTER 3: MEMORIES

"The belonging you seek is not behind you. It is ahead": *Star Wars: Episode VII The Force Awakens.* 2015. [film] Directed by J. J. Abrams. United States: Walt Disney Studios Motion Pictures.

"Mister Trouble never hangs around
When he hears this mighty sound.
"Here I come to save the day"
That means that Mighty Mouse is on the way.
Yes sir, when there is wrong to right
Mighty Mouse will join the fight.
On the sea or on the land
He gets the situation well in hand":

Marshall Barer & Philip A. Scheib. "Mighty Mouse Theme (Here I Come to Save the Day)." Terrytoons cartoons. Copyright: 1944 [under investigation].

CHAPTER 4: AND SO, TO SCHOOL

"Truly wonderful, the mind of a child is": *Star Wars: Episode II Attack of the Clones.* 2002. [film] Directed by G. Lucas. United States: 20th Century Fox.

CHAPTER 5: FATHER VITUS

"I need someone to show me my place in all this": *Star Wars: Episode VIII The Last Jedi.* 2017. [film] Directed by R. Johnson. United States: Walt Disney Studios Motion Pictures.

CHAPTER 6: FLYING

"I'm going to be a pilot. Best in the galaxy": *Solo: A Star Wars Story.* [film] Directed by R. Howard. 2018. United States: Walt Disney Studios Motion Pictures.

CHAPTER 7: THE WRATH OF IGNATIOUS

"Let me give you some advice. Assume everyone will betray you, and you'll never be disappointed": *Solo: A Star Wars Story.* 2018. [film] Directed by R. Howard. United States: Walt Disney Studios Motion Pictures.

CHAPTER 8: SURVIVING THE STRAP

"In a dark place we find ourselves ... a little more knowledge might light our way": *Star Wars: Episode III Revenge of the Sith.* 2005. [film] Directed by G. Lucas. United States: 20th Century Fox.

CHAPTER 9: GROOMING

"It's a trap!": *Star Wars: Episode VI Return of the Jedi.* 1983. [film] Directed by R. Marquand. United States: 20th Century Fox.

"In Dublin's fair city,
Where the girls are so pretty
I first set my eyes on sweet Molly Malone ...":

James Yorkston. "Molly Malone." Edinburgh, 1883.

CHAPTER 10: WINTER IS COMING

"R2 says that the chances of survival are seven hundred seventy-five ... to one. Actually, R2 has been known to make mistakes ... from time to time": *Star Wars: Episode V The Empire Strikes Back.* 1980. [film] Directed by I. Kershner. United States: 20th Century Fox.

CHAPTER 11: TAKING SHOTS AND GETTING SKUNKED

"He was the best star pilot in the galaxy, and a cunning warrior ... And he was a good friend": *Star Wars: Episode IV A New Hope*. 1977. [film] Directed by G. Lucas. United States: 20th Century Fox.

CHAPTER 12: WINTER HAS COME

"If once you start down the dark path, forever will it dominate your destiny ...": *Star Wars: Episode V The Empire Strikes Back*. 1980. [film] Directed by I. Kershner. United States: 20th Century Fox.

CHAPTER 13: MISERABLE MEMORIES

"Fear leads to anger ... anger leads to hate ... hate leads to suffering": *Star Wars: Episode I The Phantom Menace*. 1999. [film] Directed by G. Lucas. United States: 20th Century Fox.

CHAPTER 14: MORE CHOCOLATE, FAT BOY?

"It's not a problem if you don't look up": *Rogue One*. 2016. [film] Directed by G. Edwards. United States: Walt Disney Studios Motion Pictures.

CHAPTER 15: MUSIC, THE FOOD OF LOVE

"I felt a great disturbance in the Force ... as if millions of voices suddenly cried out in terror and were suddenly silenced. I fear something terrible has happened": *Star Wars: Episode IV A New Hope*. 1977. [film] Directed by G. Lucas. United States: 20th Century Fox.

"She died of a fever
And sure, no one could save her
And that was the end of sweet Molly Malone ...":

James Yorkston. "Molly Malone." Edinburgh, 1883.

CHAPTER 16: THE HOLY TRINITY OF TERROR

"We seem to be made to suffer. It's our lot in life": *Star Wars: Episode IV A New Hope.* 1977. [film] Directed by G. Lucas. United States: 20th Century Fox.

"And now, Your Highness, we will discuss the location of your hidden Rebel base": *Star Wars: Episode IV A New Hope.* 1977. [film] Directed by G. Lucas. United States: 20th Century Fox.

CHAPTER 17: THE ART OF PRECIOUS SCARS

"The Force is strong with this one": *Star Wars: Episode IV A New Hope.* 1977. [film] Directed by G. Lucas. United States: 20th Century Fox.

CHAPTER 18: MRS. REED

"We're doomed": *Star Wars: Episode IV A New Hope.* 1977. [film] Directed by G. Lucas. United States: 20th Century Fox.

CHAPTER 19: MOM

"Mom ... you said that the biggest problem in the universe is no one helps each other": *Star Wars: Episode I The Phantom Menace.* 1999. [film] Directed by G. Lucas. United States: 20th Century Fox.

CHAPTER 20: NEW KID ON THE BLOCK

"Confronting fear is the destiny of a Jedi": *Star Wars: Episode IX The Rise of Skywalker.* 2019. [film] Directed by J. J. Abrams. United States: Walt Disney Studios Motion Pictures.

CHAPTER 21: FEED ME

"You look absolutely beautiful": *Star Wars: Episode V The Empire Strikes Back.* 1980. [film] Directed by I. Kershner. United States: 20th Century Fox.

CHAPTER 22: OF BRONCOS AND EAGLES

"Get your head out of your cockpit": *Star Wars: Episode VIII The Last Jedi.* 2017. [film] Directed by R. Johnson. United States: Walt Disney Studios Motion Pictures.

CHAPTER 23: SMOKEY AND THE TRASH CAN

"This is not going to go the way you think": *Star Wars: Episode VIII The Last Jedi.* 2017. [film] Directed by R. Johnson. United States: Walt Disney Studios Motion Pictures.

"A long time ago in a galaxy far, far away ... STAR WARS": *Star Wars: Episode IV A New Hope.* 1977. [film] Directed by G. Lucas. United States: 20th Century Fox.

CHAPTER 24: A LONG TIME AGO

"That's good. You have taken your first step into a larger world": *Star Wars: Episode IV A New Hope.* 1977. [film] Directed by G. Lucas. United States: 20th Century Fox.

"We seem to be made to suffer. It's our lot in life": *Star Wars: Episode IV A New Hope.* 1977. [film] Directed by G. Lucas. United States: 20th Century Fox.

"If you strike me down, I shall become more powerful than you can possibly imagine": *Star Wars: Episode IV A New Hope.* 1977. [film] Directed by G. Lucas. United States: 20th Century Fox.

CHAPTER 25: A WHOLE NEW WORLD

"Something inside of me has always been there. And now it's awake": *Star Wars: Episode VIII The Last Jedi.* 2017. [film] Directed by R. Johnson. United States: Walt Disney Studios Motion Pictures.

"A long time ago in a galaxy far, far away ...": *Star Wars: Episode IV A New Hope.* 1977. [film] Directed by G. Lucas. United States: 20th Century Fox.

CHAPTER 26: DROID STORY

"Be-boop": *Star Wars: Episode IV A New Hope.* 1977. [film] Directed by G. Lucas. United States: 20th Century Fox.

CHAPTER 27: CONGRATULATIONS

"Great kid! Don't get cocky": *Star Wars: Episode IV A New Hope.* 1977. [film] Directed by G. Lucas. United States: 20th Century Fox.

"That's not how the Force works": *Star Wars: Episode VII The Force Awakens.* 2015. [film] Directed by J. J. Abrams. United States: Walt Disney Studios Motion Pictures.

CHAPTER 29: SICKNESS

"I have a very bad feeling about this": *Star Wars: Episode IV A New Hope.* 1977. [film] Directed by G. Lucas. United States: 20th Century Fox.

CHAPTER 30: TEMPTATION

"I sense great fear in you, Skywalker. You have hate. You have anger. But you don't use them": *Star Wars: Episode III Revenge of the Sith.* 2005. [film] Directed by G. Lucas. United States: 20th Century Fox.

"Maxima debeteur puero reverentia": Juvenal. *Satires 14:47.*

CHAPTER 31: RETURN OF THE WINTER

"There isn't enough life on this ice cube to fill a space cruiser": *Star Wars: Episode V The Empire Strikes Back.* 1980. [film] Directed by I. Kershner. United States: 20th Century Fox.

"You will go to the Dagobah System ... Dagobah System ... There you will learn from Yoda, the Jedi Master who instructed me ...": *Star Wars: Episode V The Empire Strikes Back.* 1980. [film] Directed by I. Kershner. United States: 20th Century Fox.

CHAPTER 32: THE HAPPIEST PLACE ON EARTH

"I'm just a simple man trying to make my way in the universe": *Star Wars: Episode II Attack of the Clones.* 2002. [film] Directed by G. Lucas. United States: 20th Century Fox.

CHAPTER 33: EMERGENCY 911

"That is why you fail ...": *Star Wars: Episode V The Empire Strikes Back.* 1980. [film] Directed by I. Kershner. United States: 20th Century Fox.

CHAPTER 34: I'M WITH THE BAND

"My disappointment in your performance cannot be overstated": *Star Wars: Episode VIII The Last Jedi.* 2017. [film] Directed by R. Johnson. United States: Walt Disney Studios Motion Pictures.

CHAPTER 35: SILENT BUT DEADLY

"Choose what is right, not what is easy": Volpe, Giancarlo, dir. "The Zillo Beast." *Clone Wars*, season 2, episode 18, Cartoon Network, 2010.

CHAPTER 36: TO DATE OR NOT TO DATE

"I wish I could put my fist through this whole lousy, beautiful town": *Star Wars: Episode VIII The Last Jedi.* 2017. [film] Directed by R. Johnson. United States: Walt Disney Studios Motion Pictures.

"It's a cruel, cruel summer
Leaving me here on my own
It's a cruel, cruel summer
Now you're gone
You're the only one":

Bananarama, "Cruel Summer." Recorded April 1983.

CHAPTER 37: OF KENDO AND JEDI

"Hokey religions and ancient weapons are no match for a good blaster at your side": *Star Wars: Episode IV A New Hope.* 1977. [film] Directed by G. Lucas. United States: 20th Century Fox.

"A Jedi's strength flows from the Force. But beware of the dark side. Anger ... Fear ... Aggression. The dark side of the Force are they. Easily they flow, quick to join you in a fight. If once you start down the dark path, forever will it dominate your destiny, consume you it will, as it did Obi-Wan's apprentice ... For my ally is the Force. And a powerful ally it is. Life

creates it, makes it grow. Its energy surrounds us and binds us. Luminous beings are we ... not this crude matter. You must feel the Force around you. Here, between you ... me ... the tree ... the rock ... everywhere": *Star Wars: Episode V The Empire Strikes Back*. 1980. [film] Directed by I. Kershner. United States: 20th Century Fox.

"Control, control, you must learn control": *Star Wars: Episode V The Empire Strikes Back*. 1980. [film] Directed by I. Kershner. United States: 20th Century Fox.

CHAPTER 38: UNIVERSITY

"It's a chance for you to make a fresh start": *Rogue One*. 2016. [film] Directed by G. Edwards. United States: Walt Disney Studios Motion Pictures.

"It's a trap!": *Star Wars: Episode VI Return of the Jedi*. 1983. [film] Directed by R. Marquand. United States: 20th Century Fox.

"Run, Luke, run!": *Star Wars: Episode IV A New Hope*. 1977. [film] Directed by G. Lucas. United States: 20th Century Fox.

"... beware of the dark side. Anger ... Fear ... Aggression—the dark side of the Force are they": *Star Wars: Episode V The Empire Strikes Back*. 1980. [film] Directed by I. Kershner. United States: 20th Century Fox.

CHAPTER 39: IT'S ALL AN ILLUSION

"Your eyes can deceive you. Don't trust them": *Star Wars: Episode IV A New Hope*. 1977. [film] Directed by G. Lucas. United States: 20th Century Fox.

CHAPTER 40: THE MASTER'S DEGREE

"I cannot teach him, the boy has no patience": *Star Wars: Episode V The Empire Strikes Back*. 1980. [film] Directed by I. Kershner. United States: 20th Century Fox.

CHAPTER 41: SNOW FALLING ON CEDARS

"We're gonna do this": *Star Wars: Episode VII The Force Awakens*. 2015. [film] Directed by J. J. Abrams. United States: Walt Disney Studios Motion Pictures.

CHAPTER 42: CAN I LET YOU IN ON A SECRET?

"Help me Obi-Wan Kenobi, you're my only hope": *Star Wars: Episode IV A New Hope*. 1977. [film] Directed by G. Lucas. United States: 20th Century Fox.

"You must unlearn what you have learned ... Feel the Force": *Star Wars: Episode V The Empire Strikes Back*. 1980. [film] Directed by I. Kershner. United States: 20th Century Fox.

CHAPTER 43: OUT IN THE OPEN

"The more you tighten your grip, Tarkin, the more star systems will slip through your fingers": *Star Wars: Episode IV A New Hope*. 1977. [film] Directed by G. Lucas. United States: 20th Century Fox.

"Say on target ...": *Star Wars: Episode IV A New Hope*. 1977. [film] Directed by G. Lucas. United States: 20th Century Fox.

CHAPTER 44: INCOMING RADIO TRANSMISSION

"I am fluent in six million forms of communication": *Star Wars: Episode V The Empire Strikes Back*. 1980. [film] Directed by I. Kershner. United States: 20th Century Fox.

CHAPTER 45: DISCOVERY

"Do. Or do not. There is no try": *Star Wars: Episode V The Empire Strikes Back*. 1980. [film] Directed by I. Kershner. United States: 20th Century Fox.

CHAPTER 46: GOODBYE

"The Force will be with you ... always": *Star Wars: Episode IV A New Hope*. 1977. [film] Directed by G. Lucas. United States: 20th Century Fox.

"Do. Or do not. There is not try": *Star Wars: Episode V The Empire Strikes Back*. 1980. [film] Directed by I. Kershner. United States: 20th Century Fox.

"That face you make. Look I so old to young eyes?": *Star Wars: Episode VI Return of the Jedi*. 1983. [film] Directed by R. Marquand. United States: 20th Century Fox.

CHAPTER 47: BREAK A LEG

"Into the garbage chute, fly boy": Star Wars: Episode IV A New Hope. 1977. [film] Directed by G. Lucas. United States: 20th Century Fox.

"I have a very bad feeling about this": *Star Wars: Episode IV A New Hope.* 1977. [film] Directed by G. Lucas. United States: 20th Century Fox.

"This deal is getting worse all the time": *Star Wars: Episode V The Empire Strikes Back.* 1980. [film] Directed by I. Kershner. United States: 20th Century Fox.

CHAPTER 48: A NEW HOPE

"Let's keep a little optimism here": *Star Wars: Episode VI Return of the Jedi.* 1983. [film] Directed by R. Marquand. United States: 20th Century Fox.

CHAPTER 49: BAD GUYS DOING GOOD

"Save the dream!": *Rogue One.* 2016. [film] Directed by G. Edwards. United States: Walt Disney Studios Motion Pictures.

"This will be a day long remembered": *Star Wars: Episode IV A New Hope.* 1977. [film] Directed by G. Lucas. United States: 20th Century Fox.

"Join me, and together we shall rule the galaxy as ...": *Star Wars: Episode V The Empire Strikes Back.* 1980. [film] Directed by I. Kershner. United States: 20th Century Fox.

"Do. Or do not": *Star Wars: Episode V The Empire Strikes Back.* 1980. [film] Directed by I. Kershner. United States: 20th Century Fox.

CHAPTER 50: JEDI SCHOOL DROPOUT

"Oh, no, my young Jedi. You will find that it is you who are mistaken ... about a great many things": *Star Wars: Episode VI Return of the Jedi.* 1983. [film] Directed by R. Marquand. United States: 20th Century Fox.

"Control, control, you must learn control": *Star Wars: Episode V The Empire Strikes Back.* 1980. [film] Directed by I. Kershner. United States: 20th Century Fox.

"Use your aggressive feelings, boy. Let the hate flow through you": *Star Wars: Episode VI Return of the Jedi.* 1983. [film] Directed by R. Marquand. United States: 20th Century Fox.

"Strike me down …": *Star Wars: Episode VI Return of the Jedi.* 1983. [film] Directed by R. Marquand. United States: 20th Century Fox.

"Control, control, you must learn control": *Star Wars: Episode V The Empire Strikes Back.* 1980. [film] Directed by I. Kershner. United States: 20th Century Fox.

CHAPTER 51: REMNANTS

"Luminous beings are we, not this crude matter": *Star Wars: Episode V The Empire Strikes Back.* 1980. [film] Directed by I. Kershner. United States: 20th Century Fox.

EPILOGUE

"Confronting fear is the destiny of a Jedi. Your destiny": *Star Wars: Episode IX The Rise of Skywalker.* 2019. [film] Directed by J. J. Abrams. United States: Walt Disney Studios Motion Pictures.

"This is Master Obi-Wan Kenobi. I regret to report that both our Jedi Order and the Republic have fallen, with a dark shadow of the Empire rising to take their place. This message is a warning and a reminder for any surviving Jedi: Trust in the Force. Do not return to the Temple. That time has passed, and our future is uncertain. We will each be challenged. Our trust. Our faith. Our friendships. But we must persevere. And in time, a new hope will emerge. May the Force be with you. Always": Lee, Steward, and Steven G. Lee, dirs. "Spark of Rebellion." *Star Wars Rebels*, season 1, episode 1 and 2, Lucasfilm Animation, 2014.

AUTHOR BIO

Nicholas Harrison is a writer, actor, director, swordsman, fight director, playwright, and educator. As a professional actor and stunt performer in film and television, he has appeared in many popular films and series such as *Scooby-Doo 2, Supernatural, Stargate,* DC's *Legends of Tomorrow,* and the popular *Air Bud* franchise; his autobiographical play, *How Star Wars Saved My Life,* premiered in 2017. Nicholas studied at the London Academy of Performing Arts, holds both a master's degree from the University of Victoria and a PhD from the University of British Columbia, and is currently an instructor at Capilano University. He resides in the traditional, ancestral, and unceded territories of the Tsawwassen and Musqueam Peoples.

CPSIA information can be obtained
at www.ICGtesting.com
Printed in the USA
BVHW070731150222
629036BV00007B/77/J